After the Siege

After the Siege

A Social History of Boston
1775–1800

JACQUELINE
BARBARA CARR

Northeastern University Press
BOSTON

Northeastern University Press

Copyright 2005 by Jacqueline Barbara Carr

Library of Congress Cataloging-in-Publication Data
Carr, Jacqueline Barbara, 1954–
After the siege : a social history of Boston, 1775–1800 /
Jacqueline Barbara Carr.
p.   cm.
Includes bibliographical references (p.   ) and index.
ISBN 1-55553-629-8 (acid-free paper)
1. Boston (Mass.)—History—18th century. 2. Boston
(Mass.)—Social conditions—18th century. 3. Boston
(Mass.)—History—Siege, 1775–1776. 4. United
States—History—Revolution, 1775–1783—Influence. I. Title.
F73.44.C37   2005
974.4'6102—dc22   2004006712

Materials from William Donnison account book, 1790–1833
(Mss A 786) and Allen Crocker letter, 25 September 1778, to
Joseph Crocker (in Hannah Mather Crocker's *Reminiscences
and Traditions of Boston*, Mss 219, p. 277) are reprinted courtesy
of the R. Stanton Avery Special Collections Department of
the New England Historic Genealogical Society.

Materials from the Boston Taking Books, 1780–1799
(Ms. Bos.); Boston Town Papers; Adlow Papers (Ms. Adl. J.D1–25);
System of Public Education (H.189.148); Thomas Davis letter
to sister, 30 July 1794 (Ms.2635.6); and Report of the Committee
Chairman (Ms.fBos.795.1) are Boston Public Library/Rare
Books Department. Courtesy of the Trustees.

Designed by Graciela Galup

Composed in Janson by Coghill Composition in Richmond, Virginia.
Printed and bound by Thomson-Shore, Inc., in Dexter, Michigan.
The paper is Nature's Natural, an acid-free sheet.

For my husband, Paul Henry Frobose,
my mentor and friend Robert Middlekauff,
and in memory of James H. Kettner

Contents

Illustrations

Preface

THE VISITOR TO BOSTON TODAY sees very little of the town as it looked in the eighteenth century. Landfill has transformed the original peninsula, making its former shape indistinguishable. Paul Revere's house in the North End provides an image of what some of the town's wooden houses looked like, but the charming brick structures that line the streets of the North End and the elegant brownstone buildings throughout other parts of town are of post–eighteenth-century origin. Despite the changes brought about by the passage of time there is a sense in which one may, with the use of imagination, re-create the Revolutionary-era town in one's mind. Somehow, despite all that has disappeared from the landscape, and all that has been added, Boston's past seems to infuse itself into the present-day cityscape.

The approximate perimeter of the old North End can still be walked if one follows sections of Commercial Street, and with a few good maps and a lot of patience it is possible to trace the town's outline and stand approximately where the fortifications and gallows greeted visitors crossing Boston Neck. Today, the visitor or resident can walk along Snow Hill or Beacon Hill on a bitter winter's day and imagine eighteenth-century children sliding down hills and taunting each other in snowball fights, in defiance of Boston's bylaws of the day intended to prevent such activities. Other streets, particularly in the North End, still traverse the same path that they did more than two hundred years ago. Old North Church, Old South Meeting House, and Faneuil Hall, now standing amidst concrete and traffic, still evoke reflections of the past. One can stand on Boston Common and think about the Haymarket, the ropewalks, and the British soldiers camped there that bitter winter of the siege in 1775–1776. The burying grounds, such as Copp's Hill in the North End, quietly preserve the names of those long dead on their slate and granite tombstones: young children taken in their infancy, men and boys who fought in the American Revolution, and others who lived to an old age, each represents a part of the community's history. This book is, in a sense, dedicated to all those who went before, especially those whose names or lives are lost to us now but who lived, loved, laughed, played, worked, and eventually died in the town by the Bay.

Acknowledgments

I AM DEEPLY INDEBTED to Robert Middlekauff and the late James Kettner, whose recent death is an irreplaceable loss. A student could not hope for more supportive mentors. I am extremely grateful for the ways in which both of them guided me in my work. Bob's ongoing friendship is a source of great joy, intellectual inspiration, and support. The loss of Jim was deeply felt as I completed this manuscript. His influence and friendship will never be forgotten.

Cornelia Hughes Dayton, David Conroy, and Thomas O'Connor each offered a close, thoughtful, and encouraging written critique of my manuscript. Although two of my readers at Northeastern University Press remain anonymous, I would like to extend my thanks for their detailed and enthusiastic reviews of the initial manuscript. I deeply appreciate and value the ideas of each of these historians, which have helped shape this final work. Any inadequacies or errors that remain are mine, not theirs.

Two dear friends and academic colleagues with whom I shared graduate school, the dissertation process, research trips, and the trials, tribulations, and joys of this manuscript are Diane Hill and Caroline Cox. Their support came in more ways than can be acknowledged, and their friendship is priceless.

Parts of this book appeared previously as an article in the *New England Quarterly*. Linda Smith Rhoads's editing suggestions for the article were very helpful. I presented a synthesis of various sections of this book at two conferences, the 1996 Mid-America Conference and the American Studies division of the Western Social Science Association Conference in 2001. Thank you to Bob Frye for his comments and to Richard Rohrs, who encouraged me to think about the political aspects of the theater debate in ways I had not previously considered. Various colleagues at the Bay Area Seminar in Early American History and Culture, including Dee Andrews and the late Jacqueline Reinier, also provided encouragement for which I am appreciative. I also extend special thanks to David Lieberman and Bonnie Reid Roman for their suggestions, Bob Richardson for the ward map, and to Madeline Carr.

I am indebted to John Weingartner, former senior editor of Northeastern University Press. After reading my article in the *New England Quarterly*, he inquired about my dissertation and believed in its possibilities as a book. I owe a special thanks to Robert Gormley, the current editor, Amy Roeder, Jill Bahcall, and Emily McKeigue, my production editor who has fine-tuned this work with skill and precision. It has been a pleasure working with each of them, and their expertise has made the process of getting from manuscript to finished product immeasurably easier. I extend my appreciation and thanks to the librarians and staff at the Rare Book Department of the Boston Public Library, the Massachusetts Historical Society, and the New England Historic Genealogical Society for their assistance. Funding from the Mellon Foundation, the Phi Beta Kappa Dissertation Fellowship, the University of California, Berkeley's Hotchkis Fellowship, and a Humanities Graduate Research Fellowship made research during the dissertation stage possible.

Finally, I want to acknowledge my deep appreciation to my husband, Paul Frobose, for his support of my academic pursuits throughout the years. His belief in my goals of teaching and writing were instrumental in bringing both to fruition. As a fellow historian, excellent editor, and patient friend, his help and companionship have proved invaluable. My mother, Joan Carr, volunteered her time to search through town records with me and spent many hours cataloguing materials. She has been a great friend throughout this process, always full of encouragement and rich in imagination. I will always remember fondly the summer we pounded the pavements of downtown Boston with old maps in hand retracing the landscape of the late-eighteenth-century community. Perhaps the greatest gifts each of them has offered are the ability to keep me laughing and their belief in the value of my work.

My mother and my father, John Carr, whether they realize it or not, instilled in me a love of history at an early age. The day trips and summer holidays spent visiting historical sites while growing up in England, and later Delaware, sparked my imagination from childhood onward. When we first arrived in the United States they encouraged their children to learn about its history. My photo album and my heart are full of wonderful memories. This book is a product of those early years.

After the Siege

Prologue

In the years immediately following the American Revolution Butterfield and Clarissa Scotland arrived in Boston, Massachusetts, having begun their journey in their native city of Philadelphia. Whether their path took them directly from Pennsylvania to Boston or there were other stops along the way is unknown. Were they enslaved African-Americans escaping bondage in Philadelphia or were they free individuals simply searching for a better life? This is also unknown. It is a fact that they were among the thousands of men and women who were on the move during the 1780s and 1790s, part of "a society in flux" wherein at least "40 percent of the population" moved every "few years." As the largest urban area in New England, Boston was the destination for a substantial number of migrants, and Butterfield and Clarissa were not alone in perhaps hoping that this urban seaport could provide work opportunities.[1]

By spring of 1788 the Scotlands resided in one room of a house located in Ward 4 of the North End. Living in cramped quarters was not unusual, as a number of the town's residents lived in dwellings that housed two or more families. Individuals and families might be on record as having lived in "one end" of a house, or in the "back end"; not uncommonly a house served as a place of residence and work. In the North End of Boston among wharves, shipyards, "manufactory" establishments, and small shops, wooden houses stood weathered by wind and sea spray. The Scotlands' neighbors were artisans, fishermen, truckmen, carters, sailors, and many laborers like Butterfield. Perhaps the Scotlands were drawn to the North End because of low rents or hopes that Butterfield would find work around the docks, for the town's maritime economy had started showing signs of recovery by the late 1780s. As African-Americans the Scotland family may have chosen to settle in the North End because a number of black Bostonians lived there. In a town of approximately 18,000 persons in 1790, where the African-American population numbered less than eight hundred, the friendship and support they might find in what was sometimes referred to in the eighteenth century as the North End's "New Guinea" would be welcoming.[2]

As with many Bostonians during these years, the Scotlands made frequent moves around the town. By 1790 they had relocated to Ward 12 in the South End near Hill's Wharf, where they shared "black Jack's house" with two white men, John Frangel, a "poor Dutchman," and Thomas Dalton, a "poor laborer." Shared living arrangements among unskilled workers, artisans, and tradesmen were not an unusual practice. One year later the family moved again, to Ward 6, where they remained for at least two years. It was during these years that they appear to have fallen upon even harder times than before, for the town's tax assessor now added the notation "poor" in his "Taking Book" next to Butterfield's occupation

as a laborer. In 1792 the town's overseers of the poor listed Butterfield Scotland among more than two thousand names in the "warning out" records following the decision of the selectmen and overseers the previous year to remove "Paupers to the Towns to which
they belong." Under these circumstances the family could remain
in Boston, but they were not eligible for poor relief if needed. Responsibility for the care of the indigent fell to an individual's town
of legal inhabitancy, and Boston could barely take care of its own.[3]

Perhaps Boston was beginning to feel like home for the Scotland family. They now attended Trinity Church, located on Summer Street in the South End, where the congregation consisted of
white and black Bostonians: artisans, tradesmen, laborers, and some
of Boston's leading citizens, such as attorney Perez Morton and
Selectman and architect Charles Bulfinch. At this church three important events in the lives of the family took place between 1793
and 1795. In May 1793 the Scotlands baptized their son Prince
Watts Scotland, their daughter Elizabeth in the early summer of
1794, and their son Samuel in the late spring of 1795. Prince's
namesake and sponsor was fifty-seven-year-old church member
Prince Watts, a soap boiler and property owner from the West End
who had lived in Boston since his infancy. During his adult years
Watts witnessed many changes in the community, including events
leading up to the American Revolution, the siege of Boston, and in
1783 the end of slavery.[4]

Between 1793 and 1799, during the six years following their
older son's baptism, the Scotlands relocated two more times before
finally settling in the West End a few doors down from their elderly
friend Prince Watts. Circumstances had also improved for Butterfield and Clarissa, at least financially. By 1794 the Boston assessors
had determined that they were liable for taxes. Living in Ward 7 of
the West End, Prince, Elizabeth, and Samuel could attend the new
school founded by black Bostonians for their children, who were

experiencing discrimination in the town's public free schools. Here, too, the whole Scotland family formed part of the small but growing black community taking shape in Ward 7 by the late 1790s. A number of these families would constitute the politically and socially active black middle class in nineteenth-century Boston.[5]

Over the course of a dozen or so years, in the face of much hardship, the Scotlands had made a home for themselves in Boston. Many of their experiences would no doubt have been unique to African-Americans, and perhaps even unpleasant. After 1783 slavery was outlawed in Boston, but that did not automatically bring an end to prejudice and discrimination. The Scotlands' story, though, is also typical in many ways. They were newcomers to the rapidly growing port town. Butterfield Scotland secured work, but there were also periods of unemployment. The family was mobile, moving from ward to ward within the town during the course of a little more than a decade. Butterfield and Clarissa experienced a variety of living situations, encountered hard times, made friends, attended a local church, celebrated life, and raised a family.

Perhaps Butterfield, Clarissa, and their children were among the hundreds of Bostonians who poured into the streets to witness the three-day festivities and great parade when Massachusetts ratified the United States Constitution. Maybe they watched the grand procession through town to the triumphal arch and attended the public speeches when George Washington visited Boston. What did these events mean to the Scotlands? Was Butterfield one of the hundreds of laborers who helped build the new public structures in Boston during the last decade of the century? The full dimensions of the Scotlands' lives will most likely never be known, but even the limited framework that can be reconstructed represents an important part of Boston's history in the late eighteenth century.

Annie Haven Thwing noted in her now classic work written in 1920, *The Crooked and Narrow Streets of the Town of Boston, 1630–1822*, that the history of Boston "from the close of the war [for independence] until she became a city in 1822 is largely political."[6] Attention has been paid to Boston's political history because of the town's central role in the Revolutionary Era and the emergence of Federalism during the period of confederation and the early republic. However, between 1775 and 1800 there was more to the town's history than politics. Day in and day out, men and women handled the immediate concerns of the day, feeding their families, earning a living, visiting neighbors, and dealing with the hour-to-hour issues of existence. People went about their lives making rope, hammering out tin, cobbling shoes, building chairs, selling goods, evading the town's bylaws, and complaining to its selectmen about their neighbors who did the same. They attended town meetings, raised money for the poor, argued about the moral worth of public entertainments, gathered in taverns and coffeehouses, planned parades, and complained about their taxes. In short, their lives consisted of the thousand and one things that people do on a day-to-day basis.

During the late 1770s Bostonians struggled to recover from the physical, moral, demographic, and economic devastation wrought by the British occupation and the ensuing siege of the town by the Continental Army. Discovering that a town of approximately fifteen thousand civilians plummeted in a matter of months, if not weeks, to less than three thousand after the events at Lexington and Concord on April 19, 1775, piqued my curiosity and became the original seed from which this book emerged. As I began to read letters, journals, and newspaper accounts of the terrible suffering and sadness people experienced, these events struck an emotional chord and also led me to wonder how the community ever rebuilt itself.

By 1780 Boston's population had climbed to only ten thousand, and the town's economy teetered on the edge of complete collapse. In the wake of the American Revolution the town faced many of the same problems that it had during the war years. Although it was the largest urban area in New England during the colonial period, by 1776 the town could easily have become a backwater, falling to second place behind Salem, for example. In contrast to New York or Philadelphia, Boston had already experienced both demographic and economic stagnation before the American Revolution. The events of 1774, 1775, and early 1776 almost sealed the fate of the community.

Throughout the last twenty-five years of the eighteenth century various forces propelled change, but there existed a mixture of the old and the new. The *old* consisted of traditional institutions of government, the economy, and the communal spirit (an ethic of work and responsibility instilled by the Puritan religion), and the *new* arose from the needs of recovery and growth as well as long-standing individualism, coupled with the enlightened revolutionary thought found in New England culture. Demonstrating an indefatigable perseverance, Bostonians were clearly determined to rebuild their community. The pervasiveness of republican ideology in the new nation and the way it shaped American perceptions and actions, combined with the Puritan ethic, also led many Bostonians to place an emphasis upon the necessity of achieving a virtuous community. To this end, poor relief, public education, the just market, and the presence of the theater in Boston, among other issues, became central concerns. The people of Boston often disagreed more than they agreed on how to go about the process of rebuilding their community and maintaining a collective moral life, but I'm not sure that most Bostonians ever really questioned whether or not their town should hold anything but a central role in the new nation.

The purpose of my study is to provide a social portrait of Boston between 1775 and 1800 focusing on the lives of lower- and middle-income groups and emphasizing how the community functioned in the wake of Revolution. Although it is beyond the scope of this work to draw detailed comparisons between Boston and other cities, one may wonder whether the experiences of the town and its residents were similar or dissimilar to those found in other urban centers during the same period. It is hoped that this study of Boston will contribute to the historical discussion concerning late-eighteenth-century cities and provide a building block for future work in comparative early American urban history.[7]

After the Siege rests upon a number of primary sources, but a critical foundation of the work is the collection of assessment records called the Boston Taking Books now housed in the Rare Book Department of the Boston Public Library. The story of Butterfield Scotland began as a name among thousands scrawled upon the pages of a late-eighteenth-century Boston tax assessment book. Beginning with that one entry, more than two hundred years later the bare bones of slightly over a decade in the life of this ordinary individual, long lost to history, began to emerge from the records. Each year during the months of April and May, Boston's assessors meandered through their assigned wards in the North End, South End, and West End, knocking on the doors of houses and businesses and interviewing the male, and sometimes female, heads of household. Their job was to collect and record specific information in their "tax-taking books," known simply as the Taking Books. Despite the dislike that some Bostonians probably showed the tax-taking man, there were those among the assessors who clearly maintained a sense of humor. In 1794 Ward 11 assessor Samuel Ruggles noted "pretty well known by the assessor" when he came to his own house.[8]

When I first started to examine the Taking Books, I realized the wealth of information that they contained. A handful of historians had worked with select parts of various books, but to my knowledge no one had attempted to compile and analyze the data in its entirety from the five Taking Books between 1780 and 1799 that contain all twelve wards intact (1780, 1784, 1790, 1794, 1799).[9] I determined that utilizing all the facts available in the Taking Books to their best advantage required transcribing the information into a database.

The finished product was a database that contained in excess of fifteen thousand entries, and a road map for tracking in-migration and out-migration, occupational patterns, tax assessment and property ownership patterns, and the shifting spatial organization of the town's neighborhoods, wards, and districts over a twenty-year period. Combined with other primary materials, information in the Taking Books also offered a resource for understanding broader patterns of development in Boston.

Other sources that proved helpful in fleshing out the lives of Bostonians included church records, census records, birth and marriage records, town directories, and selected wards from Taking Books that no longer exist in their entirety. A portrait not only of the community but also of individual Bostonians emerged from these collective sources. Sometimes incomplete or missing sources led to dead ends, leaving parts of the portrait in the shadows. What happened to the Scotlands, the widowed tavern keeper Elizabeth Fadre, who worked to raise a family alone, and Henry Foye, the struggling shopkeeper and door attendant at the town's first legal theater?[10] Despite some unanswerable questions, the Boston Town Records, the Selectmen's Minutes, letters, private papers, and local newspapers proved invaluable in shedding light on how the town functioned on a day-to-day basis and began the process of its transformation following the American Revolution.

Beginning with the siege in chapter 1, I have examined the social history of Boston between 1775 and 1800 through numerous topics. These include a survey of the built environment and the town's neighborhoods; an analysis of town government, its impact on people's lives, and the day-to-day trials of rebuilding and managing the community; a consideration of the postwar economy as it shaped work and daily life; and finally an account of how Bostonians played and entertained themselves, or what I have called, in chapter 5, "the politics of leisure." Primarily, *After the Siege* tells about those who in eighteenth-century terms were called the "middling sort" and "lower sort." It does not retell the history of Boston's leading families, the elite, the lawyers, or the politicians. It is about laborers such as Butterfield Scotland, widows like Elizabeth Fadre, artisans and mechanics, seamen and tradesmen. It is about what one historian termed "the plain people of Boston."[11]

Many stories of those long dead and long forgotten began to emerge as I sifted through archival records and pages of published primary sources. The majority of these were bits and pieces, incomplete or broken threads. It was often very frustrating to find that somebody simply disappeared from the records without a trace. I believed they were probably still part of the community, but as the ordinary folk (a number of whom most likely possessed little or no education) they had left few if any trails of their lives. However, as I began to take these broken threads and weave them together, the fabric of the community began to take on hues, detail, and patterns, as I hope it will do for my readers.

A View of the Town of Boston with Several Ships of War in the Harbour. (Royal American Magazine, 1774.)

I

The Siege of Boston

TEMPERS FLARED IN BOSTON during the hot summer months of
1774. Not only did townspeople find themselves dealing with hostile British soldiers stationed in their midst, but on May 13 General
Gage, commander-in-chief of the British forces in America, had
replaced Thomas Hutchinson as the governor of Massachusetts.[1]
Martial law soon followed, as did the arrival of more British Regulars. June began with the enforcement of the Boston Port Act,
whereby Parliament ordered the harbor closed to all shipping until
the town made reparations for the tea destroyed six months earlier
at the Boston Tea Party.[2] The Act was a commercial death knell for
the community, and the consequences soon manifested themselves
during the months that followed. By year's end events would turn
the city into a shadow of its former self.

When news of the parliamentary legislation first reached the port, responses included a pledge not to buy or sell English goods, but this Solemn League and Covenant was not universally agreed upon. A substantial portion of the merchant community in Boston refused to sign the document.[3] Supporters and opponents both vehemently stood their ground, leading one merchant to observe that "Animosities run higher than ever," with "each party charging the other as bringing ruin upon their country."[4] Hardware merchant Samuel Salisbury finally joined the committee supporting the Covenant only because he believed he had "already incurred their displeasure" by repeatedly refusing to do so. When nearly eight hundred tradesmen met on June 15 to address the general distress of the town, they were so "much Divided in Sentiment" that they accomplished nothing.[5] Later meetings brought residents no closer to unanimity concerning the appropriate response to Britain's hated Act. A town meeting on June 27 drew such a large crowd that the townspeople adjourned to Old South Meeting House to accommodate the large number of attendees. The meeting, lasting all day, still produced no resolution. Unable to stop the Covenant, the opposition instead circulated a petition denouncing it as "a base, wicked, illegal Measure, calculated to distress and ruin many Merchants, Shopkeepers and others" and create "unhappy divisions in towns and families." One inhabitant wrote to a friend that civil war seemed imminent if matters were not soon resolved.[6]

The consequences of the Port Act and the Covenant quickly manifested themselves in other ways besides divisions among inhabitants. Wharves sat deserted with "not a topsail vessel to be seen either there or in the harbour, save the ships of war and transport." Strolling around the wharves after church one Sunday in mid-June, John Rowe experienced a sense of futility regarding "the Distressed Situation of this Poor Town."[7] Gradually over a period of several months a haunting quietness replaced the bustling and noisy atmosphere of the once busy port, as the adz and mallet of the shipwright fell silent and the din of waterfront sailors, artisans, and hawkers diminished. When several ministers recommended a day of fasting "on Account of the Miserable Situation," Rowe believed that paying for the tea would do greater justice by the people of Boston "instead of losing a Day by fasting."[8] Certainly Rowe did not stand alone in his frustration. Angry at Britain for its tyrannical actions, John Andrews, a moderate Patriot, also expressed outrage toward those responsible for enforcing the Covenant, "the authors of all our evils . . . [who] by their injudicious conduct seem determin'd to bring total destruction upon us." His concern extended beyond himself and other merchants, for he realized that economic collapse would bring great suffering to the indigent.[9]

Sailors, shipwrights, and mechanics (manual workers), who represented a sizable portion of the town's working force, found little or no employment. Shipyards lay vacant, and advertisements in the *Boston Gazette* dwindled as shopkeepers and merchants closed their doors.[10] William Townshend hoped to sell his entire stock in October for cash only at the lowest possible prices, as he was "determined to remove into . . . the Country, *very soon.*" Retailer Nathan Frazier and coopers Newhall and Hichborn decided to remove their businesses to Salem.[11] Lack of business and failure to collect debts owing to them ruined merchants, shopkeepers, and tradesmen alike. John Hunt, a brazier located on Cornhill, had all his "goods and effects" seized for indebtedness. He had "two thousand sterling due to him," which he was unable to collect and therefore could not pay even his own smallest debts. A "general stagnation" had so seized the community that hard times fell upon many.[12]

As the situation worsened, local authorities proposed several municipal building projects to provide work for the unemployed and needy, including digging new wells, paving, repairing, and cleaning public streets and docks.[13] Digging a public well in Dock Square not only benefited the unemployed, it also provided "for the farther Preservation of the Town from Fire" and made water more easily accessible to residents in the immediate vicinity. The manufacture of bricks employed the "distressed, industrious Poor" and their sale provided wages and helped raise money for other public expenditures.[14] Despite such efforts, the town spiraled further into economic decline. Public money became less and less available for such projects. In an age lacking a central system of state welfare, the relief provided by Boston's selectmen rested solely upon tax revenue, fines collected, and private donations, each of which became increasingly difficult to acquire.

In a spirit of goodwill, assistance to the beleaguered town in the form of food and clothing donations began to arrive in midsummer from "Sister Colonies."[15] Marblehead sent "eleven carts loaded with meat [and] fish" while South Carolina sent two cargoes of rice. As "no goods of any kind are suffered to be waterborne within a circle of 60 miles," delivery of these goods overland from nearby seaports and by way of the isthmus, known as Boston Neck, proved an expensive and arduous undertaking.[16] Nevertheless, donations of flour, grain, wood, vegetables, livestock, dry goods, and even money continued to arrive. A committee of twenty-four men, from the north, central, and southern parts of town, then distributed the money and goods to ensure that those in need received supplies.[17]

By the end of summer community divisions, stagnant commerce, unemployment, and dwindling food supplies were not Boston's only worries. In September 1774 General Gage started fortifying the town and began construction of a fort at Boston Neck, creating further suspicion and fear among the townspeople. Already Boston Common had become a campground for the British army. Now British guards began detaining persons who attempted to pass peaceably in and out of town, including the "market people" necessary for Boston's supply of fresh vegetables, meat, and dairy products. This also threatened to hamper the delivery of donated goods from other towns and colonies, but the British were impervious to any new hardships their actions imposed on the colonists. When in early August certain townspeople had approached the British Commissioners as to the severe plight caused by lack of supplies, they were informed that these consequences were "the design of the act," and it was "not their intent to lessen these difficulties."[18]

Fears were compounded when during the autumn months outbreaks of "fever" and "distemper" followed by incidents of smallpox in November took a number of lives.[19] The constant arrival of new British regiments further increased health risks, as a large number had to be housed in damp, unclean distilleries owing to lack of adequate housing, Boston Common already being covered in tents. At one of the distilleries "a quantity of stagnated water in a reservoir under the floor" caused an outbreak of "a malignant spotted fever" that took the lives of several men. The smell of the water was so putrid that soldiers pumping out the reservoirs experienced "fits."[20] An outbreak of smallpox, first reported in November, was a further cause for alarm. By January, "scarce a day passe[d] without three or four soldier's [*sic*] funerals." Their bodies were laid in "a spot of ground at the bottom of the common" that had already been "improv'd for upwards a hundred."[21] Not surprisingly, desertions increased during the winter of 1774–1775, and tension within the ranks and between soldier and civilian led to hostile confrontations.

Maintaining peace between the British soldiers and Boston's inhabitants proved difficult and sometimes costly. Altercations occurred regularly between the soldiers and civilians. At town meetings residents raised their concerns as to how to "prevent Bickerings and Disputes with the Troops" in town. To this end the town increased the number of men in each watch duty and in each watch house, directing them to patrol the streets throughout the entire night during the winter season. It was recommended that the masters of families keep their children and servants close to home and indoors by nine o'clock at night "unless on necessary business." The selectmen enjoined taverners and retailers to "strictly conform to the Laws of the Province relating to disorderly Persons," but animosities between Bostonians and the British Regulars ran deep and there persisted a "Great Uneasiness in Town."[22] Since the 1760s Bostonians had resented the presence of a standing army in their midst, while British Regulars held the townsmen to be "licentious and riotous" in their "disposition." The reference to the townsmen as "Vagrants" was one of the more polite insults. One British officer considered them "the most designing, Artfull Villians [*sic*] in the World."[23]

In light of these animosities, an evening spent in the local tavern or grog shop could easily exacerbate the state of affairs. In late July fifteen officers, after wining and dining, caused a large crowd to gather when "they committed all manner of enormous indecencies, by exposing their anteriors, as well as their posteriors, at the open windows and doors, to the full view of the people . . . that happened to pass by." They accompanied their actions with "opprobrious language" and threats to fire their pistols amongst the gathered crowd. Not content with their display, two of the drunken officers began to harass an old woman in her apple shop, turning her goods onto the ground while insulting passersby and then pulling their swords on Abra Hunt the wine cooper, "a well built, nervous fellow," and his wife, whom they proceeded to abuse. Defending his wife, Hunt struck one of the officers, cutting open his head. Four other men, including a chairmaker named Fullerton and a black man, managed to disarm the soldiers, but not before doing much damage and each sustaining injuries.[24] Several months later, when two soldiers claimed they had been insulted by the local watch, they showed up late one night threatening to blow out the brains of the town watchmen. The incident resulted in "one of the Watch los[ing] a nose, another a Thumb." Simple pranks or violent fights involving brawling, cutlasses, pistols, bricks, and wood bats caused serious injury, unnerved inhabitants, and fueled the growing mutual hatred.[25]

Attempting to establish order between townspeople and the British Regulars, General Gage increased the frequency and severity of punishments for soldiers, but this proved to little avail other than to elicit feelings of even greater resentment on the part of some soldiers. John Barker privately disagreed with Gage's solution, "to seize all military Men found engaged in any disturbance, whether Aggressors or not . . . 'till the matter is enquired into." Barker wondered who would do the enquiring: "Villians that woul'd not censure one of their own Vagrants, even if He attempted the life of a Soldier?"[26] Did Barker have a point? Controlling civilians could prove equally difficult. When a fellow from the country attempted to purchase a gun from a British soldier, a group of townspeople tarred, feathered, and paraded him through town in a cart.[27] Social, political, and economic tensions, combined with idle hours of boredom and frustration, created an environment where soldier and civilian alike found mischief to engage in and scapegoats for their problems.

By contemporary accounts an air of sadness and foreboding pervaded Boston by the early months of 1775. "It is now a very gloomy place," wrote Anne Hulton to her friends in England, with "the Streets almost empty, many families have [departed] . . . & the Inhabitants are divided into several parties, at variance, & quarreling with each other, some appear desponding, others full of rage."[28] Fortifications at the Neck and the blockaded harbor led many to believe that their community would soon be severed entirely from connection with the outside world by land or sea. Regardless of recommendations by the Continental Congress against evacuation and the cold and disagreeable weather that made travel difficult, every day inhabitants fled the town.[29] Here "the streets and Neck [are] lin'd with waggons carrying off the effects of the inhabitants, who are either affraid, mad, crazy or infatuated . . . imagining themselves . . . liable to every evil that can be enumerated, if they tarry in town," reported John Andrews to his brother-in-law in Philadelphia on April 11, 1775.[30] Bostonians had not yet witnessed the worst.

Eight days after Andrews wrote his letter, British soldiers and colonists exchanged gunfire at Lexington and Concord, marking the first shots of open warfare. John Rowe recorded in his journal, "this Unhappy affair is a Shocking Introduction to all the Miseries of a Civil War."[31] One day after the shots were fired on April 19, 1775, a letter issued by the Massachusetts Committee of Safety advised towns throughout the colony and in Connecticut and New Hampshire that the events of the preceding day mandated the immediate raising of an army.[32] During the ensuing week an estimated twenty thousand colonial militiamen gathered anxiously outside of Boston in what would mark the beginning of an eleven-month siege of the town.[33] As British troops continued to arrive in Boston harbor, the level of panic among civilians increased. Believing himself best rid of troublemakers who had "hostile intentions against his Majesty's troops," General Gage at first moved to accelerate the evacuation of the city. In a meeting on April 22 between Gage and town officials, both sides agreed that "the women and children, with all their effects, shall have safe conduct without the garrison" and that male inhabitants "upon condition . . . that they will not take up arms against the king's troops" would also be permitted to leave.[34] In the event military engagements occurred within the town, "the lives and properties of the inhabitants should be protected and secured, if the inhabitants behaved peaceably."[35] To facilitate the move General Gage provided boats and permitted carriages to travel back and forth across the Neck. All possessions except plate and firearms could be taken from the town. General Gage assured those civilians desiring to stay that they would receive his protection. At a town meeting the following day the inhabitants agreed to the terms.[36]

Acquiring a pass to leave Boston was not always an easy undertaking despite the April 22 agreement between General Gage and town officials.[37] When merchant Henry Prentiss returned from a "foreign Voyage" in May 1775, he had to dock at Charlestown, where he then applied to enter Boston to collect his belongings. "The trouble & Difficulty of getting a Pass is much greater than I cou'd possibly Conceive" he informed a friend in a nearby town.[38] Just as Gage required passes for Boston residents to leave or enter the town, the Provincial Congress issued passes to Loyalists in Massachusetts to travel and enter Boston.[39]

Once received, a pass from the British commander represented freedom from the oppressive air of the occupied town. Samuel Salisbury and Samuel Barrett managed to acquire passes for their families and sent them to be housed with relatives in Worcester. No doubt as others did in the same situation, both gentlemen found it a "great satisfaction" to know that when they saw their "dear ones" departing on the Charlestown Ferry "they were going directly to the care of those in whom we could place confidence." The women carried with them important business records, cash, and "a few valuables, with such furniture" as they were permitted to remove from the town. Barrett and Salisbury chose to remain behind. Despite appeals from his brother Stephen in Worcester, Samuel Salisbury informed him on June 6, "I cant be reconciled to leave at present. I think it is my duty to take care of our interests and although I cant defend it in case of attack, it is at present in my power to protect it from thieves and robbers which we are surrounded with. Empty houses are broken open, goods are stolen and some destroyed."[40]

The families of Samuel Barrett and Samuel Salisbury were fortunate in that guards permitted them to leave Boston with certain possessions. Not every evacuating inhabitant had this good fortune, as guards at the exit points made it increasingly difficult to leave with possessions. At the Charlestown Ferry, guards severely scrutinized all packages, boxes, and trunks. In order to remove any merchandise that he knew would be seized at the patrol gates, James Lovell opened packages previously sealed by a man who had already departed Boston. As a consequence of the inspections, and in some cases seizures, some took to hiding furniture in their cellars before departing. Residents hurriedly packed goods and carted them to the house of neighbors who were remaining behind.[41] Homeowners might even offer their residence rent free to a tenant, with the hope that an occupied dwelling would provide a deterrent to vandalism. At least there existed the chance of the tenant looking after the property.[42] People waited anxiously for passes until some reached a point where they no longer cared about their furniture but only about escaping the town.

Between late April and early June a mass exodus occurred. Within eight weeks approximately ten thousand inhabitants fled Boston. Confused, terrified, uncertain as to the state of events, inhabitants gathered what possessions they could. Now refugees, they fled along the crowded roads throughout the surrounding countryside seeking places of refuge. With communication completely broken off between town and country it was "impossible to learn any particulars."[43] Those on the outside knew little of what was actually taking place in the town. Entering or leaving Boston without permission was forbidden, and the "Confusion distress & difficulty of the times" made success in sending letters or reports to those outside intermittent.[44] To this end Nathan Bushnell, a former Connecticut post-rider, joined with Elijah Willoughby in June 1775 to ride "as often as practicable, to Boston, to convey letters" and "other mail."[45] The reports coming out of the town were bleak, leading John Adams in Philadelphia to write to his wife Abigail, in Braintree, the "Description of the Mellancholly of the Town . . . [is] enough to melt a Stone."[46]

The decision whether to stay or remove oneself and one's family from the occupied town was often difficult. In April Simon Tufts wrote to a friend in Medford "that amidst the Confusion distress & difficulty of the times" he still chose to stay in town.[47] Some individuals remained out of necessity, while others chose not to join the evacuation so as to help family, friends, and neighbors. At times the inability to leave provided the opportunity to be of assistance to others. When ordered by his doctor not to go "into the trenches" because of a serious case of diarrhea, James Lovell, a member of the Sons of Liberty, determined the other way to serve was to "tarry" in town even "if 10 Seiges take place" and be of what assistance he could to those in need. He believed his staying to be "a Duty which I owe the Cause & the Friends of it," and he was "perfectly fearless of the Consequences." Thus serving his friends by keeping at bay "a Set of Villains who would willingly destroy what those Friends leave behind them" was to Lovell the only right decision.[48] Fearful of losing all that he had, John Andrews saw no option but to "submit to such living" as Boston now offered, "or risque the little all I have in the world . . . as its said without scruple that those who leave the town, forfeit all the effects they leave behind." In staying, Andrews safeguarded the property of those friends who had departed.[49] Those who joined the evacuation left their community uncertain of what might become of their friends, homes, and businesses. The assurances of General Gage that no pillaging of private property would occur proved little comfort amid such hostility.

As thousands of terrified Bostonians fled the town, Loyalist refugees from throughout Massachusetts, clinging to entry passes issued by the Provincial Congress, poured into Boston seeking refuge in an otherwise hostile world. Many left behind pillaged homes, the remnants of months of persecution from their Whig neighbors. Across the narrow Neck of the Boston peninsula, in the shadow of the town gallows and the fort that British soldiers were busily erecting, both Whig and Tory sympathizers passed. One might only imagine the mixture of anger, resentment, fear, and melancholy that each of them faced as they looked at the thousands around them pulling carts and carrying in their arms and on their backs the few possessions with which they were allowed to depart.[50] "You can have no conception of the distresses [of] the people," wrote one observer. "You'll see parents that are lucky enough to procure papers, with bundles in one hand and a string of children in the other, wandering out of the town . . . not knowing whither they'll go." The previous day he informed a friend, "if I can escape with the skin of my teeth, [I] shall be glad, as I don't expect to be able to take more than a change of apparell with me."[51]

Lives were turned upside down: some would never see their homes again. Others had already experienced the pain and heartbreak of divided families, alienated neighbors, and lost friends. To assist with the crisis the clergy who remained behind aided all whom they could. One congregation that lost its minister "prevailed" upon Reverend Andrew Eliot of the Congregational Fifth Church "to officiate" at their church services.[52] One clergyman advised his flock to consider greater matters at hand. "In the day of prosperity be joyful, but in the day of adversity," he admonished, "consider: God also hath set the one over against the other, to the end that man should find nothing after him."[53] One may only speculate if parishioners found solace in these words, as hopelessness and gloom veiled the port town. Selectman John Scollay informed a fellow town officer that "it is too painfull to attempt to discribe" what was happening to Boston.[54] Capturing the sadness of the moment, Andrew Eliot wrote of "Grass growing in the public walks & streets of this once populous & flourishing place. Shops . . . Shut up business at an end every one in anxiety & distress. . . . I cannot Stand it long."[55]

As the number of citizens leaving Boston increased, approximately two hundred Loyalist tradesmen and merchants, who had earlier pledged their support to Gage, began to question the wisdom of allowing the departure of so many inhabitants.[56] They realized that if only the British army and the Loyalists remained in the town, the rebels sitting on the other side of Boston Neck might not hesitate to burn the town to the ground. The presence of hostages and private property, they argued, assured protection from assault. The merchants and tradesmen pressed Gage with their concerns, even going so far as threatening to abandon him if he did not stop the exodus of the town's inhabitants. Gage knew that he was in a weak position strategically because the Boston peninsula, surrounded by water and connected to the mainland by a thin isthmus, was so easily blockaded.[57] This unpleasant reality perhaps convinced him of the wisdom of the Loyalists' concerns, leading him to disregard the agreement made with the committee of Boston citizens on April 22.[58] Thus by July the *New York Journal* reported that a "number" of Boston's inhabitants were "not permitted to come out on any terms" and those granted passes were denied permission to take any possessions. Gage now became "our Modern Pharaoh" who would "not let the People go," but he faced problems more pressing than his image in rebel newspapers.[59]

One of the reasons the British commander had originally agreed to let the inhabitants of Boston leave was the limited supply of food and necessary provisions available in the town. With supply lines into the town cut off, circumstances in April 1775 were not good, and as the weeks progressed conditions quickly worsened. Some civilians had earlier attempted to lay in a "store of Provision against a Siege," but these provisions went quickly.[60] Vegetables and fresh foods disappeared first. Meat, now rarely available, sold at prohibitive prices and its origins were sometimes questionable. Animal carcasses were "offer'd for sale in the market, which formerly we would not have pick'd up in the street," noted one inhabitant. Food prices soared, making items financially out of the reach of poorer inhabitants and those who now found themselves without income. A threepenny loaf of bread quadrupled in price, the cost of potatoes, butter, and cheese became exorbitant, and milk remained unavailable for months.[61] One newspaper reported in late May that the lack of provisions and consequent suffering of the town's inhabitants was "shocking." A British soldier wrote to his parents, "There is no Market in Boston, the Inhabitants all starving, the soldiers live on salt Provisions" that "rendered" some "unfit for service."[62] In the regimental hospital in Boston fresh meat was provided to wounded soldiers only when absolutely necessary, with salt pork remaining the staple so as to abide by the rationing of food.[63] Under these circumstances attempts were soon being made to find alternatives, including forays and supplies obtained from Loyalist supporters outside of the besieged town.

British soldiers made forays up nearby creeks to try and take sheep and cattle, but the Americans were quick to prevent such activities whenever possible. John Hancock ordered that all livestock be taken from islands in the vicinity.[64] Consequently, the Patriot forces under General Israel Putnam raided Hog Island on May 27. Occasionally British forays proved successful, as in August 1775, when a royal fleet plundered over one hundred head of oxen and approximately eighteen hundred sheep in the vicinity of New London. Gage recorded that this "will be some relief to the troops in general, and of great benefit to the hospitals."[65]

Loyalists living in Boston and the surrounding areas soon found that attempting to supply the besieged community could prove a risky undertaking. A group of Plymouth men smuggling eight hundred barrels of flour into Boston in Nantucket whaling boats were intercepted at sea.[66] A supply sloop bound for Boston in February 1776 was "taken by a small privateer, and carried into Plymouth" by the provincials.[67] Likewise, the plans of Boston merchant Henry Lloyd met with failure. In May 1775 Lloyd proposed to John Stevenson that he freight a two-hundred-ton vessel "with flour for the West Indies commanded by a person" who was trustworthy, as the ship would instead be sailing to Boston. Lloyd would handle the bills through a middleman and arrange the "permit at the light house." Despite precautions and a warning to Stevenson "to write me by conveyance that your letter may not fall into the hands of the provincials," that is exactly what occurred.[68] When called before the Committee of Safety, Stevenson identified Henry Lloyd, claimed that he had not received the letter, and stated that he would "not have executed the order, nor will I execute any order of the kind from any person whatsoever, contrary to the resolves of the Continental Congress, or Provincial Convention." As for Henry Lloyd, the Committee resolved that no constituents should have any "commercial intercourse" with him. That Lloyd was indeed a Loyalist proved true when in March 1776 he sailed with the British fleet for Halifax, Nova Scotia.[69]

Feeding the army soon necessitated that the British government ship food supplies to Boston. General Gage informed the War Office as early as May that the Americans had cut off supplies and that the "only resource we have for Flour, is Quebec." Despite requests, none was forthcoming from the British stationed there. As meat could be found nowhere, "it is Absolutely Necessary," he determined, that "A supply should be Immediately sent to this place as the Troops are increasing, and all the Avenues for procuring Provisions in this Country shut up."[70] Only one vessel sent by the English government ever reached its destination. A ship bound for Boston from Le Havre carrying "beef, hay, potatoes, and turnips" made its journey across the Atlantic only to end up at Barnstable after being captured by four whale boats under the command of a Captain House.[71] Provisioning Boston with food remained a serious problem throughout the siege.

Besides the threat of famine, numerous illnesses and diseases plagued the military and civilian population, including "diarrhea, dysentery, food poisoning, malnutrition, pleuritical disorders, respiratory infections, arthritis, rheumatism, scurvy, and typhoid-typhus." There was also "the added burden of caring for hundreds of seriously wounded men." By far the greatest terror was smallpox. During the previous winter of 1774–1775, a number of the town's inhabitants had contracted the disease and many now feared its return. Throughout the fall and winter General Howe gave orders for the inoculation of soldiers and offered the same to civilians. Despite precautions, by mid-May an outbreak of smallpox erupted and by December it had become virulent. In midsummer dysentery also plagued the population. In one week alone during the month of August "thirty whites and two blacks were buried in the town of Boston."[72]

To care for the civilian and military population, Jonathan Mallett, a hospital surgeon from London, turned the Manufactury House near the King's Chapel and the Old Granary burial ground into a hospital. In late June the workhouse and almshouse also became hospitals. As the number of the sick rapidly increased during the summer months, these hospitals, already overcrowded with the wounded from Charlestown Heights in June, became increasingly overburdened, compounding the problems of inadequate medical supplies and lack of food provisions. A further threat to the growing public health problems was the accumulating waste and filth in the town. Despite orders by General Howe for the streets and camps to be kept clean, and the employment of blacks in the town "in cleaning the streets," the sanitation problems never abated during the siege.[73]

To help "lessen the opportunity for contagion" and reduce the number of mouths already dependent on a small food supply, General Howe permitted several hundred inhabitants to leave the town in July and August. Fearing that these refugees might be carriers of smallpox, the Patriots escorted them to Salem instead of the Continental Army camp at Cambridge. In Salem they were cared for accordingly in the hospital and in homes left vacant.[74] With the town's resources still overburdened, during the last week of November General Howe sent three hundred of the town's poorest men, women, and children to Chelsea without anything to subsist on. The poor souls were "destitute almost of everything. . . . one of them was dead, and two more expiring, and the whole in the most miserable and piteous condition." General Washington sent assistance to them but forbade them to come to Cambridge for fear "of their communicating the small-pox, as it is rife in Boston." Another three hundred inhabitants crossed the Neck in early December, and in January General Gage released another five hundred men, women, and children from the distressed town.[75]

Rumors that had previously circulated concerning alleged attempts by Gage to deliberately send smallpox victims into the Continental Army and civilian population of Massachusetts suddenly seemed true when "sworn testimony" by a refugee appeared in the *Boston Gazette* in February 1776. As one historian points out, "A more plausible explanation is that [Howe] simply allowed Boston's civilians to come out indiscriminately and let the Patriots worry about any difficulties they might present."[76] Considering the desperate situation—inadequate food and medical supplies, problems controlling the civilian population, tensions between soldiers and residents—this is most likely, especially when the extremely weak strategic position of the British is taken into account.[77]

Although the oppressive heat of summer contributed to the crisis at hand, understandably many feared the onset of the "cold season" for the "complete . . . state of misery and distress it would bring."[78] Both military journals and personal letters complain of the biting cold and dampness during the winter months. As he sat by the fireside, William Carter experienced great difficulty writing a letter home on December 31. "The cold is so intense," he explained, "that the ink freezes in the pen whilst I write."[79] The shortage of housing for barracks meant that in December amid snow and biting winds a number of soldiers still lived in tents on Boston Common.[80] In a calculated act of survival British soldiers received orders to tear down old buildings, fences, and ropewalks to provide firewood. There was also the need for cooking fuel. As early as August soldiers had been under order to raid the cellars of houses for "washing tubs, empty casks, and all the wood they could find to make fire and cook with." This included collecting wood from the ruins of Charlestown.[81] By September they "Began taking down houses at the South end, to build a new line of Works," and orders were issued to take down "the old North meeting house and 100 old wooden dwelling houses and other buildings to make use of for fuel."[82] One deserter informed newspapers outside Boston that the mill bridge, the draw bridge, and the wooden pavements were taken for firewood. Selectman Timothy Newell watched his barn and wharf "pulled down by order of General Robinson" and carried off for fuel.[83] The wood garnered from the destruction of public and private properties still proved inadequate. In December those soldiers who were deemed "fittest" and knew how to use an axe were put to work dismantling more "Wharfs, houses, [and] old Ships" and cutting down "trees" until the "Garrison" had adequate fuel. Those undertaking this job were "allow'd 5 Shill[ings] Sterl[in]g for each Cord" they collected and stacked.[84]

Amidst the chaos and suffering inhabitants lived in constant fear of alarms as the Continental Army continued to cannonade the town. "We are frequently Serenaded here with 13 Inch Mortars and 24 Pounders," wrote one Loyalist.[85] During the month of August 1775, from their fortifications at Roxbury, the Patriots were able to throw "cannon shot and some bomb shells" into Boston every day. Captain Pawlett, while standing in the guard room at Boston Neck eating breakfast, lost his leg when an eighteen-pound ball came through the building. By October the American troops were throwing "their Shot, beyond the Hay Market" and injuring "the South part of the Town."[86] Both sides worked at a constant pace strengthening redoubts and erecting new ones, transforming Boston and the surrounding countryside as they went. Where beautiful country and "pleasure gardens" once appeared, "nothing but fortifications now rise to our view," wrote a British lieutenant.[87] The horror and desolation of the war was equaled only by "the Havock made by the pestilence."[88]

Throughout the siege inhabitants both inside and outside Boston expressed understandable concern as to the protection of their property. Between late April 1775 and March 1776, when the Continental Army marched into Boston, reports circulated outside the town by newspaper, letter, and word of mouth as to the destruction of property from cannonading, soldiers, and fire. The deserted houses of those who had fled the British occupation were particularly easy targets for marauding soldiers and civilians.[89] General Gage and General Howe both issued repeated orders against robbery and vandalism, and the latter ordered that no persons were to enter any of the houses in town without "leave from the Proprietor" or the person "in Charge unless permission be granted on proper application."[90] Punishments were severe. Court-martialed in early 1776, the "private soldier" Thomas McMahon and his wife Isabella were found guilty "for receiving sundry Stoln goods knowing them to be such." He "receive[d] 1000 Lashes on the bare back with a Cat of Nine Tails," and she "100 Lashes on the bare back at a Cart's tail in different portions in the most conspicuous part of the Town." Both were "imprison'd for 3 Months." For stealing goods and having "forceably enter'd a dwelling house," two other soldiers received "800 Lashes each." Stealing "a piece of Linen" and "a Shirt" from a shopkeeper brought another individual "500 Lashes." Perhaps some stole for food, as when two privates took "a Quantity of Flour" in August from a town shopkeeper, but others simply committed acts of violence. When soldier Timothy Spillman assaulted one Mrs. Moore, "beating her almost to death," he, too, "receive[d] 1000 Lashes." No doubt private John Henesy and his wife Ann, accused of "having broken open a house" and committing theft, breathed a sigh of relief when the military court found them innocent.[91] Despite severe punishments, the temptation to steal from unprotected houses and stores overwhelmed some. Sheriff Loring and the provost carried their plunder to the prison-house, where, in plain view of all of the prisoners, they proceeded to hold a "(mock) vendue" with the sheriff as the auctioneer and the provost, his son, and a prison guard as the bidders.[92] Thus, threat of punishment did not necessarily act as a deterrent, and plunder and vandalism represented an ongoing problem.

British Regulars were not the only plunderers, as indicated by the notice placed in the *Boston Gazette* by the Committee of Safety. There were those who took "Advantage of the Confusions occasioned by the Battles of Lexington and Charlestown" by looting and plundering "sundry Goods and Household furniture, belonging to some of the unhappy sufferers of Boston and Charlestown." The Committee sent notices to officers in a number of towns describing stolen goods and asking assistance in returning these goods to "the true and rightful Proprietors."[93] Meanwhile, Loyalists who had taken refuge in Boston with British troops knew by midsummer of 1775 that the Massachusetts Provincial Congress had begun to confiscate their unprotected property.[94]

Natural disasters also took their toll on public and private property. A fierce December storm severely damaged many houses and even blew some down, but fire presented the gravest of threats.[95] At approximately eight-thirty on the morning of May 17, 1775, a fire broke out and spread quickly along the docks, destroying a great number of buildings. Close to thirty stores burned to the ground, some of which contained food supplies, including fifty barrels of flour. Upon the discovery of the fire the chaos that ensued turned what could have been a relatively minor occurrence into a serious matter. "Instead of ringing the bells as usual, the soldiers beat to arms, by which the people were in great confusion, not being used to such signal in time of fire." To make matters worse the men could not find the fire engines, which "were in possession of the General, who had some time before seized them." By the time the fire engines were in place the conflagration had been raging for three hours. Even when the engines arrived, the delay continued as the newly appointed captains and military firewards didn't know how to command or how to obey in such an emergency. As one observer pointed out, had this fire occurred in the middle of town,

Boston would soon have been laid to ashes.[96] Conflicting reports circulated outside of town with no one certain as to the exact nature of events or the consequences. "There has been a great fire at Boston last night," one civilian wrote to a friend, "but don't yet learn the particulars but in generall that it broke out near draw-bridge & consumed many buildings; some say 30, some say 100, oh poor Boston!"[97] By winter General Howe presented the town with strict orders to be observed by all in the case of fire. Bells were to ring, but not for longer than a quarter of an hour, and he expected all inhabitants to show up at the fire with their buckets. To this end, soldiers collected fire buckets from deserted houses and distributed them to those residents who did not have any. The orders required inhabitants to obey firewards and engine masters at all times, and paid "a premium of twenty shillings sterling" to the first engine at the scene of the fire.[98] Fortunately, fire did not break out again in Boston until the end of the siege as Washington's forces moved to take the town, but the May fire proved extensive enough to leave its mark on the community in physical, financial, and psychological damage.

Although daily life challenged the very fiber of those inhabitants still trapped in the city, their responses were often ones of resistance and not resignation. This was the case of those who found themselves imprisoned by the British for suspicious activities, as in the case of a father, son, daughter, and maid who were charged with "blowing up [flares] in the evening, . . . [and] giving signals this way to the army without.[99] James Lovell, who had remained behind to assist "the Cause" when his doctor forbade him to go "into the trenches," John Leach, and Peter Edes, the son of the *Boston Gazette* printer Benjamin, who was now residing in Watertown, found themselves imprisoned in June 1775 on various charges of subversive activities against the enemy. Confronted in his father's printing office one morning, Edes made a quick escape out the back door pursued by three officers and a group of sailors until he found himself at the receiving end of an officer's cutlass. After numerous threats and insults they hauled him off to prison.[100] Ten days later Edes acquired two cell mates, John Leach and James Lovell. No "court of inquiry" was held, but one month later they happened "by chance" to learn their crimes when informed by a guard.[101] Edes was charged with "concealing fire arms," Leach for "being a spy, and suspected of taking plans," and Lovell of "being a Spy, and giving intelligence to the Rebels." Three weeks later, John Gill, printer and partner of Peter Edes's father, became a cell mate for "printing sedition, treason . . . libel."[102] Edes and Leach remained in prison for over three months, during two of which they subsisted on bread and water. They were allotted only one hour of fresh air daily when guards opened the cell door. Malnutrition, unsanitary conditions compounded by the summer heat, and close confinement made illness and disease a constant threat. One half of the prisoners brought in during the summer of 1775 died.[103] Visitors received a shower of such "Oaths, Curses, Debauchery, and the most horrid Blasphemy, Committed by the Provost Marshal, his Deputy and Soldiers . . . Soldier prisoners, and sundry soldier Women" that the few times the Marshal permitted Leach's wife and son to visit he was hesitant about encouraging them to return.[104]

While in jail Leach witnessed the imprisonment of inhabitants for offenses of questionable authenticity and numerous incidents of abusive treatment of other civilian prisoners. On August 17, soldiers seized and imprisoned an elderly Dutchman, a baker by the name of Hyster, "for Complaining of the soldiers for Robbing his Garden, which was his whole living." As he did not have a dollar to pay a required fee when discharged, "the soldiers on Guard were ordered, Each to give him a kick as he went away." Various prisoners kept for different periods of time without food or water were discharged after paying fees and falling on their "knees to the Provost in the yard" to say "God bless the King." If the prisoner did not have specie, goods were accepted, both of which seem to have stayed in the personal possession of the provost and guards. One prisoner, James Dickey, paid with a pistareen and a silver brooch. The pistareen found its way into a guard's pocket, and the brooch into the possession of the provost.[105]

In reality all Bostonians were prisoners, trapped in a town under siege with a hostile occupying army. This made them essentially helpless in preventing physical and psychological abuse, the plundering of their homes and possessions, and the destruction of their town. The inherent tensions experienced by captive and captor alike could become explosive, finding its release in pranks, mischief, and violence between inhabitants and soldiers. Sometimes the innocent found themselves as scapegoats, as did one unfortunate black man whom the provost viciously caned for pushing his wheelbarrow in the middle of the street instead of on the side.[106] While under martial law "No Man dared now to be seen talking to his friend in the Street," wrote Abigail Adams to her husband in Philadelphia, adding that "they were obliged to be within every evening at ten o clock . . . nor could any inhabitant walk any street in Town after that time without a pass."[107] As one civilian noted, "All the sufferings of the poor for the want of provisions were not equal to the dreadful scorn, derision and contempt from [the Tories]."[108] Concurrent with these troubles, civilians and soldiers alike endured the bombardments of the town by General Washington's forces.

Beginning in March 1776, the Continental Army sharply increased its cannonading of Boston, hoping to divert British attention while building fortifications at crucial points surrounding the town. In Braintree, Abigail Adams recorded sleepless nights. On Sunday, March 2, she "went to bed after twelve, but got no rest: the cannon continued firing, and my heart beat pace with them all night."[109] The attack finally ceased Monday morning, but "soon after candlelight, came on a most terrible bombardment and cannonade, on both sides, as if heaven and earth were engaged." Selectman Timothy Newell noted extensive damage occurring to several houses when "Five or six 18 and 24 lb. shot struck." Some inhabitants and soldiers sustained injuries, including a young boy found with a broken leg. The following night was once again a sleepless one for Abigail, who went to bed at midnight and got up one hour later. "I could no more sleep," she noted, "than if I had been in the engagement; the rattling of the windows, the jar of the house, the continual roar of twenty-four-pounders, and the bursting of shells" was, she believed, slowly leaving Boston in ruins. Adding to the terror of the constant bombardment, fire broke out.[110] Amid the deluge of shells and cannon fire, inhabitants and soldiers fought to extinguish the flames. The town sustained extensive physical damage from the cannonading and the fire, but no casualties resulted.[111]

"Blessed be God our redemption draws nigh," recorded selectman Timothy Newell in his journal on March 5, 1776, when he woke to see the Continental Army camped on Dorchester Heights overlooking Boston.[112] As destructive as the American diversion had been to the town, it enabled General Washington to accomplish his goal of retaking Boston. Now Continental soldiers, heavy artillery, and fortifications sat commanding town and harbor. Plagued by discontent among his soldiers, Loyalists demanding protection of their lives and property, no news from England in months, and now American forces strategically camped on Dorchester Heights, General Howe made the decision to evacuate Boston.[113] He granted permission to the selectmen John Scollay, Timothy Newell, Samuel Austin, and Thomas Marshall to leave and seek an agreement of cease-fire from Washington. In turn, Howe would agree not to burn Boston to the ground.[114] This agreement no doubt spared Boston an even worse fate than it had already undergone. The British began preparation for departure.

For the Patriots trapped in Boston during the past eleven months the final week proved particularly taxing. What order previously existed all but collapsed as looters, both Loyalists and British Regulars, quickly took advantage of the opportunity at hand. John Andrews found caring for his friends' possessions proved increasingly difficult as the "wantonness and destruction made by the soldiers" increased daily. At times he found this period more fatiguing and perplexing than any other during the siege. He made daily rounds "without any cessation, and scarce ever fail'd of finding depredations made upon some one or other of [his friends' properties]." Finally he hired several men to sleep in the homes and stores for the two weeks the evacuation took place, but was outraged at the exorbitant rate they charged for such services. Still, Andrews lost some of his possessions and some of those of his friends.[115] General Howe's strict orders that any soldier "caught plundering, will be hanged on the Spot," seemed forgotten during the closing days of occupation. Soldiers pillaged evacuated houses, destroyed furniture, and looted stores.[116]

Bands of Loyalists, led by Crean Brush, also engaged in pillage. Brush, a New York Tory, mercilessly abused his position of authority during the last days of the occupation. In October 1775, General Gage had commissioned Brush "to receive for safe keeping such goods as the people might voluntarily intrust to him," if they chose to leave Boston, as he did not want any goods that could possibly aid the rebels being taken from the town. General Howe renewed this commission on March 10, 1776, to prevent the American forces from acquiring any goods of the departing Loyalists that might assist them after the British evacuation. Howe ordered that all Loyalists should deliver their possessions to Brush, who in turn would issue a certificate and place the goods on board one of the British vessels. Loyalists not abiding by the ruling were considered as "abettors of rebels." Brush used this commission to ransack stores and homes of Whig inhabitants, whether occupied or not. To the joy of Bostonians, "that *cursed* villain, Crean Brush," was later captured by an American brig, "with [a] great part of the plunder he rob'd."[117]

Finally, on March 17 the British departed with more than nine hundred Loyalists, a number of them Bostonians.[118] They included a wide variety of individuals traveling in families and alone. Just as royal officials, merchants, doctors, lawyers, and clergymen fled, so did artisans, shopkeepers, widows, and laborers.[119] A few later returned, such as John Gore, father of the future Massachusetts governor and senator, after spending nine years in exile. Most were not welcome.[120] To this end Massachusetts passed a Banishment Act in 1778, "to prevent the return to this state of certain persons."[121] Confiscation of Loyalist property left little for most to return to in any event. How many knew that cold, blustery winter's day in March as they sailed away from Boston harbor that they were saying good-bye to homes, friends, and sometimes family forever?

Three days after Howe's departure on March 17, 1776, with "drums beating and colors flying" several regiments of the Continental Army marched across the Neck and into Boston to the tune of "Yankee Doodle Dandy." As the American soldiers "traversed the town from end to end," former hostages threw open their doors and windows to gaze upon the victorious army. Lingering fears of smallpox did not prevent people from crowding into the town seeking friends and loved ones. Those long separated shared "tender interviews" and "fond embraces." Despite the joy the townspeople demonstrated over their liberation from the British, a "melancholy gloom" caused by the horrors of the preceding months hung in the air.[122] The conditions under which the men, women, and children had lived during the occupation evidenced themselves in the bleak surroundings. A surgeon in one of the regiments noted the "deplorable desolation and wretchedness."[123] Although the retaking of Boston had not cost the "river of Blood" expected by Abigail Adams, it had exacted a heavy price in physical and emotional suffering.[124]

Bostonians dispossessed of their homes for eleven months now returned to the town anxious to survey the damage of the British occupation, reclaim their homes, resume their day-to-day routines, and attempt to pick up the pieces of their lives. The scene that lay before them was one of widespread devastation. The community lay in shambles. Many homes were unrecognizable. Instead of the season's bounty, gardens boasted weeds. Fences were missing, doors and window shutters swung loose on their hinges, and paint peeled from the walls of deserted, formerly elegant homes. Some lots glared emptily at their owners, the houses and outbuildings torn down. In the South End some inhabitants found fortifications where their houses once stood, and in the North End others found their homes turned into barracks. Old South Meeting House, converted into a riding school by General Howe, now stood an empty shell, and West Church stood without its steeple, another victim of the demand for firewood. A number of churches suffered the wear from serving as barracks and barns. The British had fortified so many streets as to make the town "almost impregnable." Artillery carts, powder wagons, and other abandoned military supplies lay about the streets and occupied public buildings. Limbs of trees from the Common were strewn across the principal entries to the town, animal dung littered main streets, and caltrops, iron balls covered in spikes to injure the feet of horses and men, had been scattered along the roads to prevent an American pursuit at the time of British evacuation. In the houses standing along the main road into town and near major fortifications soldiers found "loaded Shells with trains of Powder covered with straw." For returning Bostonians these reminders of military occupation, "the empty lots where houses had once stood, untended gardens, the broken windows, the silent empty stores and windswept docks," surely brought grief and anger.[125]

Personal property loss and damage ran into enormous sums of money for some. Not only were houses and stores destroyed, but in some instances the fleeing British "destroyed the furniture of the houses, broke the windows, chairs, desks, tables, &c. They loaded their vessels so deep that they threw overboard much of their lumber, which floats on the water."[126] A general merchant who had escaped to Woburn returned to find his store completely ransacked and all of the merchandise carried off. To help recover some of his financial losses he advertised in the *New England Chronicle* for all debtors to make speedy payment. Houses occupied by the generals, other high-ranking officers, and wealthy Loyalists received far better treatment than those occupied by the Regulars. Many suffered great losses, however. Eldad Taylor, an "eye witness" to the last days of occupation and the evacuation, wrote to his wife on March 18 that "The selectmen say the town is in a most dreadful condition; houses torn, streets nasty, [the] town empty."[127]

In March 1776 Boston was a war-torn community weakened economically, physically, politically, and socially. The community lay in a physical shambles, denuded of people, and with a warped and almost extinct economic and social life. When Bostonians began to assess the physical destruction wrought by the occupation and siege, the cost to repair and rebuild their town was measurable. By contrast the psychological damage suffered by those torn from family, friends, homes, and businesses that perhaps had taken a lifetime to build was incalculable.

One year earlier, in the spring and summer of 1775 when Bostonians began to flee the occupied town, some believed that within a short period of time they would be safely back in their homes. To this end they remained in close proximity to Boston, choosing to settle in Braintree, Weymouth, and Watertown, which became the capital of Massachusetts and home of the Provincial Congress for the duration of the siege. Others went farther afield or departed the Bay Colony for New Hampshire, Rhode Island, Connecticut, or New York. If they had the means to do so, men and women continued in their trades, as did Polly and Lucy Allen, who performed all "Kinds of Millinery and Mantuamaking" at their new residence in

Providence.[128] William Dall, an employee of the public schools in Boston for several years, started a "Writing & Arithmetick" school in New Haven in June 1775. By October of the same year he was thanking the local residents for their support and opening a second school that offered evening classes. Thomas Tileston, Boston hatmaker, established himself in Windham, while James Lamb and Son from Boston opened a dry goods shop in Middletown. One young Bostonian "who was educated by one of the most eminent School-Masters in that Place" offered to set up a school in any town in the neighborhood of Hartford, where the public so desired him to do. Numerous advertisements such as these and Peter Verstille's, addressed to "old friends and customers," suggest that sizable emigrant communities probably existed in these towns.[129]

The Provincial Congress ordered that towns not treat Boston's refugees as wandering poor, and newspapers throughout New England requested that people assist those who had left "their unhappy Situations in the Town of Boston." People were urged to "rent their Houses," help the refugees "with Teams for their Removal, Provisions for their Support, & all other Necessaries upon as easy and cheap terms as they can possibly Afford."[130] Fortunate individuals found the means to secure a living, a residence of their own, or a home to share with others. The less fortunate roamed from town to town, refugees of the ensuing war. By July of 1775 it became increasingly difficult to find a house to rent in most areas close to Boston, and many homes essentially became barracks as people opened their doors to two or three additional families. "Every Town is fill'd with the distressd inhabitants of Boston," Abigail Adams informed her husband John. "It would make your heart ake to see what difficulties and distresses the poor Boston people are driven to."[131] William Dall and James Lamb eventually returned to Boston, but many others like Polly and Lucy Allen did not.[132]

Permanently severed from their homes and community were the more than nine hundred Bostonians who departed with the

British for Halifax, Nova Scotia. Their exodus truly defined the nature of the bloody conflict as a civil war. Whether the reason was political allegiance to the Crown or fear of persecution, most did not return to Boston. Confiscation of Loyalist property under the Massachusetts Banishment Act of 1778 left little for most to return to in any case. Royal officials, merchants, doctors, lawyers, and clergymen fled. High social standing or substantial economic position in the community did not always characterize the Boston Loyalist, whose numbers included tradesmen and artisans such as tailors, carters, housewrights, barbers, and blacksmiths. Families, friends, bachelors, widows, and spinsters piled onto the British ships. Cast from their homeland how many realized that a large majority of them would spend their lives as refugees, forgotten by the Crown and rebuked by the Americans?[133]

Whether the final destination was Nova Scotia, New Hampshire, or Connecticut, in the exodus from Boston thousands left behind family, friends, homes, jobs, businesses, and a lifetime of memories. The disruption brought about by the events of 1775 and 1776 tore the social fabric of the community and seriously disrupted the town's morale. For Bostonians the closing two decades of the eighteenth century would mark a period of readjustment and rebuilding of their lives and their community. In the shattered remains of Boston, a new town would begin to take shape. It would be a town built upon the efforts of inhabitants who had survived the siege, those who were forced out by the British occupation and who found the strength and resolve to return and begin anew, and a large number of new citizens, who would arrive from many different places seeking new opportunities. Together they would participate in the rebirth of New England's most important and vital urban center. Though damaged by the British occupation, the town was not dead. In 1776, the town was just beginning to start over.

2

The Character of
the Town

EACH PASSING DAY AND MONTH brought more Bostonians back to
their homes, and in the ensuing years the seaport town drew a host
of new faces. Seven months after the end of the siege, William Bant
reported to John Hancock in Philadelphia that "Town Matters
begin to wear a better face" since "many of the Inhabitants have
lately returned."[1] Despite the shock of witnessing the destruction
wrought by the occupation and siege, some felt relieved that matters were not worse. In writing to her husband in late March 1776,
Abigail Adams noted the "abominable Ravages" committed upon
Boston, but still believed that "the Town in General is left in a
better state than we expected."[2] In order to determine the extent of
the damage and the losses to the town's people, "Sixty Persons"

were "chosen, as a Committee Five for each Ward," to walk and survey the town.[3] The men walked through narrow congested streets, along country lanes, past churches, taverns, docks, and shops. They passed closely set weatherboarded wooden buildings with shingled roofs, brick houses set on spacious lots, gardens, barns, and pastures. Many of the winding crooked streets and lanes they walked eventually found their way to the wharves and ship-yards, the symbols of this seafaring commercial town. As the men looked in public buildings, knocked on doors, and stopped to talk to fellow townsmen, much of what they saw would have been recognizable to their fathers, grandfathers, and perhaps even great-grandfathers. Still retaining much of its seventeenth-century character more than a hundred years later, the community represented one of visual continuity with its past. Change to the built landscape was barely perceptible until the closing years of the 1790s.

Almost twenty years after the devastation of the Port Act and the siege had finally passed, one visitor to the bustling port was reminded of "an old-fashioned town in England." In thinking about his homeland, he went on to liken Philadelphia to London, New York to Liverpool, and Boston to Bristol.[4] The wider streets, the "houses better in style," and the "broad footways" of New York "paved with a curb to separate them from the road" put him much more in mind of a city than did Boston, where many streets remained unpaved, simply "pitched with pebbles," and only a "post and gutter" separating the footway from the roadway.[5] During the winter season these narrow, poorly paved, dirt thoroughfares often became quagmires presenting many problems, especially when they were "rendered in some places almost impassable . . . by the large drifts of snow."[6] But overall, travelers commented favorably on Boston, despite its provincialism when compared to New York or Philadelphia. "We have been very much pleased with Boston [for] the situation is beautiful . . . the town is irregularly built but there are many fine situations for gentlemans houses," wrote Barbara Vaughn in a letter to a friend during her travels in 1785.[7]

Throughout its 150 years of existence Boston had grown organically, shaping itself to the natural topography with winding narrow streets and alleyways, having no particular plan or organization. At the time of settlement, the need for defense determined the community's location on the peninsula. Rapid growth, almost seven thousand people between 1630 and 1690, played a role in fostering this irregular development. Seventeenth-century townsmen laid out the town based on "English precedent." The absence of town planning and minimal innovation in building practices during the seventeenth and eighteenth centuries created a town in the "late medieval tradition of the City of London."[8] The town existed for almost sixty years before inhabitants officially began naming the streets. Streets were known instead by such descriptions as "the High wayes from Jacob Eliots Barne to the fardest gate bye Roxsbery Towns end" or "The broad Street or Way from the Old Fortification on the Neck, leading into the Town as far as the late Deacon Eliot's corner." Finally in the late 1790s, inhabitants began to "conceive [that] the public convenience would be greatly promoted, by the placing of sign boards at the corners of the Streets, Lanes, Alleys, Courts & Squares."[9] As the town matured in the eighteenth century it retained this medieval ambience. Despite its position as a major port town in the Anglo-American community, limited geographical access fostered the community's provincial qualities.

Boston stood on the Shawmut Peninsula, an irregularly shaped landmass of less than one thousand acres, "at the bottom of Massachusetts Bay," joined to the mainland by a narrow isthmus referred to as "the Neck." The nearly thirteen thousand Bostonians dwelling there in 1784 divided their peninsula into three geographic regions, the West End, South End, and North End, which collectively consisted of twelve wards. The distance from the town gate on the Neck to the most northerly point of the peninsula, the

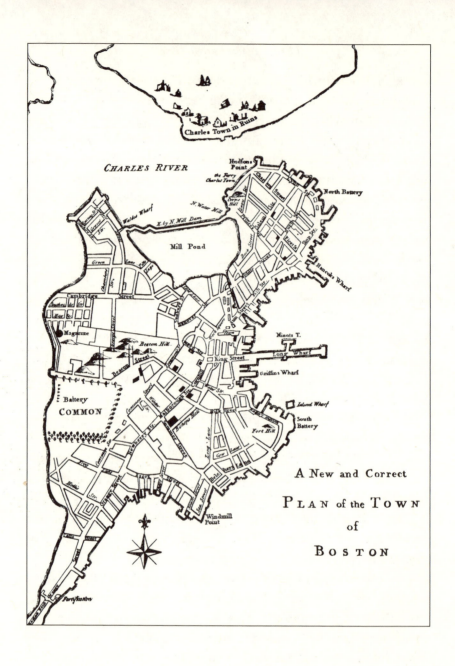

Boston in 1789.
(*Boston City Directory, 1789*, published by John Norman.)

North End district, was approximately two miles. At its widest point, from Barton's Point east to Fort Hill, the peninsula's breadth was approximately one and one-quarter miles.[10]

Just beyond the Neck, the wharves that jutted from the land along the northern, eastern, and southern shoreline began at the southernmost point of the peninsula with Gibbons Wharf. On the western side lay Roxbury Flats, dry at low tide, and the Charles River. The South End comprised the largest area of land, from the old fortification gates on the Neck north to Mill Creek, which marked the beginning of the North End. It included Boston Common in the west and spread eastward to Fort Hill. On the western side of the peninsula, north of Boston Common, rose the three-domed mountain named Trimountain. From this topographic landmark west to the Charles River and north to the Mill Pond lay the West End, a rural area with relatively few dwellings during most of the eighteenth century. By comparison, the North End was the most densely packed region of the entire peninsula.[11]

The north bank of Mill Creek marked the boundary to this district, which was accessible by two bridges, one on Middle Street and the other on Ann Street. Here, in the northeastern tip of the town, sat Copp's Hill, from where one could command a view of Charlestown. Before the building of the Charles River Bridge in 1786 and the West Boston Bridge in 1793, the only access to Boston besides traveling by land across the Neck was by water. Both ferry services in the town, the Charlestown Ferry and the Winnisimmet Ferry, docked in the North End.

The twelve wards, which had existed since 1735, served municipal and civic purposes. The first division of the town into districts occurred during the 1630s by order of the General Court for the purpose of keeping a watch consisting of "a trainband, a constable, and a tithing-man."[12] In 1662 five wards existed, and by 1715 Boston's inhabitants voted to divide their town into "Eight distinct Wards for purposes of inspection." Finally in 1735 the townspeople requested the Overseers of the Poor "to Divide the Town into Twelve Wards." In 1630, the wards served the primary objective of military protection. Over time they took on greater importance as administrative divisions for such purposes as allocation of poor relief and fire engines, and assignment of police officers, tax assessors, and various other public officials whose job consisted of monitoring a specific ward.[13] Wards 1 through 5 comprised the North End, Ward 7 the West End, and the remaining wards the South End. Within the South End Wards 6, 8, and the northernmost edge of 9 constituted the central business district of the town. What was the appearance and character of late-eighteenth-century Boston?

Boston Neck

Reaching the town of Boston by land before the building of the Charles River Bridge in 1786 meant crossing the swampy, mile-long, fifty-yard-wide isthmus that connected the peninsula to the mainland.[14] All those seeking access to the town who did not arrive by oceangoing vessel made their way along this "bleak unpleasant road" or took the Charlestown ferry, which one traveler found "not a pleasant alternative."[15] Barbara Vaughn found this singular "way out of the city" by land the "one very unpleasing circumstance respecting Boston."[16] Boston Neck, "soggy at high tide and spray-blown in a storm," could prove a fatal crossing during inclement weather.[17] Violent "Winds and Waves" pounded the land and sometimes destroyed the roadway during winter storms. The land lay so low that spring tides washed across the rough road, preventing carriages from passing, and spring rains often forced horses pulling wagons and carriages to traverse the dangerous road knee deep in water.[18] For over 150 years this dreary stretch of land in the South End had offered a less-than-welcome entrance to Boston. Except for cows grazing on portions of the marshland it was a deso-

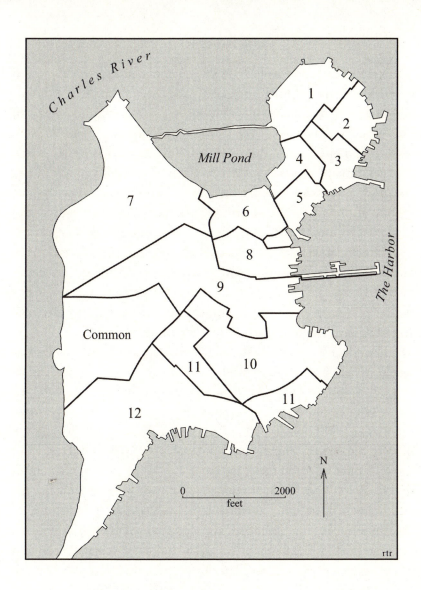

Boston ward map in 1775.
(Rendered by Robert Richardson, 2004.)

late strip of ground, broken only by a few native trees, the town gallows, and the old fortification.

The brick fortification, with a "deep ditch on the side next [to] the Neck," had two gates, one for foot passengers and one for carriages. First built soon "after the settlement of the town," the fortification initially afforded protection from "any sudden attack by the Indians." After hostilities ceased, it fell into disrepair and was not rebuilt until 1710, when a "more substantial" wall of "stone and brick, with a breast work of earth and proper gates" was completed. In 1760 the town again repaired and enlarged the "Fortification Gates."[19] The fortifications built by the British during their occupation of Boston in 1775–1776 added further defensive structures to the narrow strip of land.[20] Eventually the gates fell into disrepair and finally the town destroyed the remaining ruins.

The town government found profitable uses for the Neck's deserted stretch of low-lying marshlands. Before the 1790s, with a few exceptions, the town used it primarily as grazing land. At different times inhabitants offered proposals for use of the Neck to town officials, as did Hugh Floyd and Jonathan Hall in 1763 when they made a request to rent the land for making "Brick and Tyle." But the selectmen rejected the proposal as not being "for the benefit of the Town."[21] The Neck, therefore, remained grazing land for another eleven years until town officials made use of the area during the economically and politically trying decade of the 1770s. Following the Boston Port Act in 1774, the Committee of Ways and Means selected the site to "lay out a Brick Yard" to employ the needy in "the making of Bricks" to raise funds for the purchase of food and other necessities.[22]

The town leased land on the Neck to Bostonians and nonresidents as a way of generating revenue. During the late 1770s two men from Newton rented marshy pastures for grazing animals. Captain Fellow, a Boston resident, leased some of the town land for "Bull Pasture" during the early 1780s.[23] Outside the city gates on

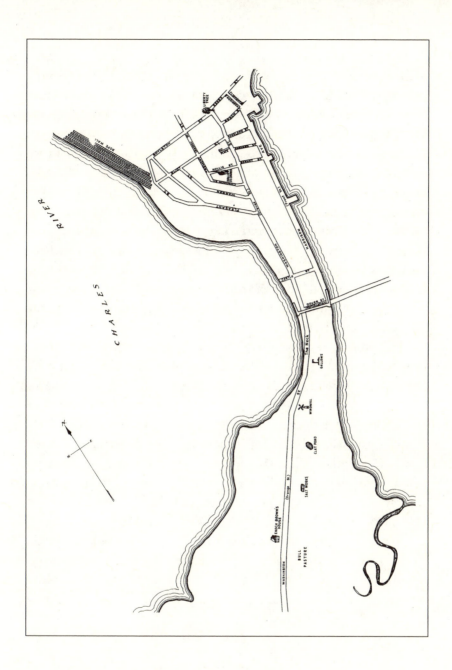

Boston Neck.
(Map by L. A. Chisholm, in Annie H. Thwing, *The Crooked and Narrow Streets of the Town of Boston*, Boston, 1920.)

the southeast side of the Neck, two townsmen held a ninety-nine-year lease on a piece of land where the selectmen permitted them to build a small house and a wharf, as long as they also built and kept in good repair a seawall to help protect the Neck.[24] However, officials disallowed other uses. When a resident of Westman inquired as to renting some of this town grazing land to "build a Dwelling House and a Coopers Shop," the selectmen refused.[25] Excluding the rented land, the selectmen permitted only town cattle on the Neck. Joshua Sever, caretaker of town lands, had the responsibility of enforcing this order, a difficult assignment.[26] The Roxbury cows were no respecters of borders, and they liked Boston Common. Finally in 1784 the selectmen appointed a man "to stand upon the Neck and prevent the Cows coming from Roxbury into the Commons of this Town."[27]

Individuals trespassing on the Neck, either by tearing up the ground, leaving "Incumbrances or Nuisances" there, or firing guns, faced prosecution. Despite the 1786 renewal of a town bylaw dating back to 1713 that carried the punishment of a twenty-shilling fine and seizure of the firearms, unlawful use of "guns or pistols" on the Neck continued.[28] This illegal sport flourished during the warm summer months. The law forbade the shooting of firearms throughout the entire town because of the obvious dangers to inhabitants, but the distant proximity of the Neck to the densely settled parts of town made it a place where an offender risked less chance of detection. In an attempt to ensure enforcement, the selectmen hired various men to patrol the area, but eventually ordered constable Shubael Hews to "notice and inform" them of offenders. Problems persisted as long as the Neck remained desolate and virtually uninhabited.[29]

The South End

Walking northward from Boston Neck in the direction of the Back Bay, one passed through sparsely inhabited countryside before reaching Boston Common, "a pleasant green field, with a gradual ascent from the seashore, till it ends in Beacon Hill."[30] On the Common's forty-five acres cows grazed, children played, and residents strolled on warm summer evenings beneath the avenues of trees planted along the eastern periphery called the Mall.[31] One female traveler in 1785 found the Mall to be "the best on the continent."[32] From here was a "pleasing prospect" of the Charles River, which bordered the bottom side of the Common, and "hills" rising "gradually on the western side."[33]

The town permitted residents to graze cows on this public land for a small fee, which went to support the upkeep of the town bulls.[34] Carriages, chaises, carts, and horses frequently cut across the Common, and sometimes even the burying ground on the southern side, "to the detriment of the Land & diminishing of the feed." Finally the selectmen determined to fence both the burying ground and the Common, and place rails around the trees.[35] In a contemporary print rendered in approximately 1800, Tremont Street Mall has the appearance of a country lane, with trees and fencing lining the left side of the road, marking the entrance to the Common.[36] The scales located on the Common for farmers to bring their cartloads of hay for weighing, the grazing cows, wooden fences, dirt roads, scattered dwellings, taverns, and shops "gave a bucolic air to the region."[37]

From the late 1780s onward the South End received increased attention from town officials and inhabitants. Townspeople made attempts to turn the causeway leading onto the Neck into a highway of sorts by planting trees on the sides of the road.[38] In 1789, Bostonians named this entryway into the town Washington Street in honor of the route President Washington traveled during his visit to the town. Beyond the former site of the old fortification, Washington became Orange Street, the main thoroughfare across much of the peninsula. It continued to traverse the peninsula first as New-

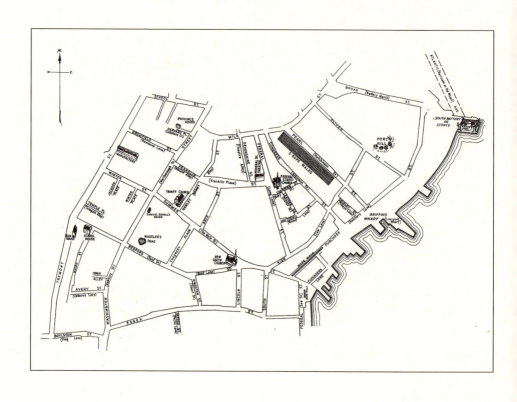

The South End.
(Map by L. A. Chisholm, in Annie H. Thwing, *The Crooked and Narrow Streets of the Town of Boston*. Boston, 1920.)

bury, then Marlborough, then Cornhill, finally ending at the central location of Dock Square.

To further incorporate the South End into the town proper, the town meeting voted in March 1788 to rename streets and assign names to those that were unidentified.[39] For example, the road formerly referred to as running "from Orange Street Westerly by Mrs. Inches House and crossing Nassau Street to Pleasant Street" now became Eliots Street.[40] Town officials assigned street names to nine roads intersecting with the main thoroughfare, Orange Street. The identification of these and other unnamed streets was an instrumental component in the development of the South End that would begin by the turn of the century.

Between 1789 and 1794 the town divided the land on either side of Orange Street into parcels and began selling them to those interested in building "dwelling houses and stores on each side of the street."[41] Although townspeople gradually erected buildings, the neighborhood still offered an unobstructed view "across open fields to the Back Bay in the west, and to the harbor in the east."[42] The region was dotted with horse pastures, grazing cows, and almost two hundred barns.[43] One such residence was that of John Waldo, a merchant of some means, who lived on Newbury Street near the Lamb Tavern. His property consisted of a house "with a large commodious Shop . . . Store, large Garden [and] Barn." Taverners often had barns on their property for stabling a traveler's horse while he or she partook of the establishment's food, drink, and in some cases, lodging.[44]

In October 1783 Levi Pease and his partner Reuben Sykes opened a business at the sign of the "Coach and Horse," near the corner of Winter and Common Streets. From here they ran "two convenient wagons" between Boston and Hartford on the Upper Boston Post Road. Soon they offered a one-day line to Worcester, and by the early 1790s, Levi Pease's Boston–New York Stage rumbled along the main thoroughfare of the town three days a week during the summer months. Passengers arrived in New York in only three and one-half days at the price of four cents per mile. For the "genteel" passenger Pease offered a coach *"in which but four inside passengers will be admitted,* with smart, good Horses, and experienced careful drivers." For those wanting a cheaper but less "genteel" journey, Pease continued to run his "Old Line" to New York for three and one-half cents per mile.[45] By the 1790s travelers could depart from Boston six days a week for any number of destinations.

The traveler or the inhabitant seeking the company of friends or a place to transact business might visit one of the taverns in the South End. Many public houses stood along the Orange–Newbury thoroughfare, it being the main route into and out of town. These included the Lamb, the Washington, the Swan, the Grand Turk, and the George taverns. On Beach Street, which ran between Orange and Wainer's Wharf on the east side of the peninsula, stood the White Horse tavern, known as a "Negro House."[46] Offering some of the cheapest housing in town, the Fort Hill area where the "Negro House" stood, was home to a number of black Bostonians. At the White Horse they might gather and drink their rum to ward off the chill of a cold December day or find refreshment on a hot summer afternoon.[47]

The Central District

North of Fort Hill lay the busiest part of the South End, the Central District. Here the main market, local government offices, and the hive of business activity were concentrated. The atmosphere of the Central District was decidedly urban compared to the rural stretches of the rest of the South End. In Ward 9, on the northeast corner of Boston Common, sat the almshouse, workhouse, bridewell, and the town granary. Close by on the corner of School and Tremont Streets stood King's Chapel, the town's first Anglican church, founded in 1688. After the Revolution, King's became the town's first Unitarian church. Within several blocks, on Marlborough and Milk Streets, stood Old South Meeting House, the place where Samuel Adams and the Sons of Liberty often rallied Bostonians in the cause against Parliament. Walking north on Marlborough, which became Cornhill, led one directly into the more crowded "downtown" area of Dock Square and Faneuil Hall. Here was the center of commercial and administrative activity. The seat of municipal government, known as the State House, stood in this part of town, as did the prison, the courthouse, and the principal shops and businesses.[48]

Private individuals owned each of Boston's wharves, the proprietors appointing "a wharfinger to collect the dockage and wharfage, and superintend all matters relative to the wharf."[49] Of the dozens of wharves resting on their weathered pilings, none had quite the distinction of Long Wharf, where "the principal navigation of the town" took place. Those disembarking from their ships met with a magnificent view as they gazed along State Street, formerly King Street.[50] At the top of the street clearly visible for all visitors and residents to see stood the symbol of government power, the State House. Before the Revolution this had been the Provincial House, the seat of British colonial authority in Boston. Wooden shops and warehouses lined the length of the north side of Long Wharf, which extended more than seventeen hundred feet into the harbor. The town issued annual licenses to a certain number of townsmen and women to run retail businesses where shoppers could purchase a variety of goods on the wharf including Madeira wine, West India rum, fresh lemons, figs, gunpowder, snuff, linens, cordage, and canvas.[51]

The town almost lost Long Wharf in the autumn of 1780 when a fire broke out early one afternoon. Fortunately, the high tide, help from the inhabitants, and the hasty response of Engine Number Five prevented the "raging Flames" from consuming the entire structure. The conflagration did destroy warehouses, the Commis-

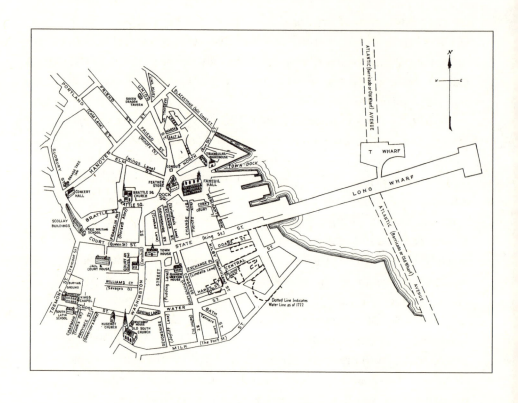

The Central District.
(Map by L. A. Chisholm, in Annie H. Thwing, *The Crooked and Narrow Streets of the Town of Boston*, Boston, 1920.)

sary, stores, and several other buildings at a considerable financial loss. The looting that followed the fire made matters worse.[52] Although the wharf proprietors struggled to get back on their feet, Long Wharf soon became, as before, one of the most frequented parts of town.[53]

Proceeding back up State Street from Long Wharf, one passed shops, taverns, and inns.[54] Just off the Long Wharf at Kilby and State, the weary traveler could find lodging at the Bunch of Grapes Tavern. At two o'clock in the afternoon the proprietor served a meal of "salmon, veal, beef, mutton, fowl, ham, roots, pudding, and . . . Madeira" at a "long table covered with dishes, and plates" for lodgers and local inhabitants seeking a midday dinner. The close proximity of Bunch of Grapes to the main wharf meant a diverse and interesting clientele. One English visitor noted dining with several French immigrants, a Philadelphian, and a man from Newburyport, among others. The Bunch of Grapes also served as an important gathering place for business meetings, auctions, and organizational affairs such as the annual meeting of the "Members of the Society of the Cincinnati" on July 4.[55] If the Bunch of Grapes did not appeal to the traveler, he might visit the American, formerly the British, Coffee-House "at the sign of the Golden Eagle." Many of Boston's merchants gathered here, where between the hours of "seven to ten in the morning, and from five to eight in the evening" the proprietor Daniel Jones served coffee.[56]

Before the building of the Charles River Bridge stagecoaches ran from the bustling center of town across Boston Neck taking passengers to the North Shore of Massachusetts and New Hampshire. For the cost of six dollars, travelers could journey to Portsmouth within two days on John Greenleaf's stagecoach, which departed from Catherine Gray's boardinghouse, next door to the American Coffee-House. Jonathan Plummer, who operated a stage line from Boston to Newburyport, also departed from Catherine Gray's establishment. By the 1790s, when travel was eased somewhat by the Charles River Bridge, stagecoaches also departed town by an alternate route through the North End. Greenleaf and Plummer now had competition from John Staver's Portsmouth and Boston Stage, which departed from the American Coffee-House at least twice a week and arrived in Portsmouth in only one day for the bargain price of only four dollars. Thus Stavers undercut Greenleaf by two dollars in cost and one day in travel time. As the number of stage lines increased so did the competition, evidenced by the advertising of "Careful Drivers, good Horses," best rates, and even which line drove the best New England roads.[57]

In 1794, State Street was a broad, eight-hundred-foot-long avenue. Depicted in that year as the "most noted and spacious street" in Boston it stood in stark contrast to a large number of other streets and lanes in town.[58] It "affords a picturesque scene" where "everything [is] charming to the eye and gratifying to the imagination," noted one admirer.[59] In an engraving of the Old State House printed in *Massachusetts Magazine* in 1793, the viewer looks down State Street toward Long Wharf from Cornhill. The street is a rush of activity evidenced by the carriages, chaises, carts, people on horseback, and pedestrians moving about. Three-story brick Georgian row-buildings neatly line the street, with open, ground-floor windows tempting passersby with a grand assortment of goods for sale including English imports, calicoes, broadcloth, hats, ribbons, teas, wines, silks, gauzes, and countless other merchandise.[60] On the corner across from the State House, Nicholas Bowes sold an "elegant Assortment of Stationary" and a wide variety of books.[61] Occupants used these buildings as "dwelling houses, publick offices, warehouses, and auction offices."[62] Private space and public space merged amid the bustle of domestic activity and business enterprise combined under one roof.

State Street also offered the inhabitant and visitor a scene of stark contrast to the busy world of commerce. Here, as on Boston Common, the local and state governments might choose to exhibit those convicted of crimes by the Supreme Judicial Court of Massachusetts. Before being "confined to hard labour on *Castle-Island*" in Boston harbor, fourteen men convicted of various crimes in the spring of 1791 each received punishments "for the purpose of discipline," as they were "offenders against the peace and dignity of the Commonwealth." For "housebreaking and theft" two men had "both cheeks" branded, others received whippings ranging from twenty to thirty-nine stripes and varied amounts of time "on the gallows." The town's "large whipping post, painted red" also stood centrally located in a "conspicuous" position on State Street, "under the windows of a great writing-school." Here the general public witnessed a variety of punishments, although hangings were restricted to the gallows on "Boston Neck." Such scenes may have disturbed some, but as part of eighteenth-century life they were considered by others the normal events of any given day, perhaps even providing a moment's entertainment.[63]

North of State Street, Dock Square and Faneuil Hall served as central gathering places for business, social, and political activity. The town used the upstairs of Faneuil Hall for a variety of events from the entertaining of foreign dignitaries to the exercising of the light infantry on Wednesday evenings. Five hundred guests gathered there in 1778 to greet the Count d'Estaing and enjoy an evening of "magnificent entertainment," and in 1784 the merchants used the hall to give Lafayette a dinner.[64] With far less pomp and circumstance, Mr. Vandale once used the hall to "deliver an oration in French to his Pupils."[65] All uses of the hall required prior permission of the selectmen, who occupied a chamber on the same floor as the public hall. The tax assessors kept their office above the selectmen's chamber. Defaced by the British during the winter of occupation in 1775 and 1776, Faneuil Hall was soon restored to its original stature by the town.[66]

The ground floor of Faneuil Hall served as a public market for butchers, and close by in Dock Square was a general market. Under the supervision of the selectmen, the Clerk of the Market carefully monitored both. In these markets inhabitants purchased pork, beef, mutton, poultry, fresh seafood, vegetables from West Boston gardens, and dairy products.[67] Each day people from the rural areas surrounding Boston and the South End drove their carts to market along the main thoroughfare (Orange to Newbury to Cornhill). The heavily loaded carts and trucks rolled through the dirt and gravel streets chased by barking dogs and children, and tearing up the pavement to the dismay of town officials.[68] Sometimes peddlers made their way to Dock Square but quickly found themselves run off by the Clerk. Town law did not permit "Sellers of Small Wares in a pedling way" to do business at Dock Square.[69]

The market rapidly filled up with stalls, people, carts, horses, and refuse—waste from live animals, as well as dead animals, discarded produce, and human garbage. The visual, auditory, and olfactory senses were no doubt overwhelmed by day's end, especially during the hot months of summer. The selectmen controlled the size of the market through the rental of a specific number of stalls. Those desiring to sell in the market had to apply to the selectmen and wait for an available stall. In 1775 the town planned to fill in the dock to make room "for the Standing of Horses Hacks of those Country People, who bring Provisions for sale to the Market."[70] Landfill in this area eliminated the need for the old swing bridge.[71]

Despite town regulation of stalls and hawkers, the marketplace continued to present problems. Overcrowding created the major problem on market days. In 1783 a "Committee Appointed to devise the Necessary Means of removing the disorders of the market and other Nuisances" presented a lengthy report to those convened at the March 25 town meeting. They recommended that specific "places be Assigned for the different Markets for Wood, Hay, &c." as the area "contigueous to Faneuil Hall" was "for the great market of Flesh" and "Vegetables." The committee suggested that the town select a town officer whose sole responsibility would be enforcement of the "Laws and Orders of the Town . . . as they respect the Marketts." The report called upon the town's scavengers to deal with the filth in the market streets, which, if not removed, would "contribute to produce the Most fatal disorders among the Inhabitants." Since the "Carts, Teams, Sleds, Sleighs, Waggons & Horses" daily presented a threat to the "Lives and Limbs" of all townspeople visiting the market, the committee recommended that the laws to keep the streets clear of such standing traffic be enforced and designated parking areas be established. Stopping in the street on the way to market to sell one's meat, vegetables, or other articles, or blocking the streets resulted in a fine. The town proceeded to approve these and all other recommendations made in the committee's report, but the problems did not abate for long as the appearance of complaints in the newspapers and town records attests.[72]

Adding to the din and congestion of the market area, the Dock Square shops, houses, taverns, and inns stood around the periphery of the open-air market. The shops offered as varied an assortment of goods as any in town, including "Iron hollow Ware" at John Kennedy's store, English goods at Nathaniel Greenough's, and wines "at the lowest prices" at Joshua Blanchard Jr.'s shop.[73] Of twenty-five people known to have received licenses between 1776 and 1786 permitting them to do business in Dock Square (not including stall licenses), sixteen had a license to sell spirits, either as a retailer, innholder, or taverner.[74] Residents sometimes used their houses as taverns or inns.[75] A common house style was a two-story wood or brick structure consisting of a kitchen and a small front room on the bottom floor with chambers on the floor above.[76] These homes served well for bottom-floor shops with living quarters above renting to one or more families.

Leaving Dock Square and walking north along Union Street one passed the Green Dragon Tavern and the Union Coffee-House, "a House of Entertainment," that accommodated "Gentlemen, in large and small parties; fire-clubs, and other societies," who would "find plenty of Room; Dinners; Suppers, . . . [and] Good attendance." Both the local businessman and the traveler could find a "constant supply of best London Porter, English Cheese and Oysters" at this busy downtown establishment.[77] At the north end of Union Street and to the right on Hanover one short block led to the Mill Bridge. Here, Hanover became Middle Street and the boundary between the South End and North End.

THE NORTH END

From the Central District one entered the North End over one of two small bridges that crossed a manmade creek running between the harbor and the Mill Pond. Both of the town gristmills, the North Mill and the one at Mill Bridge, sat here. Three major thoroughfares traversed the North End. The first, Back Street and Prince Street ran along the western edge of the district connecting the Mill Pond and the foot of Copp's Hill, where one could command an excellent view of the Charles River. Atop Copp's Hill lay the town's North Burial Ground, where such Boston notables as Cotton Mather rested. Prince Street led directly to the Charlestown Ferry and, after 1786, the Charles River Bridge. In 1789 the town widened this thoroughfare to accommodate the additional bridge traffic. The second thoroughfare ran through the center of the district beginning with Middle Street. On the eastern side of the district the third major thoroughfare wrapped itself around the perimeter of the North End along the wharves. This was Fish Street which became Ship, Lynn, and then Ferry. Shops and houses crowded along these streets, with the exception of Lynn Street, where "great desolation" had occurred during "the time of the Late war." The town decided, in 1787, to widen Lynn Street from the Globe Tavern, which stood on the corner of Lynn and North, as far as Ferry Way on the west side of the peninsula to better accommodate traffic.[78]

Before the building of the Charles River Bridge in 1785–1786, departure from the north end of the peninsula depended upon the Charlestown Ferry across the Charles River and the Winnisimmet Ferry across the Mystick River to the Marblehead and Salem Road.[79] After the building of the bridge, only the Winnisimmet Ferry remained a necessity. Ferryman Joseph Oliver held a twelve-year lease from the town, to whom he paid a small monthly fee for the privilege of running the ferry, as long as he maintained it in good repair.[80] The boat passage across the water to the beginning of the Marblehead and Salem Road took about twenty minutes in fair weather, leaving the traveler with approximately a sixteen-mile ride through rugged country to Salem.[81]

The Charles River Bridge spanned 1,053 feet over the river to connect Boston to Charlestown. "Six feet walkways" extended on either side of a center road for carriages, carts, and horses, and at night forty lamps lit the structure. While building the bridge the town repaired Prince Street, laying out a "proper street" from the bridge to the Winnisimmet Ferry and building a stone seawall, 470 feet in length, along Ferry Street between the ferry house and Goodings Wharf.[82] The completion of the bridge, and the accompanying changes, in June 1786 brought cause for a great celebration with parades, great fanfare, and public entertainments.[83] These major points of departure from, and arrival to, the peninsula, the Charlestown Ferry and later the Charles River Bridge, and the Winnisimmet Ferry, made the North End a heavily traveled area.

The five North End wards consisted of a clutter of shipyards, shops, warehouses, and closely situated houses and garden plots clustered along a maze of crooked streets mixed with the elegant and spacious homes of many of the former Loyalist elite who fled with the British in 1776. Their departure from the district left a vacuum that was not filled by the new monied families coming into Boston who preferred other parts of town "as the tides of fashion turned southward and westward." As late as the 1780s the area still

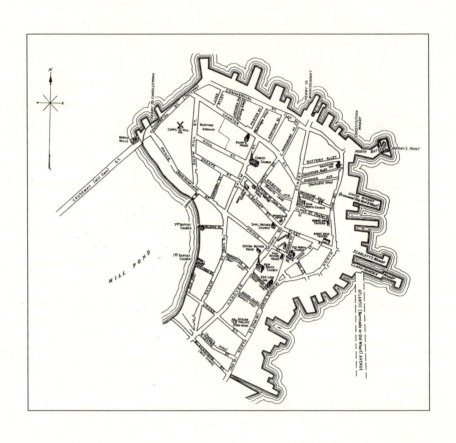

The North End.
(Map by L. A. Chisholm, in Annie H. Thwing, *The Crooked and Narrow Streets of the Town of Boston*, Boston, 1920.)

housed some of Boston's leading citizens, but by the middle of the 1790s they, too, began to move to the South End and, particularly, the West End.[84]

The North End was the most densely populated region of the peninsula. Although it comprised less than 25 percent of the peninsula, eleven of the town's eighteen churches stood here. By comparison to the South End, the North End was so congested with buildings in certain neighborhoods that at points sunlight was barely visible through the overhanging roofs and upper floors of buildings. In the crowded neighborhood markets sellers found little room to "stand by their produce" and buyers [were] unable to "find room to . . . pass each other."[85] Occasionally gardens punctuated the closely set buildings, and open areas such as North Square and Copp's Hill also provided space amid the congestion of predominantly late-Elizabethan architecture.

As with the South End, the neighborhoods in Wards 1 through 5 of the North End were visually eclectic. In the same area one might find two-story Georgian brick buildings graced with many windows, two-story wooden dwellings built in the Postmedieval English style, and simple one-story wooden dwellings whose few windows barely admitted light. The dark two-story wooden houses sometimes had steeply pitched roofs and an overhanging second story typical of seventeenth-century domestic architecture, making them heavy in appearance. Interspersed among these diverse structures were blacksmith shops, bake houses, distilleries, and the occasional barn. Domestic space and business space often overlapped in dwellings that housed a family and a shop or tavern. Benjamin Goodwin owned a two-story house in Ward 1, with an adjoining one-story wooden bake house. James Kirkwood's house had "one shop adjoining for soap works." In Back Street, Ward 4, close to the Mill Pond, sat a "distill-house" with a large, adjoining double house that had four rooms to a floor, a convenient shop, and "Accommodations for two Families."[86]

After the Revolution the exodus of the elite out of the North End, once "the court end of town," led to the loss of the region's "former prestige" and created the "unquestionable evidence of decay and unpopularity."[87] Neither the Clark-Frankland mansion on North Square nor the splendid home of former governor Thomas Hutchinson remained as prestigious residences. Increasingly, these five wards housed some of Boston's more poverty stricken. "Willon's lane, Exchange lane, and Fitch's alley—through Fore Street as far as Winnisimmet ferry" were dark, stench-ridden places, according to one critic.[88] Still, inhabitants of middling rank, and not just the poor and destitute, continued to call the North End home during the years prior to the massive influx of immigrants in the nineteenth century that would permanently transform Boston's North End.

THE WEST END

Like the South End, the West End remained sparsely settled throughout most of the eighteenth century. In 1784 the area had only one meetinghouse, the West Church, or Lynde Street Meeting House, and relatively few residents compared to the other areas of the peninsula. Slightly fewer than two hundred heads of household lived in Ward 7, which comprised the entire West End, compared to more than eleven hundred in the North End, and eighteen hundred in the South End.[89] The main businesses were the ropewalks set on the far edge of the ward against the Back Bay. Unlike the South End, the West End was isolated from the main flow of traffic across the peninsula. The area would remain pastoral for some years to come. Even when the town constructed the new State House between 1796 and 1798, the stately, neoclassical structure gazed out over cows grazing on Boston Common.

On the side of Beacon Hill overlooking the Common prior to the 1780s were a few elegant homes of the Boston elite like Han-

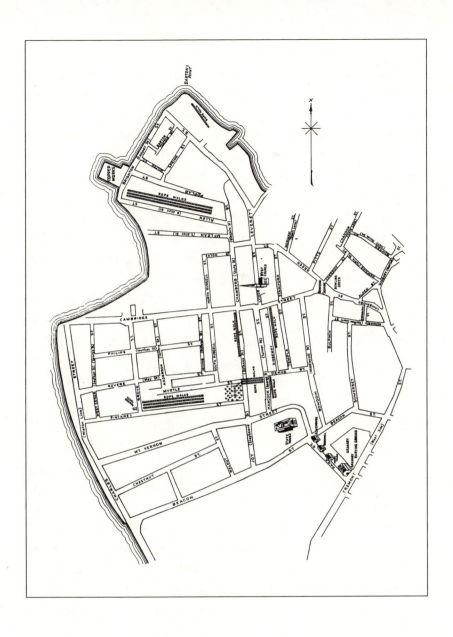

The West End.
(Map by L. A. Chisholm, in Annie H. Thwing, *The Crooked and Narrow Streets of the Town of Boston*, Boston, 1920.)

cock and Faneuil, and the land and farms of John Singleton Copley. The Bromfield home was an impressive, three-story Georgian structure with "three steep flights of stone steps ascend[ing] from Beacon Street to the front of the mansion." In the terraced gardens, full of flowers and fruit trees, stood an elevated summer house that "commanded a panoramic view of the harbor and environs."[90]

The West End was "a very pleasant and healthy part of the town" where one found "plenty of agreeable inland breezes" and protection "from the easterly winds." Consequently, inhabitants visited the area "for air and pastime" and their general "health."[91] These pleasing circumstances also appealed to prosperous merchants, especially the new elite emerging after the Revolution. It was in the 1790s that the area began to develop, as homes built around Beacon Hill created a genteel world separate from the distasteful aspects of the growing town.[92]

In 1795 the Mount Vernon Proprietors purchased the property of John Singleton Copley, which lay northwest of the Common, bordering on the Charles River, for the purpose of erecting stately residences. Impressed with the vision and designs of Charles Bulfinch, the newcomers built an array of neoclassical homes displaying his architectural innovations.[93] The houses here, noted one visitor, differed from those in other areas of town in that they were "all neat and elegant, (of brick) with handsome entrances and door cases, and a flight of steps."[94] Another commentator noted how the "eye rests with pleasure on fine airy buildings, interspersed with delightful gardens."[95] The acquisition of the Copley estate, the "largest land transaction" in Boston to date, marked the many changes that lay ahead, such as the leveling of Trimountain that began in 1799.[96] Compared to the North End, the Southern and Western regions remained sparsely settled until the 1790s, when rapid population increase began to slowly transform the two regions.

At the outbreak of the American Revolution the majority of Bostonians still clustered in the same areas of the peninsula occupied for the preceding 150 years. The twelve wards varied in population density and growth rate. During the last two decades of the century town records show on average 243 heads of household living in Ward 5 of the North End. Ward 11 in the South End showed 273 for the same period. Yet, Ward 5 was considerably smaller in area than Ward 11, making it more congested. Further adding to the overall congestion of the North End relative to the remainder of the town was the fact that the number of heads of household in Wards 1 and 2 doubled over the twenty-year period. These two North End wards were among the smallest in the town. Observations made by contemporaries speak to this pattern of growth for the region. In 1784, out of 3,265 heads of household, 35 percent (1,151) lived in the North End, 9 percent (297) lived in the West End, 22 percent (702) lived in the Central District, and 34 percent in the South End. The largest region of the peninsula, the South End, contained approximately the same percentage of heads of household as did the smaller North End.[97]

Besides the arrival of new faces in Boston, extensive intramobility from ward to ward continually reshaped the demographic picture in each part of town. Of 1,227 heads of household tracked between 1784 and 1794, approximately 40 percent of those who had resided in Boston for at least four consecutive years had relocated within the town one or more times during that period and a handful three or more times. Laborers exhibited the lowest rate of persistence in any given ward and the highest rate of intramobility. More than 50 percent of the laborers had relocated within the community at least once (89 percent of the total number of laborers had lived in Boston for less than four years). Difficulty finding work, low pay, and poor housing certainly had a role in the frequent turnover. By contrast, housewrights had the highest persistence level among all occupational groups. Only 2 percent relocated within the community during the decade between 1784 and 1794. Between the two extremes of the high rate of persistence found among house-wrights and low rate of persistence found among laborers ranged other occupational categories. The average persistence level of all other occupational groups was 35 percent. Clearly for a large number of Bostonians the postwar years involved at least one change of residence within the community.[98]

By 1799 the distribution of the population throughout the peninsula showed signs of change. Compared to the rest of Boston, the North End remained a densely settled area while the South End, with more than 42 percent of the town's heads of household, represented the fastest-growing region of the peninsula. The number of "new houses" and "half-finished" residences recorded by the Ward 12 assessor in 1799 attests to this development and suggests the pattern of rapid growth in the southern end of the peninsula that would unfold in the new century.[99]

Throughout Boston, neighborhoods were eclectic and dynamic in their composition. Although economic distinctions may have long separated Bostonians into different social groupings, the town lacked the segregated neighborhoods that would come to mark the nineteenth century. Residency patterns did not reflect sharply demarcated economic and racial divisions. Homes frequently served as places of work, and mixed land-use patterns often meant that shops, houses, distilleries, blacksmiths, shipyards, and the like could be found in the same neighborhood.[100]

Fort Hill, a low-rent area housing a number of poor blacks and whites, was visually, socially, and economically different from the more prestigious northwest side of Boston Common, but this did not exclude within each of those areas neighborhoods, streets, and blocks that were dynamically integrated. Throughout the town in each of the wards the wealthy merchant, the artisan, the common laborer, Bostonians both black and white, lived in close quarters. Walking along Lynn Street as it hugged the northernmost perimeter of the peninsula in the North End, one passed the dwellings of Benjamin Gooding, Thomas Harris, David Cobbet, Samuel Ash, and Andrew Leach: a grocer, blacksmith, cooper, journeyman truckman, and wealthy merchant, respectively. Within a few doors lived poor laborers and fishermen. In 1799 Leach, who owned a store downtown on State Street and a wharf, was in the process of building a "Large New H[ouse]," a contrast to some of his neighbors who lived in only one room or part of a dwelling.[101] At the far end of the peninsula in Ward 12, the mason Nicholas Pierce had a new house under construction on Beach Street. His neighbors included white journeymen, black laborers, a sea captain who also had a "large new House," and two wealthy merchants who dealt in West India goods.[102]

For the majority of people in the eighteenth century, houses were generally small. Domestic living arrangements were frequently cramped, and the presence of a wide variety of people in a dwelling that might also serve as a place of business afforded little privacy. On average 1.6 heads of household lived in each "dwelling-house and tenement" in Boston in 1784.[103] In addition to the heads of household there were the family members and perhaps others. The "domestic unit" or family could be quite diverse, including a husband, wife, children, servants, apprentices, journeymen, or in-laws. The composition of the household was also fluid, changing at any given time depending on births, deaths, marriages, and the arrival or departure of kin, servants, or other workers such as apprentices.[104] In some instances a household consisted of only one parent, such as a widow, or a single adult, male or female, who might live alone or with a sibling, relative, or friend. Nuclear family size varied, with families consisting of as many as twelve children, although five to six appears to have been the average. Extended family groupings combined with live-in employees could make a household quite large. Samuel Parkman presided over a household of twenty-two family members, eleven of whom were his children.[105]

Multiple households in single dwellings created numerous types of living arrangements. Edward Holyoke, a scribe, shared half of a house with two pewterers, John Skinner and his son. The laborer John Spear shared a house with six other men. Laborers, coopers, tailors, shoemakers, carpenters, or a variety of other artisans, either alone or with their families or friends, occupied part of a house, such as one room, "1 end," the "back end," "front end," or a "chamber."[106] John Fillebrown, owner of an "India goods" store with Thomas Williams, occupied one half of a house with his wife and eight children. William Parkman, a poor cooper with seven children, dwelt in one end of a shared residence. Down the road from Parkman journeyman shoemaker William Silvester lived in one room with the elderly mother for whom he cared.[107]

Some individuals resided in a boarding establishment. Widows, single men, and families with available space in their homes took in boarders. Between 1785 and 1795 more than thirty widowed and single women operated boardinghouses in town, such as Widow Snow, who offered room and board to ladies only. Between 1795 and 1799, the number of people listing their occupation as the keeper of a boardinghouse increased by one-third. Many more residents kept boarders, although they did not list themselves as operating a boardinghouse, as with Mary Lobb, who kept "no Boarders only 2 French Priests." No doubt the increase reflected the demand for housing among the growing population. Besides offering an economical and perhaps efficient way to live, especially if one was single, boardinghouses could provide company for those who did not wish to live alone. When Lemuel Cravath's wife Catherine died, he became a boarder in the home of another family. The proprietors ranged as widely in their financial status as their boarders did. Boarding was not simply an inexpensive living arrangement for those unable to afford any other domestic arrangement. Residence in boardinghouses was a popular living arrangement, as demonstrated by their large number of occupants.[108]

Homeowners and tenants frequently divided their place of residence into home and shop, or work area. A two-story wood or brick tenement with "two rooms on a floor" provided an excellent arrangement for an artisan or shopkeeper and his family. Either the upstairs or back room served as a residence, with the shop occupying a downstairs front room facing the street. The residence of shopkeeper Joseph Crocker and his family of eight also served as Crocker's place of business. Tallow chandler James Raymer lived in a "large dwelling-house" that included a shop fronting on Marlborough Street in Ward 8. A hatter and his family lived next door to Raymer, in "a small tenement" also partly used as a shop.[109]

The lack of distinct, racially separated neighborhoods during the 1780s and 1790s meant that white and black Bostonians found themselves not only living side by side but also at times sharing living space. The neighbors next door to Prince Patterson and Thomas Williams, two black property owners living on Unity Street in the North End in 1799, included a number of poor white laborers but also a founder of comfortable means who owned his residence and shop. Next to Peter Dalton's "Elegant House" on Water Street in the South End three black laborers shared "a small tenement." Living quarters for black Bostonians, as for white, varied, including "one room," a "chamber," a "small tenement" "1 End," or the "upper" part of a house. As with a large number of white Bostonians, living conditions could prove cramped. The poorest inhabitants suffered the most, such as the four men living in the South End's Fort Hill area described by the assessor as "Blacks as poor as the Devil." These four men and their families totaled nineteen individuals living in a single house. Such circumstances were conducive to the spread of disease, especially during epidemics. Despite similarities between their living situations and those of white Bostonians, most black residents lived in the poorer areas of town such as Fort Hill in the South End, the waterfront regions of the North End, and by the 1790s parts of the West End.[110]

By the 1790s the West End was becoming home to an increasing number of black Bostonians, although some had lived there since the 1760s. The town's black population had declined throughout most of the second half of the eighteenth century, but it began to increase once more during the 1790s. These men, women, and children experienced some of the most significant changes of any Bostonians during the late eighteenth century, for by 1783 the Quock Walker court case, and its resulting decision handed down by Chief Justice Cushing, ended slavery in Massachusetts.[111]

Black Bostonians at the close of the eighteenth century demonstrated as much mobility as their white neighbors, moving from ward to ward and region to region with some frequency. Fifty-six-year-old Prince Sutton, who lived in the South End in 1780, relocated to the West End, once again moving back to the South End by 1786. Individuals sometimes left town, returned, and settled in one ward only to shortly move to another. John Brown was "gone in the country" in 1784. When he came back to Boston he settled in the West End, but at some point between 1791 and 1794 moved to the South End, where he could still be found in 1799 working as a ropemaker and a laborer. In 1784 Newport Davis resided in the West End, but later moved to the South End, where he shared living quarters with Nebo Fairfield in the early 1790s, and then in 1795 went to sea.[112]

At least one-half of the black population changed their place of residence during the 1780s and 1790s, with some moving from ward to ward two or three times. At one point or another 10 percent left Boston entirely, heading for "the country," the sea, or other states and countries, as did James Titus, who headed to New York in 1784, and William Gregory, who left for England the same year. This was a highly mobile community motivated by any number of circumstances, including emancipation, work, and the desire to improve one's residence or find more affordable housing.[113]

By 1790 the African-American population in Boston surpassed that of any other town in Massachusetts as men and women from rural areas and other regions drifted toward the seaport seeking work. By 1800 the number reached 1,174 persons, creating the nucleus of the town's substantial and politically active nineteenth-century antebellum black community centered in the West End.[114] In the closing few years of the eighteenth century this move to the West End was in its early stages. Between 1784 and 1800 the African-American population in Boston was dispersed throughout the town, with the South End consistently housing the majority of the population.[115] In 1794 approximately 60 percent of black Bostonians lived in the southern wards compared to 20 percent in the West End. Fort Hill in the South End was a popular area, most likely because here could be found some of the city's cheapest housing.[116] Although five years later, in 1799, the beginning of the shift to the West End was evident, with more than 35 percent of black households located there, the South End still held approximately 60 percent of Boston's African-American heads of household.[117]

The West End probably drew some African-Americans in the late eighteenth century because of domestic work opportunities in the homes of Boston's white elite. Those domestic service opportunities were limited in number before 1800 as the West End had still not fully developed as the central location for Boston's wealthy upper class. In fact, as late as 1799, 80 percent of those African-Americans reported as servants by the town's assessors lived in the South End, not the West End, and of those individuals most were in Ward 12 in the southernmost region of the peninsula.[118]

The South End also housed a large number of the second-largest African-American occupational group, laborers. Although the building of the State House on Beacon Hill and the new almshouse and workhouse in the western reaches of Ward 7 could provide employment, the building boom in the South End probably offered a greater number of opportunities for laborers. In turn, the evidence suggests that this rapid development of the South End after the mid-1790s and the influx of white residents ultimately disrupted black settlement in the area as a result of increased rents and raised property prices, thus acting as a push factor in African-American movement to the West End. Simultaneously the development of a black community in the West End in the closing few years of the century acted as a pull factor that would increase in intensity by the nineteenth century.

The relative isolation of the southern reaches of the South End may have appealed to black Bostonians who found themselves treated with disrespect and frequently ostracized from white institutions. Prince Hall advised fellow black men and women "to bear up under the daily insults we meet on the streets of Boston."[119] The restrictions that the white community placed upon black Bostonians manifested themselves in a variety of ways. It took three petitions over a four-year period just to secure the permission to have "one of their Colour . . . [act] as an Undertaker at the Funerals of the Blacks" and to break ground in one of the burying places. It was not until 1792 that the selectmen finally permitted Boston's African-American community to "take care of the Funerals" of their own, and "have the care of burying the Blacks."[120] To help pay funeral expenses and "provide aid for widows and children," forty-two black citizens in 1796 founded the African Humane Society. Many self-help mutual aid societies of a similar type would become popular among Americans during the nineteenth century.[121]

Besides establishing a means to care for women and children fallen upon hard times, the town's black inhabitants also took it upon themselves to establish a place of worship after not finding equal reception in most of the city's white churches. In 1789 a number of individuals collectively applied to the selectmen for the "use of Faneuil Hall . . . to accommodate them in hearing an African

Preacher, lately arrived with a good recommendation." The selectmen granted the use of the hall for one weekday afternoon, with
the stipulation that the meeting take place during daylight hours so
"that no opportunity may be given rude Fellows to make a disturbance." Shortly thereafter, a "group of respectable inhabitants"
once again petitioned the selectmen for use of the hall one day a
week "for the purpose of public worship." This petition proved
unsuccessful, but through persistence black inhabitants secured
permission to use Mr. Vinal's school "for public worship, on the
Afternoons of the Lords Day."[122] The limitations encountered in
finding a place to worship freely no doubt led to the building of the
African Baptist Church in the West End by 1805.

Experiencing similar discrimination in the Boston school system, seven years earlier, in 1798, the small West End community,
with the assistance of some white Bostonians, had established "a
separate school for their children in the house of Primus Hall."
Rapid growth in the student body led the school to relocate to the
basement of the newly completed Baptist Church on Belknap.[123]
Institutions such as the church, the school, and the African Humane
Society offered a strong sense of community in the face of hostility
and discrimination. Accordingly these institutions could serve as a
pull factor in drawing more black men and women and their families to the West End. By the nineteenth century the lower slope of
the Hill would come to house Boston's "largest black enclave," living "in a world far removed from the wealth and power just a few
blocks away."[124]

Summarizing the circumstances for Bostonians as a whole, a far
higher number of unskilled workers, whether black or white, lived
in shared domicile arrangements as compared to skilled tradesmen,
shopkeepers, and merchants. Artisans, midsize shopkeepers, and
some professional men along with their families did live in shared
housing but in fewer numbers. Merchants fared best. Many of them
lived in houses assessed at considerable value, and many also owned

shops, stores, and carriages. Distillers, successful master artisans, a few tavern keepers, lawyers, and widows shared this fortunate position. Living arrangements comprised a diverse and complex web of familial and nonfamilial organization, maximizing the use of space and affording little or no privacy.

The relatively close proximity of certain trade and manufacturing enterprises further added to the heterogeneity and complex spatial pattern of neighborhoods. In theory "Common Nuisances" such as slaughterhouses, distilleries, or ropewalks were relegated to the less settled areas of the peninsula, but in reality this was not the case. This was particularly true as the population increased and began to spread into more sparsely settled areas. On Frog Lane, adjacent to the Common Burying Ground, sat the Duck Manufactory with its "Spinning Shed, . . . 1 Store, . . . and 3 Small Shops."[125] Distilleries operated in all three South End wards.[126]

The town government did attempt to regulate businesses that proved dangerous or inappropriate for certain parts of town. In this they followed the 1692 law passed by the Massachusetts General Court "for the prevention of Common Nuisances arising by Slaughter-Houses, Still-Houses, &c. Tallow-Chandlers, and Curriers." The act specified that the selectmen of "market Towns in the Province, with two or more Justices of the Peace, dwelling in the Town" had the responsibility of assigning places in the town where these men might "practice their respective trades and mysteries." Those engaged in their trades in any part of the town not assigned for that purpose were subject to fines. The 1692 act remained on the law books throughout the eighteenth century and appeared in the 1785 publication of the town's bylaws.[127]

In 1784, when Oliver Vose began construction of a slaughterhouse in Pleasant Street, which ran from the west side of the Common south into Orange Street in Ward 12, Robert Hews complained to the selectmen. Vose was advised by the selectmen that he had not received approval for such a structure and was to stop building or face "the penalty of the Law."[128] By contrast, the selectmen approved Edward Curtis's building a slaughterhouse on the desolate Neck in 1791, "on condition that in case it should prove disagreeable or offensive to the Neighbours or Inhabitants passing there, that . . . he shall remove or discontinue" it.[129]

The same year, when a fire consumed ropewalks that sat on Boston Common, the town took the opportunity to relegate ropewalks to the farthest distance possible and improve the Common. They received "A Peice of Marsh Land and Flats at the Bottom of the Common" that included Fox Hill on the very westerly edge of the Common. The condition for accepting this land included an agreement by the owners of the ropewalks that they would never build their rope factories in any other part of town, and that on the new land no more than six ropewalks would ever be built. Furthermore, the structures were to "be Placed at the Southerly End of the said granted Lands . . . [and] not be more than One Story in height," and each structure built of "brick & Covered with Slates."[130] In this manner, town officials and residents managed to have a degree of control over the type of structures and businesses that appeared in various neighborhoods.

During the eighteenth century, the peninsula's geographic limitations, combined with the growing population that was slowly spread across it, contributed to the close proximity of "Common Nuisances" and residential areas.[131] The grand architectural accomplishments of Bulfinch and the numerous new homes being built in the town stood nose to nose with more humble structures, and almost all occupants encountered at least some, if not most, of the same problems. Streets and lanes were frequently narrow, unpaved, and full of "dirt and dung." In walking from Long Wharf or State Street to the market at Dock Square one could pass through "nauseous alleys," just a turning away from main thoroughfares like Cornhill where adjoining brick buildings lined wide streets. Even on the wider streets that boasted handsome brick structures and finer business establishments, the carriages, carts, hackneys, horses, dogs, roaming hogs, and uncovered wells could put one's life at risk. The spatial expansion of the town to the west and south meant that the almshouse and workhouse on the northeast side of Boston Common now stood in close proximity to the elite Beacon Hill neighborhood and the Central District. That they were in a terrible state of disrepair made matters worse for those concerned about the inmates.[132]

A growing number of inhabitants in the 1790s began to raise the issue of relocating the town's almhouse, workhouse, and asylum for the "disorderly and insane." Rebuilt in 1682 after having burned down, the almshouse was the oldest of these structures. A two-story brick building, it housed the town's "aged and infirm poor." Bostonians erected the workhouse, a 120-foot, two-story brick building, in 1738 "for the reception of vagrants and idle and dissolute persons of both sexes" and the small bridewell in 1765 with a bequest from Thomas Hancock.[133] As the town grew, and the number of destitute increased, the buildings became inadequate. This had most likely been true for years but finally came to the attention of the community as people became more conscious of the structures, the location of which increasingly placed them in the center of public activity. By the turn of the nineteenth century the town had moved all three institutions to more remote locations on the peninsula.

In 1794 the town discussed "procuring better accommodations for the Town Poor in the Alms House," but townsmen determined within the year that the only solution would be "erecting new buildings." The committee assigned to research the situation recommended to the town meeting on May 21, 1795, construction of new facilities at Barton's Point, "on the north side of Leverett street" at the extreme north corner of Ward 7, adjacent to the Charles River. This location represented the most desolate region of the West End. The buildings, with their disturbing noises, odors, and inmates' cries to passersby through iron gates, would be removed from sight, earshot, and smell, an important consideration since Centry and Beacon were the main streets connecting the newly developing wealthy district in the West End with the Central District. In order to acquire the land at Barton's Point, the committee recommended the selling of house lots owned by the town "opposite the Mall," which ran along the east side of Boston Common, in addition to the land where the present almshouse and workhouse stood. Sale of these lands by the town would prevent "burthening the Inhabitants with a tax." The proposal "Passed in the affirmative unanimously."[134]

Citizens voiced concerns in the 1790s over the seemingly endless problems the town faced. They spoke out about widening the streets, creating a police force, maintaining a cleaner city, and a host of other municipal issues and proposed projects. The constant flow of carts into the town brought dirt and increased traffic congestion. "There is more dirt and dung brought into Boston, by teams from the country in one day, than in New-York in one year," complained "A Bostonian" in a local newspaper.[135] Another concerned Bostonian informed his fellow townsmen that in this "time of rapid improvements" the town seriously needed a new major thoroughfare in the central business district. State Street alone was insufficient.[136]

By 1796, traffic congestion had become such a serious problem that after numerous complaints the selectmen passed a bylaw regulating hackney carriages. The law required licensing of all persons providing carriage transportation services. The selectmen established "stands" at different locations around town where passengers could hire a carriage. Hackneys were numbered and fines issued to those blocking traffic, operating without a license, or not clearly displaying their assigned number on the side of their carriage. Still, alleyways "designed for foot traffic" became throughways for carriages, leading one group of citizens to propose that the town "put up posts to stop carriage use" in such unsuitable places. Around Union Street and "in the vicinity of the Market," carts, carriages, horses, and cattle blocked the streets, preventing townspeople from "a free passage to their . . . stores & dwellings and . . . their customers from that free & safe access which invites & facilitates business."[137] Besides the problems of traffic and insufficient, poorly laid out roads, there was the question of where within the developed areas of town to erect more public and private buildings or, for that matter, where to bury the dead.

By the middle of the 1790s the "two central burying places" in Boston, the Common and King's Chapel, had reached capacity. One Bostonian asked, where can we find room "*to bury our dead out of our sight?*"[138] Even the common practice of reopening graves to add more bodies no longer provided adequate space as the ground had been "turned over an hundred times." Under these circumstances the town meeting acknowledged that they must find "some suitable place or places of deposit for the Dead" and elected a committee to investigate the matter. The town physicians with whom the committee consulted informed them of the inherent dangers of overcrowded grave sites around so many dwellings and the possibilities of spreading disease from the practice of opening graves. It was also pointed out by one inhabitant that the continual reopening of burial sites to add more bodies showed little respect for either the dead or the living, who might attend a funeral of a family member only to see the bones of their father lying beside the grave to make space for the newly deceased. Finally town leaders forbade any more burials at the central burial grounds. "If the town had not voted to bury no more" in the two central burial grounds, one citizen wryly noted, "the dead would." Only the South Burying Ground, which was a distance from the town center, remained open. As inclement weather might prevent the transportation of the deceased to that part of the peninsula, town officials ordered a "Vault" erected at the Chapel grounds for "temporary deposit" of bodies.[139] The lack of adequate burial grounds was exacerbated by rapid population growth and continued to present a problem into the early nineteenth century, when the town began to use sites outside Boston.

Bostonians sometimes experienced frustration as they struggled to expand within the framework of settlement patterns established more than one hundred years earlier. The irregularity of the town's street plan reflected what one resident referred to as the lack of foresight on the part of the town fathers. Unlike Philadelphia's William Penn, who this townsman believed had great vision, the "pious ancestors" of Boston had not laid the town out "upon a regular plan with open squares and streets at right angels," which in turn would have allowed "wider streets and much more land" on which "to build." This lack of foresight, he alleged, now contributed to the town's growing "evils."[140] Among other things such "evils" included the dangers of walking at night through the narrow, winding, unlit streets; inadequate housing; and the danger of disease and epidemic due to overcrowding and numerous sanitation problems. One inhabitant proposed specific municipal improvements: "widening and straitening of streets, opening squares, and new streets to communicate with older ones, . . . planting trees and grass plots, and placing wells or pumps in several streets." Such changes would promote the "general welfare" of the town's citizens and the beauty of Boston.[141] To accomplish this he proposed that an accurate plan be made of the city depicting every "street, lane, alley, and crevice." This being done, the residents could see precisely where all the open ground lay in the town, and the exact size of each lot in "acres, feet, &c."[142] Such an undertaking would then enable townsmen to wisely determine the best use for this land rather than letting it lie idle. Land would become available for housing and public buildings, the poor would not be homeless, crime rates would decrease, and disease, if not prevented, could be controlled, he claimed. The numerous municipal projects associated with the grid, improved lighting, better use of space, a drive for order and organization, all were part of the republican desire to "conquer space" and control the environment. The belief in the grid's ability to accomplish this reflects the "near-mystical qualities" the plan acquired during the early republic.[143]

Other visions for Boston included those held by Charles Bulfinch. After a Grand Tour in Europe, Bulfinch brimmed with ideas of how to transform the architecturally provincial town into a European-style neoclassical city. He began his architectural enterprises in the West End with houses designed and built during the early 1790s for several of Boston's prominent citizens. Boston's first theater, a stately neoclassical structure, and the magnificent neoclassical State House that graced Beacon Hill and overlooked the Mall and Common soon followed. In the South End around the corner from the Boston, or Federal Street, Theater stood Bulfinch's Tontine Crescent, which consisted of sixteen "handsome dwelling houses, extending four hundred and eighty feet in length." These three-story-high, neoclassical dwellings boasted the Ionic order on their exterior and curved around a three-hundred-foot grass common complete with many shade trees. "We may anticipate," noted one booster, that upon completion the Tontine Crescent would be "a favorite part of the town, and in some degree its boast."[144] Charles Bulfinch soon proved to be the individual who could imagiñe and create the urban landscape sought by the new elite. Elegant homes on spacious lots, gardens, parks, promenades with fountains and shade trees, and elegant public buildings represented in Bulfinch's mind a livable urban environment, or what James Machor identifies as the Enlightenment's "pastoral city."[145]

The building schemes of Boston's wealthy citizens did not appeal to all inhabitants. Speculations such as the Tontine Crescent and the Boston Theater, which according to some had "the system of Deviltry" accompanying them, drew criticism. The "poor laboring men" did not necessarily benefit from the plans of these "Tyrants," for mechanics sometimes remained unpaid until the wealthy realized their profits.[146] As the elite went about "ornamenting and beautifying the town," one irate mechanic wondered what the tradesmen gained. But other day-to-day concerns ultimately drew more attention.

As the town's population climbed to 18,000 in 1790 and then to 25,000 in 1800, the challenges of urban growth manifested themselves in numerous ways. Population growth presented sanitation problems from an accumulation of street refuse with an inadequate removal system and the increasing number of privies and sewers overflowing into the roads and contaminating wells. Crowded streets and the building of unapproved structures raised the danger of fire. Crime concerned a number of citizens who believed that the community lacked an adequate number of constables. Regulating the local market and addressing the need for more market space, additional schools, and the enforcement of the town's bylaws were just a few of the seemingly insurmountable problems that required constant attention. As the community rebuilt itself following the siege and coped with a plethora of difficulties in the face of war and postwar economic hardship, Bostonians turned repeatedly to their town meeting and elected town leaders as a means to create the well-ordered town.

3

A Well-Ordered Town

ON FRIDAY, MARCH 29, 1776, Bostonians assembled at the old brick meetinghouse for their annual town meeting. Proceedings actually began two weeks earlier in the Watertown meetinghouse, during the final days of the British occupation in Boston. Now, gathered once again in Boston, residents transacted the annual affairs of their town meeting much as their predecessors had for over a century. Reverend Cooper opened with a prayer followed by Thomas Cushing's "Congratulary Speech to the Inhabitants upon the Recovery of the Town out of the hands of the British Enemy, & for the present Opportunity of transacting the Affairs & Business of the Town in a free Town Meeting."[1] Neglected civic matters required immediate attention. The business at hand was repairing damages from the British occupation, the election of town officers, reopening the schools, and checking the condition of the fire engines, along with many other pressing matters.[2] As the voters returned to office the seven selectmen elected on March 13, 1775, who had diligently served during the preceding crisis, order gradually emerged from the chaos of the previous year.[3]

Unlike New York City, which remained the British headquarters for the duration of the American Revolution, Boston had experienced the horrors of warfare on its own soil for only one year, and the majority of residents had fled the town during that period. Nevertheless throughout the Revolution the social and economic impact of the war continually haunted the community. Besides the siege itself, these were the darkest hours Boston had yet faced. The town was confronted with severe food shortages, lack of clothing and wood for winter, and the constant arrival of refugees, which further strained a weakened treasury and a devastated economy. Meeting the requisition for war supplies, as set by the Massachusetts government, drained pocketbooks. Raising soldiers for the army disrupted family structures leaving women and children without husbands and fathers to provide for them.[4] Suffering abounded.

The years between 1776 and 1784 proved challenging for town officials and the overall functioning of the local government, but the end of the war did not necessarily mean that troubled times were over. The closing years of the 1780s and the decade of the 1790s brought new challenges of their own as the town grew rapidly and sought to rebuild its economic and social infrastructure. Despite periodic hardships throughout Boston's history, the closing decades of the eighteenth century tested the mettle and the resiliency of the local government, the town meeting, and the townspeople to a degree not previously encountered.

Many inhabitants were intensely involved with their town government and actively voiced their concerns. To this end they wrote to their local newspapers, spoke out at town meetings, and filed petitions with the Board of Selectmen offering both complaints and suggestions concerning problems the town faced. Petitions, personal correspondence, newspaper essays, and town meeting debates demonstrate that rarely, if ever, were all Bostonians in agreement as to the solutions for the town's problems. Yet despite these disagreements, a picture does emerge in post-Revolutionary Boston of a community attempting to unite in the face of adversity. The present chapter examines this process as it explores civic affairs in late-eighteenth-century Boston by focusing upon some of the central concerns of the town's inhabitants, including poor relief, public education, the marketplace, public safety, and public health.

Since its founding, the political, social, and economic functioning of Boston had depended upon elections held at the yearly town meeting and the participation of eligible citizens in the local government. The first settlers to the Bay Colony originated from towns and villages where the local government had "regulated economic affairs, taxed them, established whatever sanitary standards existed, governed their morals, . . . recorded their land transactions, . . . and generally governed their relations with their neighbors."[5] A century and a half later, town officers continued to play a critical role in overseeing activities in the marketplace, protecting property rights, correcting infringements of the bylaws, policing the town, monitoring the school system, keeping hogs off of the Common, and issuing building permits, to name just a few of the numerous and varied activities in which these men engaged.

At the annual March town meeting, Boston's freeholders elected men to a wide variety of offices including selectmen, overseers of the poor, firewards, sealers of weights and measures, fenceviewers, surveyors of boards and shingles, surveyors of hemp and flax, surveyors of wheat, purchasers of grain, cullers of staves and hoops, hogreeves, constables, scavengers, and tax collectors.[6] Each position was dependent on the others to varying degrees and each was integral to the functioning of the community. Consequently, when chosen candidates asked the selectmen to excuse them from office or when others simply declined the position to which they were elected, it strained the process.

In March 1781, not one of the twelve constables elected to office accepted, an indication of the difficulty of the job, particularly since town law required that those declining to serve pay a fine of £10. The moderator requested that the voters make a second selection. This time eight of the men elected refused the office. The town finally filled the twelve positions, but only after several more rounds of voting.[7] The danger of the job and the increased demand on time made the position unpopular and constables the least likely of all town officials to hold a second office.

Such short terms and erratic patterns of officeholding were typical during the war years. By the mid-1780s old patterns of stability such as longer terms of service began to resurface, but by then a new generation of faces had begun to replace the old. Between 1770 and the late 1790s more than half of all town officers served the community for at least one year, and a small percentage of these men held multiple offices simultaneously. This pattern was common among the selectmen, who might jointly serve as a clerk of the market and fireward. Some also held positions as assessor, assay master, auditor, purchaser of grain, constable, or overseer of the poor. The hatter William Boardman served as selectman continuously between 1787 and 1795, doubling as a clerk of the market for two of those years, 1790 and 1791, while also a deacon in his church. In a twenty-five-year period more than two-thirds of hogreeves and firewards, one-half of sealers of leather, one-third of surveyors of boards and shingles, and one-quarter of the constables held joint offices. Captain John Ballard, owner of a livery stable and boardinghouse on the corner of Rawson's Lane and Newbury Street in the South End, served Boston as a fireward, fenceviewer, constable, scavenger, sealer of wood, and clerk of Faneuil Market.[8]

Officeholders in town government came from a variety of occupational backgrounds, particularly that of artisan. Some positions required familiarity with certain skills, as in the case of those who inspected leather and those who surveyed boards and shingles. Not surprisingly, surveyors of boards and shingles doubled as cullers of staves and as fenceviewers, and almost 90 percent of those surveyors whose occupation can be identified engaged in the woodworking trades. Likewise, approximately 80 percent of those sealers of leather whose occupation is identifiable worked in leather-related trades such as cordwainer. Selectmen, by comparison, tended to be merchants, professional men, and artisans of comfortable means, such as the upholsterer Moses Grant, the baker John Lucas, or the hatter William Boardman. Even though merchants were numerous in Boston and played an important role in key positions of leadership, they did not dominate the local government, at least in numbers.[9]

The responsibilities of selectmen required that the individual be dedicated to the welfare of the community as a whole. It was likewise essential that these men command the respect of their peers and that a majority of the freeholders and inhabitants within the community support them for the system of local government to function. Serving the community as a town official proved a time-consuming undertaking. Serving as a selectman required that the individual be able to afford time away from his business affairs for regular and sometimes significant periods of time.

Each week when the selectmen convened, the business before them varied. Inhabitants continually appeared before them to make special requests, to report the transgression of a neighbor, or to answer for having broken the law. When they met on February 3, 1790, the agenda included reviewing and approbating Abigail Woodman's application for a license to retail "Spirituous Liquors at her Shop in back Street," and considering John Lewis's request for permission to "Retail at his House in Ship Street." Two weeks later, on February 16, Zacheus Moulton and John Drisco each received approval to become innholders at their houses on Dock Square and the Royal Exchange, respectively. At the same meeting the selectmen appointed two new fire engine men to replace the two who had just resigned, and they considered when they would take "up the Complaint against Mr. Moore an Officer of the Police."[10]

At any meeting the Board of Selectmen might issue building permits or business licenses, oversee the work of other town officers, and generally engage in a wide variety of tasks. Unruly residents, roaming hogs, cows on the Neck, uncovered wells, and all types of public nuisances came under the jurisdiction of the selectmen.[11] They in turn delegated each matter to the appropriate town officer, as in May 1785, when George Hamlin, a stable keeper by trade who served as town hayward, had to remove dead carcasses from the Common at town expense, since the selectmen and constables could not discover the perpetrators.[12]

A selectman's job frequently included assessing which buildings, broken fences, damaged pavements, crumbling chimneys, and other structures might prove hazardous to inhabitants. To make these determinations they relied on their own inspection of the community, by means of "a Walk or Visitation of the Town." The "visitation" represented a regular and long-standing ritual that involved surveying the town not only to ensure compliance with safety measures but also to look into matters such as school attendance, care of the poor in the almshouse, and the condition of the marketplace. The reports of other town officers, including the fenceviewers and constables, were also an integral part of the process of managing the town. Likewise, the complaints of inhabitants concerning their neighbors helped the town monitor various daily, weekly, and monthly occurrences. When "Sigorney & Robinson" informed the selectmen that a fellow townsman was presently erecting a blacksmith's shop near North Church that could be a "danger to the Inhabitants," they quickly responded.[13]

In March 1787, the selectmen ordered the immediate repair or demolition of "an old Brick Building in Ann Street owned by Mr. John Welch and others." The structure was in such a bad state "as greatly to endanger the Limbs and Lives of those who pass by it."[14] When William Saxton broke up the pavement "by opening his Drain" and created a hazard, the selectmen ordered him to repair the damaged and now dangerous public space or face "immediate prosecution."[15] Likewise, Mr. Hudson's digging of gravel in the street left "several Pitts which in the Night Season especially indangered the Limbs of the Inhabitants." When town residents complained to the selectmen, they immediately ordered Hudson to report to their chamber.[16] Oliver Vose received orders to cease building a slaughterhouse in Pleasant Street, because it was considered a danger and offense to the surrounding homes.[17]

Town laws prevented the building of structures that might present a danger to the community without the approval of the selectmen. This included brick kilns, lime kilns, bake-houses, and chocolate mills, all considered dangerous because of their constant use of large fires. In 1786 Samuel Wallis applied to the selectmen for a license to operate his chocolate mill "for roasting Cocoa & making of Chocolate" located below Swing Bridge on the Town Dock. After an inspection, which determined that his mill was safe and presented no danger to the property or lives of inhabitants nearby, the selectmen approved his license. Not so with Edward Rumney, who applied three months later to operate his mill in Ball Lane. Inhabitants complained that such an operation presented danger, especially from fire, and consequently drew up a petition, which they presented to the selectmen. Following their routine inspection of the premises, the officials this time denied a license.[18]

Building and operating slaughterhouses and tallow works also required prior board approval. Neighborhood residents presented a petition to the selectmen in 1785 when Thomas Johnson constructed a tallow works "in a Building near Lindells Row for carrying on the business of a Tallow Chandler—without consent of the Selectmen." When he appeared before the nine officers as ordered, they "cautioned against carrying on that business" so as to "avoid the penalty of the Law," after which "the said Law was read to him."[19]

Part of a well-functioning local government was the passage

and enforcement of the town's bylaws. These represented an accumulation of "Rules, Orders and By-Laws, Made by the Freeholders and Inhabitants of the Town of Boston," which had governed the community since the seventeenth and early eighteenth centuries.[20] To remind residents of the rules and regulations of the town, the selectmen ordered the reprinting of Boston's bylaws in 1786. From the printer Edmund Freeman each constable received four hundred copies of the "Code of By Laws," which he distributed in his assigned ward to "Inhabitants as may appear to them proper to be served with them," and he recorded the names of those who received copies. The constables also put two hundred copies in the "Selectmens Chamber, to serve such Persons with as may be over looked or omitted in the above Distribution."[21]

Selectmen also reviewed all reimbursement requests from town officers for expenses incurred while carrying out their duties and approved payments from the treasury for the repair of town property. Such repairs included the town clock in the South End, which stopped "every Cold Night" and "the Cupolow and hanging . . . Bell on the North Latin School," which needed attention. Enoch May, who built "a Necessary House," hung "23 windows," built a chimney, and put up a gutter on "Master Carter's school," was fully compensated for his work after the selectmen reviewed the accounts.[22] Expenses included payment to individuals who did a variety of work for the town. Homer Lewis and Shubael Hews each billed the city for "warning town meetings."[23] Thomas Dakin took care of miscellaneous metalwork at the town market, and Elisha Ticknor submitted a bill on behalf of "Adam a negro man" who "cleaned 16 windows" on a town building.[24] The demands of the almshouse, expenses of the schools, wages to watchmen and lamplighters, and payment to the physicians who inoculated inhabitants during a smallpox epidemic represented just a small portion of the disbursements drawn from the town coffers.

Overseeing charges and payments required that the selectmen

work closely with the town clerk and the town treasurer, especially when the treasury was "drained of money" and the collectors of taxes were "deficient in collection."[25] At the mercy of a collapsed economy, men and women found it difficult to pay property and poll taxes during the 1780s. The brazier John Clough, who owned a residence in Ward 1, in the North End, appeared before the assessors in 1786 pleading for abatement because "he had 7 mouths to feed, and . . . not half a pistereen to buy a Dinner" for he had "no Business." That same year "the Widow of Captain Stephen Hull," who also lived in the North End, was "left with 8 small children" and found herself "unable to pay the Tax of the House." Widows with children, women with husbands unable to work and many mouths to feed, and those with husbands at sea constituted the greatest number of requests for abatement.[26]

Not all of those grumbling about taxes were necessarily poor. At a town meeting in 1793 a merchant claimed that "he had paid his Taxes with Chearfulness. That he was willing to Pay A reasonable Tax, but the Tax of 1791 Assessed on him was Cruel," and he "Expected an abatement, but did not Name any Sum." Another merchant also thought "himself greatly Over taxed" for the same year, while the merchant Samuel Breck Jr. wasn't certain, it seems, as to what to do. He informed the town meeting that he had "received Letters from his Father Not to pay his Tax, but that he had Very Lately received Letters from him to Pay his Taxes" for the two previous years, "Provided the Assessors would take of[f] 15 per Cent." Abatement records suggest that Breck was not alone in attempting to negotiate with town officials regarding the amount due on local taxes.[27] If the town records are any indication, the cost of running the town of Boston during the late eighteenth century frequently exceeded monies collected, adding yet another difficulty to the job of the selectmen.

The Board of Selectmen in a very real sense served as the figurative fathers of the town, attempting to ensure, to the best of their abilities, that the town functioned as a corporate community and consider the good of the whole and the needs of the many. To this end the selectmen did not work alone, for intrinsic to the success of their position was the work of the dozens of other officers elected each year at the town meeting. The overseers of the poor constituted one such group, especially during the severe hardships of the 1770s and early 1780s. Inhabitants of Boston could apply to the overseers for assistance during times of need. The constant demand upon the town funds for the care of the poor, discussed regularly in town meetings during the 1770s and 1780s, speaks to the degree of suffering many endured during those years.

The overseers of the poor worked closely with both the selectmen and the town's constables. Townsmen established the office Board of Overseers of the Poor in the town in 1690 with four officials. By 1735, owing to an increase in the number of poor and the division of the town into twelve wards, the office came to include twelve men and remained that size throughout the eighteenth century. That same year the townsmen authorized the overseers to build "a workhouse for the poor, regulate the same, and receive donations for endowing it."[28] The officers bore the additional duties of supervising the accounts and management of the almshouse and workhouse, sending "idle and indigent persons" to the latter, and advising the selectmen of those in need of admission to the almshouse. Likewise, the officers bound out poor, abandoned, and orphaned children to relieve the town of expenses and, perhaps more important, apprentice these children for a future livelihood to prevent them from becoming a burden on the community as adults.[29] Each official was responsible for the welfare and supervision of one of the twelve wards and possessed a wide range of responsibilities. Daily, weekly, or monthly duties included receiving Boston's poor warned out from other towns, determining who among the inhabitants needed relief when applied for, and through close monitoring of their wards safeguarding the community from unwanted strangers who would overburden the town's limited resources.

The war years were particularly lean ones for Bostonians, heavily burdening the town and its government. In January 1777, John Rowe recorded in his journal that at the town meeting on the morning of the 13th the inhabitants chose a committee of nine men "to consult the best methods to be taken for . . . Immediate Relief" of the town's distress resulting from a lack of food. Even when food became available, poverty meant there were those unable to afford it. One resident informed his friend, "Boston affords nothing new but complaints upon complaints. I have been credibly informed that a person who used to live well has been obliged to take the feathers out of his bed and sell them to an upholsterer to make money to buy bread." To make matters worse, the winter of 1778–1779 was very harsh and bitterly cold. Finally, in desperation, the town appealed to the General Court for assistance.[30] Adding to the severity of the problem, homeless men, women, and children, themselves victims of war and hard times, often straggled into the town seeking assistance.

With the responsibility of caring for its own already difficult, the town could little afford any additional drain to its finances. To prevent strangers from becoming a financial and social burden upon the community, the town government relied upon a system referred to as warning out. This procedure was based upon the premise that simply moving to a town did not automatically make one a legal inhabitant and therefore eligible for public support, or poor relief, a matter of significance when towns often struggled to care for their own poor. Without any safety nets in place, money for poor relief rested upon local taxes and donations from churches and private individuals, and those who might offer care and board to the indigent.

Those who were not inhabitants had no legal claim to assistance and the overseers gave "warnings" to this effect. The practice of warning out, rooted in English Elizabethan Poor Laws but shaped by American experience, had a long history in Boston, having first been used in the Bay Colony in 1636 "to keepe out such whose Lives were publickely prophane and scandalous."[31] The Massachusetts General Court in 1637 ordered that "no towne or pson [*sic*] shall receive any stranger" without permission from "some one of the counsell, or two other of the magistrates."[32]

Thirteen years later, in 1650, the court issued another law ordering that those over the age of sixteen years should be brought before the magistrates to receive permission to remain. Besides the possibility of lewd people disrupting the community, this practice prevented unwanted strangers from becoming financial and legal charges of the town.[33] Legislation in 1692 reinforced the right of town officials to warn out persons and keep a list of their names. This was followed in 1700 with an act protecting towns, which stated that unless admitted as an inhabitant, an individual could not charge the town for support unless he or she lived in the town for twelve months without being warned out.[34]

By the eighteenth century inhabitancy could be acquired in one of five ways. These were birth, consanguinity, a vote of the town meeting, approval by the selectmen, or ownership of a freehold or estate valued at a set amount. Still, inhabitancy, or even the opportunity to remain in town, required demonstration of a means of support and references testifying as to one's character. For example, Elizabeth Finnecy arrived from Cambridge with a recommendation from the selectmen of that community as to her "sober behavior, suitably qualified and provided for the exercise of the employment of a Taverner or Retailer of Spirituous Liquors." The testimony of "a number of the respectable Inhabitants" of Boston further supported her character, and she received permission to remain and operate a business.[35]

The codification of legal inhabitancy in provincial, and later state, law underwent a number of revisions during the course of the eighteenth century. A 1739 act provided that an individual might pay taxes, "perform all the duties of citizenship," and even hold office, but if warned within twelve months of arrival he or she had no legal right to demand assistance from the town.[36] Legislation dated 1767 stated that all persons seeking inhabitancy were required to have the approval of the selectmen or the town meeting.[37] The passage of these laws reinforcing existing statutes suggests periods of increased migration into Boston and concern as to the additional burden on the town's financial resources.[38]

In 1789 the Commonwealth of Massachusetts clarified the status of inhabitancy again, creating a variety of circumstances under which this legal status could be granted to "Citizens of the Commonwealth" in any town they chose. Now in addition to inhabitancy through birth or marriage and approval of the selectmen or town meeting, it included individuals who had "dwelt within the town" for at least one year before April 1767 and had not been warned during that time. Likewise, those occupying and improving a "freehold estate" that constituted a "clear annual income of three pounds" for "the space of two whole years" could claim inhabitancy. Those over the age of twenty who paid a town tax for five successive years and those who resided in the town for two successive years after June 23, 1789, without being warned during that period were also granted the status of inhabitant.[39]

In the last decade of the century laws regarding inhabitancy once again came under revision. First, the number of years of residency without a warning increased on a yearly basis beginning in 1791. That year the law changed so that three years of "settlement without being warned to depart" became the requirement for inhabitancy. This increased to four years in 1792 and five years in 1794 for those who possessed an estate valued at sixty pounds. Also in 1794, apprentices who served four years in a town and "continued to carry on the same" for five years after their bond ended at age twenty-one acquired settlement. Those who served the town in the capacity of selectmen, treasurer, overseer of the poor, assessor, constable, clerk, or tax collector for at least one year did likewise.[40] For more than 150 years Massachusetts' towns practiced warning out, which legally relieved them "from all obligation to aid . . . [individuals] if they became poor and in need of help or support."[41]

Between November 23, 1791, and February 22, 1792, Boston's overseers warned out more than 2,200 men, women, and children. More than one hundred of these adults had resided in Boston since the early 1780s. The total number warned included 740 women who were alone, 69 couples with children, 32 couples without children, and 22 women with children. All others were single males. The placement of names in the records suggests that siblings may have traveled together, as in the entries for Catherine, Polly, and Patty Goodwin and Kitty and Polly Field, all of whom arrived from Ireland. Family size and composition varied. Ann and George Hornby, with their daughter, Elizabeth, arrived from York, England, three weeks prior to receiving a warning. Susannah Maney, a native of Portsmouth, had three daughters and a son. The Moses family, who arrived from Salem, consisted of five children and a father, but no mother. Jonathan and Mary Harris arrived from Charlestown with eight children.[42] The hardship that some of these individuals and families endured must have been daunting. Often driven from community to community with little hope of employment, sometimes disabled and frequently ill or malnourished with minimal if any poor relief available to them, these people constituted the "strolling" or "wandering" poor, the most impoverished sector of eighteenth-century America.

Of the more than two thousand receiving warnings, at least three hundred remained in town despite the fact that assistance could now be denied to them. Those who had been in Boston for a few years or more before being warned may have already secured some form of employment. No matter how irregular or low-paying the work, a job offered the possibility of settlement. The case of the Scotland family, Clarissa, Butterfield, and their children, who arrived in town in the early 1780s, underscores this point.[43] By 1794, the General Court ended the practice of warning out in Massachusetts, although it continued in other New England states.[44] The 1791–1792 warnings appear to have been the last in Boston.

Before the change of law, selectmen notified the warned person's town of legal settlement of any expenses incurred either for removal of that individual or the person's medical care. Considering the number of wandering poor during the years of the Revolution and its aftermath, it is not surprising that the Massachusetts General Court admonished communities to care for their own inhabitants and not let them burden other towns in the Commonwealth. In the middle of 1775, during the crisis of the British occupation and the ensuing siege, the legislature had requested that towns throughout the Commonwealth and in adjoining colonies not treat Boston's inhabitants as wandering poor.[45] By 1776 normal procedures returned.

When Boston's freeholders assembled "at the Old Brick Meeting House" on October 30, 1776, the moderator reminded the townsmen that the General Court now required that those "Inhabitants of Boston" living in towns throughout Massachusetts and "supported at the public Expence" now "be returned to" Boston by the first day of December. Towns such as Salem, which presently housed Boston's poor in their almshouse, informed the selectmen that they intended to return such men, women, and children before the end of the month. In light of "the present distressed State of the Town" and "their being at this Time no Money in the Treasury, nor any Tax made," the meeting approved the borrowing of funds to pay the "Draughts of the Overseers of the Poor, for the Support of said Poor." The townsmen elected a committee to look into the matter.[46]

Destitute men and women in need of medical attention or unable to travel owing to weakness, inadequate clothing, or other circumstances might be given temporary care in the almshouse or boarded with an inhabitant who received remuneration from the town. The selectmen billed these costs to the pauper's town of inhabitancy. As Boston cared for the poor belonging to other communities and in turn charged their local governments, other towns did likewise.

In 1790 Issac Hobbs, the town clerk in Weston, informed the selectmen and overseers of Boston that he was returning Nancy Budge (alias Blake), who had been living in Weston under the town's care. Nancy, "a pauper Deprived of her reason," had become "troublesome and expensive to the family where she resides," and therefore Boston's officials needed to see to "her removal . . . or take such other measure for her support & comfort as her case demands."[47] Likewise, the town of Medford notified the Boston selectmen that they had Benjamin Rouse and his family and Patty Maise, who had "for some months past been in a delirious state." Medford officials had already notified the Boston selectmen that they were caring for Rouse some months earlier, but according to Medford's chairman, Ebenezer Hall, the town had not responded. With the letter sent by Hall in late summer 1790 came the stern reminder that Medford's authorities would take "legal measures" if Boston did not "take the mentioned poor from our hands."[48]

The evolution of the local legal system governing inhabitancy also addressed the responsibilities of legal residents with respect to outsiders. Town laws dating back to 1647 and 1659 forbade citizens "to rent or sell either shop or dwelling within the town's limits" to a stranger without the selectmen's permission. A newcomer could be granted admission if an inhabitant offered security that the individual would not become a burden upon the town. By 1659 laws prevented inhabitants from receiving into their "howses or employments" any individual "without liberty granted from the select men." To do so incurred a fine. The status of strangers was further defined by a town law that strictly forbade inhabitants from entertaining or receiving "in any of their houses or tenements" new residents for longer than twenty days, unless they had first received permission from the selectmen. More than one hundred years later, these laws still governed the behavior of inhabitants.[49]

In 1787, Thomas Walley duly notified the officers that he had taken in Rebeccah Bradshaw of Medford, Middlesex County, as a servant, and John Andrews gave notification "that he received into his House as a dry nurse one Margaret Orcut an inhabitant of Hingham." William Dawes Sr., a North End shopkeeper, assured the selectmen that Hannah Gray from Salem, to whom he let "a Chamber in his House," was "a virtuous Woman, who works for her living."[50] When Captain John Du Heaume arrived in Boston with thirty-eight passengers from Newfoundland, the selectmen required him "to give *Bond* that they Shall not become a charge to the Publick," which he promptly did.[51]

Determining who did and who did not belong in the town was a constant job, and to this end overseers of the poor made periodic visitations throughout the town to "enquire what Strangers are in the several Houses, and to take the names of such Persons."[52] This information was then submitted to the selectmen, who weighed each case on an individual basis to determine who should receive assistance, who should be allowed to remain in the community and for what period of time, and who should be warned back to their place of origin. To avoid any misunderstandings, inhabitants who had left Boston reported to the selectmen upon their return. The fine for the illegal harboring of "strangers" was six shillings for each day of violation, a hefty sum of money that could feed an individual for several days.[53] The laws requiring that new arrivals in town be registered made exceptions for "mere traveller[s] passing or repassing through the [town]."[54] For those in need of reminders as to town laws, these and others were periodically posted, read in meetings, or announced publicly by constables.

Among those warned, the overseers listed a number of foreign immigrants living in the port town.[55] Bridget Neagles and her child were initially placed in the almshouse at the state's expense until the selectmen eventually paid her passage back to Ireland. The immigrants listed on the overseers of the poor warning-out lists represented a culturally diverse group. About 40 percent of the total listed were Irish, with another 40 percent English, and the remaining 20 percent being Germans, French, Danish, Spanish, Dutch, and Welsh. Some traveled alone, as did Stephen Roberts from Ireland, while others such as James Owens, his wife Betsy, and their four children arrived in family groups. Overseers warned the family of Scottish immigrant Alexander Gillis, which included his wife, three daughters, and four sons, in 1791. Gillis appeared in the town records in 1790, when he worked as a laborer in a small factory in the South End, but after 1791 he disappears.[56] Large families who were not legal inhabitants of the town and fell upon hard times represented a financial burden that the community was unable to afford. The consequences for the poor were harsh, and many wandered from town to town seeking an elusive security.

Through strict enforcement of bylaws and by undertaking periodic visitations throughout the town, the selectmen, overseers of the poor, and constables collectively monitored the community. In so doing they acted as guardians against crime and civic irresponsibility and attempted to limit additional burdens on an already inadequate job market and the community's insufficient resources for the care of the indigent. With no centralized state system of assistance in place to care for the impoverished, mentally ill, and homeless, responsibility for an individual fell to the town of birth, as specified in the laws of the Commonwealth. In turn, when communities faced economic hardships to the point that they could not care for their own, warning out seemed the only viable means of handling unwanted dependent strangers. Although some attempted to care for outsiders, as in the case of Rouse and Maise, it was economic hardship and not necessarily lack of compassion that intensified the use of warning-out practices. Those who already suffered the most became the victims who found themselves driven from community to community.[57]

Not all in need were immediately turned away, as with Bridget Neagles, who first went to the almshouse until she was well enough to travel. Although conditions were usually deplorable, the almshouse provided some food and shelter for inhabitants fallen upon hard times whom the selectmen and overseers of the poor deemed needy of care until fit for travel to the town of their birth. Paul Farmer, the almshouse keeper, received orphans, mothers with children, fathers with children, and the indigent into the institution by order of the selectmen and recommendation of the overseers. In one instance, two of the officers advised the selectmen to admit two women with their children on April 3, 1777.[58] Less than a month later "Mary Vose and her six children, three of them at Birth named Hancock, Washington & Lee," joined them.[59] The length of stay in the almshouse varied greatly, and costs involved not only food but also some clothing, medical care, and perhaps funeral expenses. Robert Hinds received a shirt and "homespun jacket," his wife a pair of shoes, hose, a gown, and a petticoat, and his child two shirts. Sara Partridge needed a wooden leg, and when Matthew Bright, Richard Orchard, and the child of Fanny Jones died, there were funeral charges.[60] Unless they were inhabitants of Boston, charges were billed back to the individual's town of birth. If that could not be traced, then the Massachusetts General Court received the bill.

Conditions in the almshouse were chronically terrible. Underfunded, overcrowded, and suffering from much postponed maintenance, the facility struggled constantly to care for its charges. In response to these conditions, some inmates ran away, as did "Betty Ward and her child," and "Sarah Hill & Mary Billings."[61] According to a petition addressed to the Board of Selectmen in July 1793, there were "220 Persons in the Almshouse, which makes between 6 & 7 a room, [and] in the Winter season there are generally about

300 in the house, which crowds about 9 persons into a room."
Under such circumstances men and women were frequently housed
together, meaning that "the Ears & Eyes of the more modest are
often offended with the indecent language and more indecent actions of many of their vile companions."[62] The "suffering and almost perishing circumstances" included not only inadequate food
and clothing, but lack of proper shelter during the winter months,
and dangerously unsanitary conditions. One resident described it as
"rather a dungeon than an hospital. It can neither be ventilated nor
properly cleaned." The size of the building was usually inadequate
for the number of inmates, and the many "evils unavoidably resulting from bad air, and filth are notorious." It was determined that
neither the physician nor the overseer could prevent these "evils."[63]

The expenses of the almshouse included clothing, food, and
wood during the winter months, pay to laborers, carpenters, and
such men who made repairs and maintained the property, employees' compensation, and doctors' fees, as well as remuneration to
townspeople who took the poor into their homes to nurse them.
The two most serious problems faced, especially during the war
years, were overcrowding and lack of funds.

In the spring of 1781 the overseers of the poor informed the
town meeting "that they were in such want of Money" for the institution "that unless furnished with some immediately they must
open the Almshouse Doors to let the Poor out." They reported to
those present on the "suffering and almost perishing condition[s]"
that they attributed to lack of an "adequate supply of Money." To
help alleviate some of the suffering, it was voted that "a Committee
be appointed in each Ward to raise by Subscriptions . . . several
thousand pounds in Silver or current Money equivalent." Recon-
vening later in the day, the committee of the whole, representing
each of the wards, informed the town meeting of "the aged decri-
ped & other suffering Poor," a number of whom "had lived well
and contributed their share towards the Publick expence." There-

fore they admonished that "Neglect" of these inhabitants was "cruel" and would "justly bring [reproach] upon the Inhabitants" of Boston. Accordingly, the meeting appointed another committee to walk the wards and collect the necessary funds.[64] This was neither the first time nor the last time that Bostonians reached into their pockets and contributed to the needy.

Collections in 1781 no more provided a permanent solution to the suffering than had previous subscriptions. One year later conditions had not improved. In the spring of 1782 the almshouse poor went without bread for nearly a week until "two hundred of hard Bread was procured for them." It was an inadequate amount of food that lasted barely two days, once again leaving them with nothing but water. The master of the almshouse had already incurred such great debt "for beef and other Necessaries," which he was "unable to discharge," that he "could not get more credit." The town meeting voted to pay the almshouse whatever money was necessary from the town treasury.[65] Another means of reducing costs associated with the almshouse and a way of providing homes for younger inmates involved the established custom of indentureship.

The overseers indentured, or bound out, both infants born in the institution and the orphans left there. Boys could be indentured until the age of twenty-one and girls until eighteen years old unless they married earlier. On October 6, 1788, the overseers bound out young James Lewis the same day he arrived. The young child Hebron Matterson arrived at the institution on January 11, 1790, and was sent to his new master eighteen days later. One young infant, born at the almshouse, remained there only three months before being bound out.[66]

Between April 1785 and January 15, 1790, the overseers indentured seventy-four of the children in the almshouse. All would remain indentured servants for ten to twelve years. Only five of these children were bound out to Bostonians, although the other sixty-nine remained in Massachusetts. Three of the five youths were

bound to a hairdresser, a leather dresser, and a housewright and
cistern maker. The overseers indentured nine-year-old Elizabeth
Champlen for twelve years to the merchant Nathaniel Paine. Cordwainer David Burrill, a resident of Cambridge Street in Ward 8,
took Stephen Ingalls, the fifth orphan. After his indenture ended
eleven years later, Ingalls remained in Boston, where he earned his
living as a cordwainer, residing not far from where he spent his days
as an apprentice in Burrill's shop.[67]

The process of indenturing children required confirmation
from the selectmen as to the character of the new master or mis-
tress. This was a particularly important concern if the child's destination was other than a Boston home, where they would be out of
the jurisdiction of the selectmen. Confirmation included a signed
statement affirming that the person taking the youth was "of sober
life & Conversation & in good Circumstances" and that "both he &
his wife" were "suitable persons to be Intrusted with the Education
of any Child which may be bound to them as an apprentice." The
indentureship contract specified the length of apprenticeship and
that "sufficient Meat Drink & Lodging and Apparell" be provided
for the youth.[68] Periodically the overseer investigated the living situation of those indentured to ascertain that the child was not
abused.

Unlike an orphan bound out from the almshouse, those children bound into apprenticeship by their parents so that they might
learn a trade were more likely to have had an advocate in case of
unexpected circumstances. When Ann Currier brought a complaint
before the selectmen and overseers regarding the abuse her appren-
ticed son William received at the hands of Ebenezer Swan, the
board called Swan before them to hear his accounting of the situation. With the help of witnesses they determined Swan guilty and
immediately canceled William Currier's indentures.[69]

In theory binding out children served the orphaned and impoverished children as much as it did the town. The almshouse no

longer bore the cost, the new master gained a source of labor, and the child acquired a trade, though orphaned children did not necessarily have an advocate as did William Currier. Some children bound out from the almshouse clearly learned a trade, as did Stephen Ingalls. However, conditions could be harsh for indentured children coming from the almshouse. The number of advertisements for young runaway apprentices appearing in Boston newspapers between 1775 and 1795 may well reflect the plight of indentured youths, orphaned or not.

Records of the town meetings from the mid-1770s into the 1790s attest to the staggering portion of the town's budget devoted to caring for Boston's poor. Sometimes the town met expenses by securing private loans, thus incurring further debts. Besides through the payment of taxes, Boston inhabitants also made direct contributions to the care of the poor. The annual distribution of small sums of money to thirty-one needy widows during the winter months came from the interest earned from Mrs. Brooker's trust, willed specifically for that use. The amount was only enough to cover the very barest of necessities, and recipients varied no doubt based upon need. Some received a portion of money every year, as had Mrs. Delaplace since 1769. Others received assistance only once or twice.[70]

Churches took up collections for the poor to help buy food and provide firewood, various charity benefits raised funds, and money collected from fines went to the support of the almshouse.[71] When the town treasurer David Jeffries died, he deeded land to the city for the purpose of renting or selling it so that those rents or the profits collected from the sale could be "applied annually forever to purchase *Tea, Chocolate, & Sugar* for the refreshment of those Persons who in the Providence of God are or shall be reduced & obliged to take shelter in the Almshouse."[72]

These acts of kindness no doubt helped, but raising funds to care for the poor fell primarily to the town government. At town meetings, inhabitants were reminded of the need to allocate tax money or raise additional money for the care of the destitute in the poorhouse. In 1781 the overseers prepared a report "of the destresses of the Poor in the Almshouse" to distribute among "the Ministers of the Gospel of all denominations through the Town" so that they might inform their congregations of the plight of the poor. A town committee then walked the town ward by ward seeking donations from the inhabitants for the almshouse, which would "be discounted out of the Tax."[73]

During the last quarter of the eighteenth century, as Boston's population grew, the system of poor relief became increasingly inadequate. The conditions in the almshouse and workhouse were appalling, but this cannot be assumed to have stemmed from a lack of concern for the less fortunate. Surely there were those who remained indifferent to the plight of others, but many inhabitants demonstrated concern and compassion even though collectively as a town they frequently lacked the means to address fully the problems of poverty. In more than one instance the minutes of the Boston selectmen refer to the overseers of the poor as reaching into their own pockets to help the men, women, and children in the almshouse. Individual citizens donated money and food. Regardless of the demands upon the town budget, inhabitants repeatedly approved monies to be paid to the institution for the destitute, and raised taxes accordingly. Records indicate that the overseers and selectmen sent to the almshouse a large number of people who were not residents of the town but were strangers passing through. Whether black or white, with or without children, male or female, the almshouse took as many as it could, sometimes beyond the point of full capacity. This no doubt exacerbated the existing problems this institution faced. Both the reports of the overseers and the fact that inmates ran away attest to the horrid conditions in the almshouse. But the efforts to help the poor on the part of many

Bostonians, the town government, and town officials also demonstrated a sense of community responsibility and compassion.[74]

Besides overseeing the community's poor relief, the responsibilities of town officials extended into many other arenas of daily
life, including public education. As Boston struggled to rebuild its
community following the siege, one of the first orders of business
was the reopening of the town schools. In May 1776, two writing
schools and one grammar school began once again to accept children, but the schoolmasters were "to depend upon the generosity
of the Town for an allowance" because of the troubled financial
times. Two months later, in July 1776, another writing school re-
opened, and by November the town finally took up the issue of
schoolmasters' salaries, which included quarterly pay plus a one-
time stipend "in Consideration of the present high Price of the
Necessaries of Life."[75]

As four of the six masters teaching before April 1775 returned
to the classroom, their familiar faces and the open schools made
another contribution to a sense of normalcy and stability in the war-
torn community. Three of the masters had taught in Boston for
close to a decade, one had served for two decades, and another,
Samuel Holbrook, for thirty years. John Lovell, who had given approximately forty-five years of teaching service to the community,
departed with the British in 1776, but his son James remained and
continued to work as an usher.[76] As people returned to Boston the
demand for the schools grew, and "in Consideration of the great
Encrease of Schollars" additional ushers were assigned to the masters in mid-1777. By the following decade, the town began constructing new schools.[77]

Low pay for teachers remained a problem, as attested to by a
column appearing in the *Boston Gazette* three years later. That salaries were tied to the number of children in a master's school did not
help, as the author of this column pointed out. The "low prices"
paid for the education of a child led schoolmasters, he argued, "to

make up in *number* what is deficient in *weight*," therefore taking on more boys than could be given "proper attention." This was not the fault of the schoolmasters, who had to earn a living, but a fault of the system under which the town functioned. "Larger wages are given to men, who break and train horses and dogs," he wrote, "than to those, under whose direction children are to be formed either to good or to evil, to happiness, or misery for the rest of their days." The result of these practices, he satirically concluded, will be "tame and well ordered horses, but wild and unfortunate children; and therefore in the end, they find more pleasure in their horse, than comfort in their child."[78]

The gradual increase of Boston's population during the early 1780s led some residents to consider expanding and improving the town's school system. As it was not always possible to construct buildings owing to the chronic shortage of funds, other means were sought to provide educational facilities. When the town's children needed a school in the South End, officials determined that "Widow Holbrook had a Room which would accommodate about Seventy or Eighty Scholars," which was immediately "hired."[79]

A system of public education had long been one of Boston's priorities. This was evident not only in their maintaining an adequate number of schools so that they might be accessible to children in all areas of town, but also by the fact that under a 1720 provision, masters were required to teach male apprentices "to read and write, and the girls to read." Likewise, according to the law, parents who neglected the basic education of their children so that they were "not able to distinguish the alphabet or twenty-four Letters at the age of six years" might also find their children bound out "into good Families," who would oversee the acquisition of these basic skills.[80]

In a committee report in 1784, Bostonians clearly demonstrated their pride in having a public school system that guaranteed all children "equal Advantages and being placed upon an equal Footing" regardless of the "Circumstances of their Parents." This was not entirely true, as the parents of black children might attest. In a 1796 petition to the selectmen, more than twenty African-Americans stated that notwithstanding the admittance of "Black children as well as wite into the free schools" and the "good inteneon [*sic*]" of the School Committee in making free education available to all, the committee's action "bred a discord and hindrence." Black youth, the petition asserted, would benefit from a school of their own. The committee had either not taken into consideration or chose to ignore the discrimination the African-American children would encounter. Less than two years later Elisha Sylvester applied to "set up a School to teach the children of the Africans, at or near West Boston." Sylvester, despite his not being a native Bostonian, came well recommended by several inhabitants and had "a Certificate from the selectmen of the town to which he belongs" addressing his "abilities." In May 1798, he was granted a license "to open a School . . . for the Instruction of Youth more especially African Youth, in Reading Writing & Arithmetic."[81]

The community's goal in 1784 was to make education as accessible as possible. Accordingly, fees were abolished in an attempt to remove economic obstacles. The town voted "that the practise of the Schoolmasters in receiving Entrance & Fire Money (so called) be abolished as inconsistent with that Freedom of Education which was originally intended in the Institution of the Publick Schools." Simply put, fees meant that "Poor Children" were deprived "of the Benefit of" education. Those parents who were too poor to send their children to school could receive assistance to do so, and the town paid the schoolmasters and schoolmistresses each week "for the Instruction of . . . such Children."[82]

When some "worthy citizens" proposed establishing academies in Boston, as was being done in other parts of the state, Samuel Adams was quick to respond that although he knew there were "great advantages" to such institutions, they might prove harmful to grammar schools. "The peculiar advantage of such schools is, that the poor and the rich may derive equal benefit from them, but none excepting the more wealthy . . . can avail themselves of the benefits of the Academies." From the public schools, he pointed out, "have flowed so many great benefits." The purpose of such schooling was to create citizens "more useful to the Community" and to serve "the future Wellfare of the Community."[83]

In 1789 the committee for "reforming the present System of public Education in Boston" introduced a "Plan & Arrangement" for "a new system of education" to educate both boys and girls. The plan included one grammar school to prepare males of at least ten years of age in the "rudiments of the latin & greek languages" so that they might be "fully qualified for the Universities." The plan also called for "Writing" schools and "Reading" schools for children of both sexes from seven years of age to learn writing, arithmetic, spelling, reading, and "English Grammar & Composition." Boys would attend schools year-round and girls April through October, both until the age of fourteen.[84] In this extensive and highly detailed report, the curriculum, textbooks, school hours, holidays, "play-days," and regulations were specified by the committee in consultation with the schoolmasters. School attendance would be mandatory. To oversee the program inhabitants annually elected a committee that, along with the selectmen, "visit[ed] the Schools once in every quarter" or more frequently if "judged proper." Subcommittees also visited on a monthly basis. Finally, the plan included opening new schools.[85]

By 1790 the new program was in effect. During a visitation in July 1790, the committee counted 1,301 students attending school, 539 of whom were girls. Although in April 1790 the committee had determined that it was not presently "practicable to admit the Females to the publick schools" because of the condition of the buildings and improvements they were undergoing, the problems had obviously been resolved by late summer. The committee proudly announced to the community after their July visit that they had found "abundant testimonials of the attention and assiduity of the several Masters, and the decent decorum of the scholars."[86]

The reform program of the 1780s did not solve all of the problems in the school system. Taxes still needed to be raised to pay salaries and erect new buildings. Some parents ignored the regulations requiring that all children be in school. Concerns existed that children were "playing in the Streets" during school hours "or still worse gathering into Clusters and inuring their impressive Minds to the abominable Vice of gaming," which was the fault of the "Indulgence of Parents" and "too lax a Government in Schools."[87]

For one individual the problems lay with the schoolmasters rising above themselves. "Aristides" claimed that salaries paid schoolmasters were too high and the Thursday and Saturday afternoons off were turning some of them into "gentleman," as was "clearly seen" by the "*Tom-Cod frolicks* and excursions into the country."[88] A letter appearing in the *Boston Gazette* in 1795, written in a more serious vein, raised concerns and questions suggesting that the public school system was not running as smoothly as it had before the Revolution, when by and large masters remained in positions for extended periods of time, even decades.[89] "Senex" informed his readers that he had lived in Boston for almost eighty years and never remembered "one instance . . . of a School master being dismissed from the service of the town, until within five or six years past." Not only had two schoolmasters "been turned out" and another two "resigned their Schools," but "complaints from the School masters of difficulties" were constant and serious. This "convinces me," wrote Senex, "that things do not work right. . . . Are the School masters less faithful than formerly? Or, are they really oppressed?"[90] The minutes of the selectmen's meetings remain silent, not revealing what troubles Boston's schoolmasters may have faced.

The final part of the reform program for Boston's schools addressed private institutions. The School Committee expressed its concern in 1784 that private schools caused problems in three ways. First, they made the opportunities for education unequal because some parents could afford extra education while others could not, which had been a concern of Samuel Adams. Second, public schoolmasters teaching students after hours took resources away from their regular students. Finally, the quality of private schools was not being monitored.[91] Yet private evening schools, "Writing and Arithmetic," and "Bookkeeping and Accounting" schools, to name a few, were undoubtedly popular if the increasing number of advertisements for such is any gauge.[92] Under the new regulations proposed by the committee and voted by the town meeting, public schoolmasters were no longer allowed to run private schools after hours. To compensate these schoolmasters for the financial loss to their families, they would receive a salary increase. Hereafter, prior to opening, all private schools required the approval of the selectmen, who would also govern hours of operation, curriculum, and the quality of the schoolmasters.[93]

Selectmen did deny permission to open schools and ordered those shut whose proprietors had not first received approbation. This happened to John Nutting and Monsieur Revaut, who opened a school for reading, writing, and French only to have it promptly closed down until they had spoken with the board.[94] Overall, the selectmen approved more school applications than they denied. When Betsy and Ammy Raymer applied for permission "to keep School for teaching reading & sewing," the selectmen agreed to their undertaking, considering them "Persons of a sober life & conversation and well qualified."[95] William White, "being well recommended" and therefore acceptable, opened "a private School in State Street . . . for the instruction of Youth in Writing Arithmatick & English Grammar." Francis Nichols, with a recommendation from a town physician, received permission to open a school to instruct "young Persons in English Latin Mathematics & Natural

Philosophy."[96] In the case of Nutting and Revaut, they had not sought approval before advertising. Once these procedures were followed there were usually no difficulties. This was the situation with Mr. Duport, who advertised a dancing school without permission. Once he appeared before the selectmen and made a petition describing his intentions, which usually included providing references, the selectmen granted approval, as he was now "adheering to the Laws of the Commonwealth for the regulating [of] Schools."[97] This was the crux of the matter. As the town fathers, the selectmen bore the responsibility and obligation of knowing who was educating the town's youth and running the town's schools.

During the war years and those that followed, town officers, with the assistance of the town meeting, oversaw not only poor relief and public education but also the functioning of the local market and domestic economy. In the second half of the 1770s and early 1780s this involved the implementation of regulations. Following the war, though regulation was still attempted, Bostonians became increasingly interested in reforming and not just regulating the day-to-day operations of the marketplace.

Regulation of the market in Boston had its roots in the seventeenth century, when officials began to set "minimum standards" and fair "prices for various goods." As the town shifted from an agricultural to a commercial community, the town meeting added additional officers necessary for such an economy, including sealers of weights and measures, surveyors of boards and shingles, and sealers of leather. Still, in many ways market life was informal. Bostonians bought goods directly off ships in the harbor, and they had grown accustomed to peddlers, hucksters, and farmers from the rural surrounding areas selling freely in the streets and door-to-door rather than using a specifically designated market area with rented stalls and strict regulations. Demand for change began in the very early 1700s. By the 1730s, amidst other town reforms, the town meeting in a close vote established three public marketplaces, with regulation falling directly to the selectmen, as the town did not choose to have the markets monitored by specialized market clerks.[98]

While inhabitants remained protective of their own economic freedoms, they expected selectmen to punish engrossers (monopolizers) and those who infringed upon a sense of moral economy. The conflict in essence was one between the practice of the medieval moral economy and the emerging free-market economy. During the latter part of the century, as the community struggled to survive the shock of the Port Act, the siege, and the crippling effect of the ensuing war, the selectmen and other town officers played a dynamic role in overseeing the market. At town meetings and in petitions a substantial number of Bostonians seem to have made it clear that this was what they expected in order to create a moral economy for the purpose of the survival of residents and the town itself. While war provided opportunities for monopolizers and extortioners, it also led inhabitants to demand justice in the marketplace. Those verbally attacking the profiteers wanted full weight brought to bear on them not only for creating want and hunger but for violating the sanctity of the communal spirit and demoralizing the virtue of the community.

A petition submitted to the Board of Selectmen in 1776 demonstrates the ways in which residents expected the selectmen and their assistants to monitor the functioning of the marketplace for the protection of honest inhabitants. Following the siege, more than seventy petitioners reminded their leaders of the "many Troubles and Difficulties in being driven from . . . [their] Habitation for a long time," and the consequent loss of "all business." They had acted as virtuous citizens by making, they argued, "disinterested sacrifices . . . for the good of . . . [their] country" but still found themselves in "intolerable Distress." The "exorbitant price of firewood" resulted from engrossing by wharfingers; the "exorbitant price of provisions of all kinds" likewise was owing "to Forestallers & ingrossers." What "little business" the town had should belong to inhabitants and not "persons of abroad." The petitioners in closing reminded the selectmen that "Extortions of every kind are an abomination to God Himself & We cannot expect a blessing from the Almighty unless we bear Testimony against them & take every method in our power to prevent the poor from being oppressed."[99] These Bostonians, in demanding that the needs of "the many" and not "the few" be paramount, looked to their leaders to ensure such.

By February 1777 the town meeting had appointed a committee to deal with the ongoing concerns regarding the scarcity of "Provisions" owing to a "Number of Engrossers, who have monopolized great Quantities of Rum, Sugar, Molasses, Cotton-Wool, coffee, Cocoa, &c. & most Kinds of Cloathing." Despite the prices fixed by the General Court in a January 1777 Act "to Prevent Monopoly and Oppression," these individuals, according to the committee, now refused to abide by such mandates. The committee hastened to add that not all traders in the town were guilty of such actions. Despite the committee's "earnestly" encouraging compliance, the problem continued, as evidenced by the town records, personal correspondence, and newspaper commentaries.[100]

Shopkeeper Allen Crocker, who lived on Marlborough Street in the South End, went so far as to inform his brother and partner, Joseph, in 1778 that he was "more Affraid of the Cursed Extortion that Prevails Among Us" than of another attack from the British forces.[101] When dairy farmers across the Neck sent two-day-old milk with the cream skimmed off to the Boston market and demanded *"three Pounds of Sugar"* in exchange for *"one Pound of Butter,"* housewives in town responded with the accepted means of exposing culprits of unjust and immoral behavior in the marketplace. They published in the Boston newspaper a candid description of the offenders' activities and reminded them of Ezekiel 22:12. "And thou hast greedily gained of thy Neighbours by Extortion."[102]

By 1779 some Bostonians turned to the streets to express their anger at the appalling conditions that left them with empty stomachs.[103]

Attempting to curb "greedily gained" profit, the town meeting unanimously passed a resolution for "regulating [the] prices of Goods" on August 17, 1779. Six months earlier, in February 1779, the General Court, having repealed the 1777 act against monopolies, once again passed an act "proscribing hoarding." Although a precedent existed in Boston for market controls during the Revolutionary era and earlier, previous resolutions appear to have never been as extensive as those the town meeting discussed in 1779.[104]

Under advice of the selectmen, the townspeople agreed upon fixed wages for certain occupations and fixed prices on specific goods and services. The resolution limited the legal daily pay of ship carpenters, ship joiners, riggers, caulkers, housewrights, carpenters, masons, and laborers, who might earn up to three-quarters of what artisans earned. Dozens of tradesmen were to reduce their charges by varying degrees, such as the "twenty pc [percent]" reduction "from the Present Prices" required of printers, boatbuilders, ropemakers, cordwainers, tinmen, and coopers. The resolution determined what sailmakers could charge per "Bolt for working New Canvas and for old Work in Proportion"; what farriers might charge for shoeing horses and truckmen for the truckage of sugar, rum, and molasses; and hatters for their "beaveretts," "best Beaver hatts," and "felt Hatts," although the hatmakers complained that the prices fixed on beaver hats brought them economic difficulties. The new resolution also required innholders and "Victuallers" to reduce the price of "Victualling and Horse keeping in proportion to the Reduction of the Prices of Provisions and Hay." Tradesmen not mentioned in the list had to "reduce their Prices in an Average proportion with those of their Brethren, and the Article of Consumption."[105] This regulation of wages and prices was, in addition to the apprenticeship system, one of the few similarities to the English guild system, something that had never been successful in the colonies.

One response to allegedly corrupt trade practices resulted in the town office of hay weigher being reassessed. Believing that some farmers from surrounding areas used false weights when selling their hay at Boston Common, a number of townsmen argued that "leasing" the "Hay Engine to [the] highest bidder" each year only made matters worse. This was a job that required the same individual on a yearly basis so that the town could "be well acquainted with the disposition of persons." The hay weigher would then know "carts and drivers," and a farmer would not be able to put "a quantity of Boards under his load of hay" or conceal "a bag of salt" to make the hay weigh more and thus overcharge. A steady "good Farmer" in the job could also better "judge the quality of the hay." To this end the concerned townsmen petitioned the selectmen and met with success.[106]

Regulations aimed not only at controlling labor costs and fair prices for market goods but also at providing a more equitable opportunity for all Bostonians to acquire the necessities. The price that fishermen were legally permitted to charge for a pound of cod, haddock, or "Hallybut without entrails" was set. To oversee the setting of fair prices for necessities, selectmen ordered prices of "*good* Provisions" published in the local newspapers.[107]

Concern about the food shortages and the dependence on expensive vegetables from surrounding areas led some unnamed residents to offer the town twenty acres of rent-free land that the town meeting elected to enclose for the purpose of growing vegetables for the community. "Butchers, Tanners, Leather Dressers, Tallow Chandlers and Soap Boilers" requested that the "Town would enter upon some speedy Measures for the introduction of live Stock" with the plan that the "Butchering businesss may be again carried on in this Town as also the other branches of Manufacturers Which have been driven from us to the Neighboring Towns." To encourage this, inhabitants voted to give their "preference" to those who would establish the "Butchers buissiness" and once again sell "Beef Mutton or Lamb" in the market.[108]

To further protect local business, the selectmen discouraged the practice of residents sending their servants to neighboring towns to acquire goods unavailable in Boston. Instead, they were encouraged to purchase what was available in Boston to the advantage of the town's own shopkeepers and marketmen.[109] When it became clear that not all residents agreed with this suggestion, the town assigned twenty men to "serve in rotation as guards" at the old fortification on the Neck and at the Charlestown Ferry "to prevent people from leaving Boston to purchase provisions elsewhere."[110] If appealing to the conscience of the town did not meet with compliance from all inhabitants, the selectmen might employ alternatives that they hoped would convince them otherwise. In this vein, the Committee of Correspondence, Inspection and Safety (hereafter CCIS) and even one's own neighbors played an important part in enforcing market control resolutions.

Votes in the town meetings reflected unanimity, but in practice gaining compliance from the townspeople as they went about their everyday business was another story. As the CCIS discovered when they visited various merchants and shopkeepers the following month, there were those who did not support the new price controls, just as some residents did not agree with restricting inhabitants' access to markets in neighboring towns. Lack of consensus on economic issues was not new, as had been seen with responses to the Boston Port Act and the Solemn League and Covenant in 1774. Reminiscent of its activities prior to the onset of the American Revolution, the CCIS had the responsibility of investigating forestallers, extortionists, and anyone suspected of noncompliance in regard to price controls.

On Monday, September 27, the committee "waited upon . . . as many shopkeepers" and merchants "as . . . time would admit." John

Molineaux, a South End merchant, "was obliged to consult with his Brother William" before giving the committee an answer. Shortly after the meeting with John, the committee met up with William "& were treated by him with indelicate Language the effect of high passion." Mrs. Molly Williams and Mrs. Curles each told the committee that they did not know whether or not they might conform. Despite the uncertainty of support among some, the records indicate that the majority of shopkeepers and merchants visited by the CCIS on September 27 expressed their willingness to oblige, whether out of general concern for the well-being of their fellow townspeople or fear of consequences of noncompliance.[111]

Ignoring the town's market resolutions resulted in the printing of the offender's name in the town newspaper. It was then expected "that the Publick knowing" of the offender "may Abstain from all Trade and Conversation with them and the People at Large inflict upon them that Punishment which such Wretches deserve." In short, this meant that citizens would neither trade nor "hold any intercourse or conversation with such Persons" and that each would "keep a Vigilant Eye upon his Neighbour" with the purpose of preventing "Any infringements upon the Resolution." For those not present at the August 17 town meeting, the selectmen printed the resolutions in the town newspapers and on handbills for distribution throughout the community. Those who did not comply with controls of the marketplace were pariahs to be excommunicated from the corporate body.[112]

By the war's end in 1783, Bostonians began turning their attention to market reforms, particularly with respect to the public markets. A number of inhabitants expressed concern in March of that year about "Carts, paynyards, stalls and benches on Dock Square, and in other Publick Places" that presented serious hazards to passersby and shoppers. Consequently, they suggested providing "some suitable Place or Places . . . for the Accommodation of the Market people." Two weeks later the town meeting voted on and passed reforms that established new market procedures.[113] Now there would be designated market areas for the sale of different items, such as hay, wood, meat, grains, and fish. The sale of wood, for example, was assigned to two markets to accommodate both the north and south ends of town; one was situated in the Old North Square in Ward 2, and the other at the northeast end of the Common by the Town Granary. At these two locations it was "lawful for all Persons bringing Wood, loads of barrells Empty or full, or Hoops to Marketts to Assemble [to] stand with their teams, Carts, Sleds & Waggons for the purpose of vending" their merchandise. Oliver's Dock, south of Long Wharf in Ward 9, served as the hay market. It was permissible to sell grains, meat, and vegetables only on "the lower floor of Faneuil Hall and the Land around." Persons selling or buying any market goods in areas around town other than those designated faced substantial fines, depending upon the infraction, with the revenue collected supporting the upkeep of the markets.[114]

No sooner had the designated markets been established than Bostonians began expressing their concerns and displeasure when the marketplaces, in their opinion, were not properly supervised. The primary responsibilities of the newly created office of Inspector of the Markets included ensuring that the marketplaces about town be "continually clean and free from all kinds of filth & Dirt; and . . . Nusances."[115]

In 1784 the selectmen prepared a plan for the placement of stands in the markets, to be rented on a weekly basis with specific areas of the market assigned to specific groups of vendors, so that lemon sellers, for example, were assigned to the "Range on the North Side of the Market House." This provided a way of monitoring those in the public market who had permission to sell and those who did not. It also helped to control various types of "noxious" activities by restricting them to specific areas of the marketplace. Horses and cattle were now to be unhitched from their carts and

"fastned to the Rails on the South side [of] the Market House."
Those who stopped in the streets to sell goods and parked their
carts or animals in nondesignated areas acted "contrary to Law"
and offenders were subject to prosecution.[116] Butchers could not
sublet their stalls without permission from the selectmen. All hides,
skins, and tallow from the creatures they slaughtered had to be sold
at the market, and they were required to "constantly keep their
stalls clean" and "not pack any meat in the market."[117] Fishermen
were permitted to sell fish in Market Square providing they kept
the area clean, but fish stalls in the marketplace let "offal and filth"
run into the streets despite warnings to the contrary.[118]

Finding a location for the fish market that provided the fishermen with an appropriate area to sell but did not offend one group
of inhabitants or another was sometimes difficult. Two fishermen
petitioned the selectmen in the late 1790s "on behalf of themselves
and the Fishermen who supply the Boston Market." They informed
the officials that the town needed the "establishment of a well Regulated Fish Market" that would benefit both the fishermen and the
townspeople. When they caught "large quantities" of fish they had
to "salt them down" rather than sell fresh because there was no
place at present to set up their stalls on a regular basis. Besides "a
Regular place whereon to Vend" with "proper stalls," they wanted
built "a Sewer to convey off" the refuse. Six months later the fishermen were still without a separate fish market, but needing to
make a living they continued to sell at Oliver's Dock and other
designated places. When one group of residents requested that the
selectmen remove the fish market at Oliver's Dock, it "being Dangerous to the Health of the Inhabitants from the noxious Effluvia
Issuing from the Fish there kept," others spoke out in the fishermen's defense. Within a month after the selectmen advised the
fishermen that they must not "occupy the House on Olivers Dock
as a Fish Market untill further orders," sixty-eight inhabitants responded. They offered their support to the fishermen, especially

Solomon Hewes, who "for Forty four years past . . . had kept a fish market at Oliver's Dock, which has enabled him to maintain his Family." Not only would it "be a great Injury to his Family" to remove him, the supporters argued, but "most" of those who complained and signed the previous petition did "not live in the vicinity of the Dock" anyway.[119]

Official complaints regarding the fishermen seem to have diminished in the years that followed, and town records suggest that the selectmen did not grant the fish market requested by Joseph Stevens and Charles Cole. Five years later, in 1803, by permission of the selectmen, Joseph Stevens was occupying "the Fish Stall at the bottom of Summer Street," along with other fishermen. Standing fish stalls along the waterfront appear to have become common by the early years of the nineteenth century, although on the basis of complaints as to their raucousness, we can infer that fishermen continued to sell at the dock markets.[120]

Public safety was of paramount concern for town leaders and many, if not all, inhabitants to one degree or another. This applied not only to maintaining a well-regulated public market but to all areas of daily life where the public and private worlds intersected. Protecting the citizens of Boston meant a constant vigilance on the part of town officers and neighbors. The crowded and often closely built streets of the Central District and the North End could make this a difficult undertaking at times. Selectmen, fire wardens, and constables found themselves regularly reminding people of the by-laws and the necessity of compliance for the safety of all concerned.

As the population increased in Boston, public thoroughfares like State Street often became so congested as to be impassable. More people, more carts, more carriages, and goods overflowing from shops into "the middle of the street" all meant that damage to the "footways" ensued, carriages could not pass by, and passersby found their safety threatened by the clutter.[121] Officials regularly reminded inhabitants that these conditions, combined with refuse in the streets and unsafe building practices, created a serious fire hazard.

The constant threat of fire provided a critical reason for maintaining strict building codes and keeping streets clean and accessible. In the spring of 1780 neighborhood residents and goldsmith Thomas Simkins brought to the attention of the selectmen that Captain Newell was "erecting a Building" on the property adjoining Simkins's land. Since Newell's building was an alleged "incroachment on the Street," it was determined that two selectmen, Ebenezer Dorr and Mungo Mackay, act as the investigating committee. Upon inspection the committee of two determined that the complaint was valid, and informed Samuel Phillips Savage, the owner of the property, of Captain Newell's activities. Within the week, Savage agreed "to remove said Building back from the Street one foot."[122] As with the inspections of the chocolate mills, regular visitations of the town by the selectmen and other town officials aimed at preventing violations of bylaws and unsafe, illegal building.

The narrow streets of Boston made it essential that firemen be able to easily access houses from the rear, side, or front through the yard. Selectmen warned "tradesmen, such as ropemakers, coopers, carpenters, blockmakers, riggers, joiners, hatters, blacksmiths, chocolate-grinders etc.," not to "occupy wooden shops or sheds within the vicinity of dwelling houses" since "a cluster of them [when] contiguous to each other" presented a serious fire hazard. Selectmen routinely reminded people about the bylaws pertaining to fire prevention through announcements at town meetings, notices in the town newspapers, the distribution of broadsides, and inspections by constables and firewards. Alerting the public to their responsibilities and gaining compliance appear to have been a never-ending job.

One such common responsibility was maintaining a clean chimney. Officials reminded Bostonians of the need to clean their fireplaces before each winter season, since "Houses are frequently set on fire by sparks, from a foul chimney."[123] In November of 1757 the inhabitants of Boston passed a bylaw "For preventing Danger by Fire in the Town." The law established that under the supervision of the selectmen, inspectors would from time to time survey the chimneys in Boston to look for defects that might pose the threat of fire. The town meeting likewise established the position of chimney sweep with set wages depending upon the height of the chimney. Henceforth, only these official sweeps were permitted to clean the chimneys of Boston's houses. Keeping a "foul" chimney or refusing to repair a damaged one, having a chimney cleaned by anyone except one of the town's official sweeps, transporting fire between houses or businesses, building fires in the open air "within two Rods of any House Warehouse Wood-Pile or any other Combustible matter" resulted in fines. A number of specifics regulated the burning of fires in certain businesses, workshops, and warehouses.[124]

It was also the responsibility of neighbors to report to the selectmen faulty fireplaces or dangerous conditions that might be fire hazards. Ebenezer Simpson informed the selectmen in the winter of 1786 that Benjamin Roberts's chimney was "out of Repair and unsafe for the neighborhood." The chimneys on the houses in Dorsets Alley belonging to the absentee landlady Mrs. Richards, who lived in New York City, were so far beyond repair they required demolition. After an inspection of the south part of town the selectmen spent six months repeatedly advising Mr. Simmons that he must take down the chimney on "an old House at the So. West Corner of Frog Lane." Concerned neighbors agreed that it presented a hazard to surrounding houses. Unable to gain Simmons's compliance, the selectmen told him on October 25 that he had two days to pull down the chimney, after which they would take it down, and he "would be made to pay according to the law."[125]

In 1782, the selectmen determined to appoint a chimney committee for the purpose of preparing a report on the "Sweeping of Chimnies." Early in January 1783 the committee presented its report at the town meeting, where the inhabitants reviewed it paragraph by paragraph and made necessary changes, after which it was adopted as a town regulation. The plan gave to one man, called the Chimney Comptroller, the *"exclusive right"* to sweep all of the chimneys in Boston, the number of which was estimated at 5,400, or 1,800 houses with three funnels each. Chimneys would be swept three times per year at a fixed price, which would save the inhabitants money and, it was hoped, prevent future hazardous conditions. Rates charged by the Chimney Comptroller and his employees were fixed by the town government and varied depending on the height of a building's chimneys. The Comptroller's responsibilities also included inspecting chimneys to guarantee compliance of the residents with the new ruling. A few years later, when certain inhabitants complained to the selectmen regarding the prices chimney sweepers charged, the town officers published prices and a list of licensed sweeps.[126]

Every year fire destroyed or damaged homes and businesses. In some years, inhabitants endured a series of fires, as in 1780.[127] In April 1786 a chairmaker's shop near the Charlestown Ferry in the North End caught fire around midday. The "dry flags, used for bottoming chairs," caused the rapid spread of the flames throughout the shop and into "an adjoining dwelling-house," which suffered severe damage. Three days later "fire broke out in an outbuilding in Board Alley" in the South End. The fire completely destroyed the structure, which was full of dry hay, as well as two dwellings, a "Wheelwright's shop, improved by a young and industrious mechanick, a Carpenter's shop, and two stables." As with all major outbreaks of fire, the neighboring towns of Roxbury and Charlestown sent aid.[128]

On July 30, 1794, a terrible fire destroyed six ropewalks and forty to fifty homes in Boston. As Thomas Davis wrote to his sister, "nothing remains but the land." One hundred nineteen people sustained substantial losses. Fifteen of them lost in excess of $1,000 worth of property, including the schoolmaster John Tileston, the housewright Samuel Dillaway, and numerous widows. To assist the victims several churches organized a committee to collect donations ward by ward and from the churches in town. Bostonians opened their hearts and their purses to their fellow inhabitants who had suffered in the fire. The committee collected a total of $25,278.60.[129]

Following the fire, Bostonians called for new measures to prevent such horrors. Some citizens demanded "increasing the number of Firewards and Engines," and obtaining "an additional number of leather buckets" to help put out fires. Wooden dwellings, far more numerous than brick throughout the town, presented the greatest hindrance to preventing fires. Accordingly, by 1803 the city finally enacted laws requiring that structures "exceeding ten feet in height be built of stone or brick and be covered with slate, tile, or other non-combustible material." Between 1702 and 1794 there were fifteen conflagrations recorded that "kept the building trades busy and changed the face of the town."[130]

As Boston grew, and with it also the inherent problems of urbanization, the constables of the watch served a critical role in the community. Overcrowded and dangerous streets, increasingly dense housing, unfamiliar faces of strangers recently arrived—all served to heighten concerns about fire and police protection. By the 1790s inhabitants regularly wrote to their local newspapers complaining about repeated violations of the city's bylaws, a topic frequently taken up at town meetings. Some inhabitants demanded better regulation of gaming houses, tippling shops, taverns, and "houses of bad fame" where thieves and the "idle and profligate" gathered before turning themselves loose on Boston. During the 1790s the town meeting and the local newspapers repeatedly discussed and debated the difficulties at hand, with little agreement on solutions.

The lack of a professionally trained, permanent police department exacerbated the problem. Boston's system of justices of the peace, constables, watchmen, and town visitations, like many other aspects of the local government and ways in which the community functioned, "all derived from the English, pre-urban past."[131] As the town grew the old system did not work as efficiently as it once had. In 1791 "a considerable Number of the Inhabitants of the Town" began pushing for "A More efficient Police" force. Six years later a petition to the selectmen concerning "increasing the number of Watchmen, and taking such measures for the Safety and Security of the Town" still referred to the circumstances as an "alarming crisis."[132] Boston's move toward a full-time police force would not begin until 1802, when the position of constable became "the first of the traditional town offices to be made appointive" rather than elected at the town meeting.[133]

Constables of the watch worked from nine o'clock at night until daylight during the winter months, September to March, and from ten o'clock at night until sunrise during the rest of the year. Besides law enforcement, their responsibilities included keeping "a fair Journal" of their nightly activities and giving "the time of Night & the Weather, every 50 or 60 paces" in "an audible voice" at least twice each night. They were to always act "with decorum," remember that they must "not abuse even offenders" and that the "safety of the Town" depended upon their care.[134] Reports of the watch show that besides dealing with theft, a night's work might include jailing loud and unruly characters for the night, getting medical care for people in need, and handling situations of domestic abuse, as when "a Negro Woman" called the watch to "take her Husband for abusing her." As the watchmen "entered the Room the Black Man had a fork in his hand which he drove" into the side of one of the men, but fortunately "Little Damage" occurred.[135]

Despite the dangers the watch sometimes faced, and the fact that few wanted the job, inhabitants did not hesitate to voice their opinion to the selectmen about the alleged character of these officers. In 1787, the selectmen dismissed Jacob Gould from his "Watch at the South part of the Town . . . on complaint of a number of respectable Inhabitants, that he was not a suitable Person" for the job. Charges against the "Dock Watch" and complaints about the character of Constable Newman, who patrolled Ward 7, brought him temporary suspension. Citizens also made frequent complaints about "Constable Starr & his Men." The selectmen informed Starr's watch that "the whole of them would be dismissed unless they were circumspect in their future behavior."[136]

Where the job of the night watch ended the job of a constable began. These town officers, charged with enforcing the town's by-laws, worked seven days a week. Selectmen requested that the constables "walk the Streets . . . on the Lords Day's [*sic*] . . . as a means to prevent disorders on the Sabbath more especially in the time of Divine service."[137] Although laws were on the books regarding the Sabbath, it seemed that some Bostonians continued to gather in crowds in the streets and drive their carriages at a fast gallop, the noise of which disturbed the public. They drove their horses into the pond on the Common, the sea, or "other usual *public* place[s] for washing or watering [them] on the *Lord's Day*."[138] It was the constables' job to enforce the law and prevent these and other such disturbances. People most frequently complained to the newspapers, the selectmen, and at town meetings about the reckless driving habits of people on horseback and with carriages and sleds.

In May 1793, the master of the almshouse permitted Elizabeth Barry, a young inmate, to briefly leave the institution. Upon her return, as she walked up Beacon Street, a horse and rider came galloping along, knocked her down, "trampled . . . her, fractured her collar bone, broke four of her ribs, wounded her very badly on her breast and leg, and left her senseless—she was carried to the almshouse, and died the Saturday following." Suffolk County coroner James Prince requested that the inspector of police place the tragic story in the local newspapers along with a reminder to Bostonians about the "laws respecting driving Carriages through the Streets, and various other related complaints."[139]

In a letter to a local newspaper, a Bostonian signing his name "Civis" agreed that the worst offenders of the people's safety were "the drivers of Hackney-Coaches—the Carters and Truckmen in the town" who drove their carts, trucks, and carriages with three or four horses, when the law permitted at most two. The drivers rode their carts and carriages through the narrow streets like "balls shot out of a cannon," endangering in particular the elderly, the hard of hearing, and young children playing in the streets. Private carriages should be "entirely laid aside, unless some different regulation[s] take place," claimed "Civis." On the opening night of the new Federal Street Theater in 1794, the management ran an advertisement providing in detail carriage parking instructions so as not to obstruct traffic. A plan was devised to assist in the smooth flow of traffic to and from the theater. Constables found parking regulations and a traffic-flow plan proved difficult to enforce. The management repeatedly had to advise its clientele of the dangers of obstructing traffic. Boston's elite no more obeyed the laws regarding the proper driving and parking of their carriages than the marketmen did in regards to their horses, oxen, and carts.

Carriage and cart traffic combined with auctioneers blocking the streets; shopkeepers' and tradesmen's "Sign Boards projecting into the streets"; untethered livestock, horses, and dogs; poorly paved roads and walkways badly in need of repairs; uncovered wells; and garbage strewn about collectively created a hazardous landscape for the Boston pedestrian. The town's streets were generally unpaved. Selectmen constantly reprimanded townsmen for poor upkeep of roads and pathways in front of their property, and when funding permitted, ordered repairs to public byways. Residents threw "large quantities of dirt . . . into the streets, from cellars and yards," refusing to claim responsibility for their actions.[140] Rain quickly turned dirt streets and walkways into quagmires mixed with manure, sewage, and garbage, which presented a serious health problem.[141] Operating as quasi–public health officials, the constables found bylaws regarding sanitation no easier to enforce than traffic laws.

Boston's most serious public health crises between 1775 and 1800 consisted of three smallpox epidemics and a yellow fever epidemic. As was true of any port town, Boston was susceptible to infectious diseases brought in on arriving vessels. Any incoming ship carrying diseased persons was immediately ordered cleansed, quarantined, and cleared as safe before being granted the right to dock. At the outset of the American Revolution a smallpox epidemic hit Boston.[142] Except for isolated cases, three smallpox epidemics swept through Boston before the end of the century: the first in 1775–1776, the second in 1778, and the last in 1792. During the siege, General Washington and other authorities prevented the spread of smallpox into the surrounding countryside by isolating contaminated refugees and soldiers. With the evacuation of the British in March 1776, he then attempted to control the number of people rushing into the town, but to no avail. The excitement of returning home and seeing friends and loved ones made it "quite impossible to prevent them" from entering, even though smallpox created "more danger" than "the enemy." One inhabitant requested that his family not "come here to gaze, as there is the utmost danger of the smallpox."[143]

No sooner did inhabitants settle in their homes than the red quarantine flags signaling the dreaded disease appeared again. On May 1, 1776, the town meeting elected a twelve-man committee "to go through their several Wards" to determine which houses required "cleansing" and see that both inhabited and vacant houses were "suficiently smoaked & cleansed."[144] Inoculation of all susceptible American troops and townspeople was under way by early July, and soon eight guards stood on Boston Neck "to Prevent Persons" from entering the town "who have not had the Small Pox." Neither could anyone leave the town "untill the selectmen or the Guards are satisfied, that such persons and their Effects are free from Infection." All those in the town had to remain until further orders. Exceptions required the approval of at least two selectmen. By early August, those who had been inoculated at least three weeks prior, obtained a physician's letter saying that they were clear of the disease, and submitted their possessions to be smoked and cleansed could receive a certificate from the selectmen to leave the town and return to their homes outside of Boston. Inhabitants choosing to leave would not necessarily be readmitted, however, because of the dangers of smallpox in the surrounding countryside. The selectmen requested that all people in the town show the greatest diligence in "airing and cleansing their Houses and Effects, that this suffering Town may not continue a Hospital longer than is absolutely necessary."[145]

When the selectmen and physicians determined that information was needed on the state of the disease in the community, a "Committee of Thirty Six Persons" walked the twelve wards during the month of August gathering information. They recorded the number of persons in each dwelling, and asked the residents who had contracted smallpox "the natural Way, & by Inoculation, & how many of each have died?" In addition, they collected the names of those who had entered town since July 15 "& by whom innoculated." Finally they inquired "How many are not Sick" and had "never had smallpox?"[146]

The collected data assisted the selectmen and physicians in determining how to control the spread of the disease. On August 21 the selectmen announced "with pleasure" that "not more than seventy-eight persons" were still under the care of physicians. Within four weeks only six houses hung "red Flags" on their doors "as signals to Passengers." The selectmen ordered the guards removed from the Neck, and once again travel opened up in and out of the town. The outcome of the epidemic resulted in 304 people contracting "Small Pox in the natural Way; of which twenty-nine, or approximately 10 per cent, had died." A total of 4,988 persons had been inoculated in Boston, 2,873 being inhabitants of the town, and twenty-eight, or considerably less than 1 percent, had died.[147]

Smallpox revisited the community two years later. On the morning of March 9, 1778, the selectmen received notice from an inhabitant that "a Child of Mr. Nicholas Bows" was infected with smallpox. Refusing to allow the child to be removed from his care, the selectmen determined that "his House be fenced up & a flag put out." Two days later the selectmen received reports of infection in six more houses. All physicians were immediately called to the board's chambers and informed of the town's vote in favor of inoculation.[148]

The 1778 epidemic resulted in forty deaths out of 122 people who contracted the disease naturally, and nineteen deaths out of the 2,121 people inoculated.[149] Except isolated cases within the town and vessels arriving in the harbor with infected persons, Boston did not experience another smallpox epidemic until 1792.

The immediate and timely response of town officials to the arrival of smallpox in 1792 included inoculation, quarantines, and guards placed at Boston Neck. At the town meeting on September 28, 1792, the inhabitants elected a committee of forty-eight persons to walk the twelve wards asking the same questions of each household that they had in 1776.[150] The cooperation exhibited by the town, the number of precautionary measures, and the organization and care with which the inhabitants, physicians, and officers worked prevented the situation from becoming worse than it did.

The town paid the cost for those unable to afford inoculation, as was the case for the "two children of James Williams an African" and "Nancy Potters Three Children." By order of the selectmen and a vote of the town meeting, Boston physicians inoculated individuals from other towns and those who were not from "any Town in this State" despite the expense. The matter of when to begin inoculations, who should receive them, and who should pay for them at first caused controversy. By law smallpox had to exist in twenty families before inoculations could be administered, but Bostonians began petitioning the selectmen to begin the procedure before that number was reached. Finally agreeing to this, physicians began "a mass inoculation" of "eight thousand in four days." Of Boston's nineteen thousand inhabitants, only 248 died from the smallpox epidemic in 1792. Of those, 179 had died after inoculation and sixty-nine had died by contracting the disease "the natural way." After receiving official word from the selectmen that the "Distemper" was under control, in mid-October the townspeople "cleansed, smoked, and aired their houses, linen, woolens, and furniture." By order of the selectmen, recently inoculated persons were forbidden to come into Boston after October 22. Any person who knowingly harbored such an individual in "their families" was "declared an Enemy to the Welfare and Security" of the town and would have his or her name published in the local newspaper as such. By late November the town was safe once again from the dreaded disease.[151]

On September 10, 1792, the schooner *Neptune*, belonging to Boston residents Mungo Mackay and John Ward, arrived in Boston harbor having sailed from Martinique twenty-two days prior. The ship was without a captain, for he had died of yellow fever after fourteen days at sea, and the ship's mate was also reported as "dangerously ill." Following an onboard inspection by a town doctor, the ship was immediately ordered to Rainsford Island, where the usual procedures for "Vessells having infectious Distempers" were undertaken. Meanwhile at Faneuil Hall the selectmen were reviewing the "Resolves of the General Court, relative to preventing as far as prudence will suggest, the reception of the malignant Distemper raging at Philadelphia." The board immediately appointed Josiah Waters as "*Health Officer*," with the responsibility of inspecting all people and "their Baggage Merchandize or effects" arriving in Boston from Philadelphia or "other infected places." Those persons infected would immediately be quarantined at Rainsford Island. Within two days a "Military Guard" was posted "at the different Avenues of the Town" to prevent infected people from entering. A list of arrivals and their place of origination was daily given to the selectmen and any suspected of infection were sent to Rainsford Island. Quarantine lasted thirty days or until those infected were free of the distemper, and all vessels under quarantine, including hospital ships, were to display "a large red Flag, at least a Yard Square . . . at the Mast-Head."[152]

The reappearance of infectious diseases in seacoast cities year after year led to greatly improved sanitation measures in urban areas, including Boston. During the 1790s, the selectmen ran newspaper advertisements in early summer reminding people that "the season is now advancing in which fevers and contagious disorders are most prevalent," and encouraging residents to "clear all gutters, and have all the dirt swept into heaps at the center of the streets, early on each Tuesday and Friday morning" for cleanup. Citizens were responsible for raking manure into heaps and volunteering carts to help haul it away from town. These measures no doubt proved to some advantage, but from the numerous letters complaining of the filth in the streets, it is obvious that enforcement of laws for street cleaning proved difficult.[153]

As selectmen, constables, fire wardens, and inspectors of the market attempted to regulate daily life between 1775 and 1800 for the better functioning of the community, there existed an underlying component that played an important role in the way people acted and responded to authorities, namely the way inhabitants and visitors perceived public and private space. No matter how Bostonians attempted to control aspects of their environment by defining specific activities that were and were not acceptable in public space, in reality clear-cut divisions seldom existed between private and public space. They were often one and the same. Merchants claimed public space for private use when they moved their wares and advertising signs into the public area of the street. In some cases, as at Dock Square, vendors operated their entire business in the public street. The overlapping of private and public space, and the confusion in attempting to define and assign responsibilities to citizens regarding the use of such space, created a sense of chaos. Repeatedly individuals found themselves called before the selectmen for illegal encroachments onto public areas. Periodically selectmen ordered the reprinting of the town's bylaws, but the reality of spatial use more often than not subverted the ideal.[154]

Bostonians continually sought solutions to mounting problems in the closing years of the eighteenth century. "Living in a circumscribed community forced attention to matters of common concern which could not be ignored. . . . Fire protection, the care of streets, crime prevention, sewage disposal, water, community health, marketing facilities," and related concerns became paramount in the governing of the town. "The necessary concern with the general welfare contravened the doctrine of individualism and nourished a sense of social responsibility."[155]

The concept of the organic community with paternalistic government that focused on unity, harmony, and the "good of the many" was the ideal underlying Boston's town government. Although practice did not necessarily match theory, these notions were strongly ingrained in the ideology of the sanctity of the town meeting. The philosophy represented a fundamental tenet of the Puritan worldview concerning man and society that stretched back to the founding of the Bay Colony. Certain that these basic principles regarding the relationship between government and society had all but disappeared in Stuart England, seventeenth-century Puritans had looked backward to an idealized golden past and sought to capture this framework in the town meeting system established in New England. Regardless of changes time may have brought to

Boston since the 1630s, these concepts still provided the foundation of the town government and defined the relationship between government and citizen as manifested in the town meeting.

The very process of defending the institution of town government as it existed in Boston from those who had sought to change it throughout the eighteenth century, whether inhabitants or the British Parliament, further nurtured a passionate belief in the superiority of the system. As one historian notes of eighteenth-century Boston, the town meeting may not have been "strictly democratic or egalitarian" but it "was far more open, flexible and popular than English municipal corporations, in terms of voting, residents' rights, legislation and officeholding." The town meeting, with its annual election and rotation of officers, its "decisions by majority rule, open debates, speedy redress of grievances, . . . responsibility of officials . . . and popular participation," preserved an active and immediate role for Boston's enfranchised inhabitants in governing their own community.[156]

With close to one thousand male inhabitants holding office at various times during the twenty-five years between 1770 and 1795, a substantial portion of white male freeholders found themselves represented by local government, if not an active part of it themselves, at some point. Bostonians cherished these rights.[157]

Inhabitants knew that whatever their concerns—neighbors infringing on property, dangerous structures being erected, or contracts of apprenticeship being subverted—the problems could be brought before the selectmen sitting in Faneuil Hall. The local officers—whether hogreeves, sealers of leather, or overseers of the poor—were elected by inhabitants at the town meeting. Under town law "any matter or thing" could be "inserted in a warrant for calling a meeting" as long as requested by a minimum of ten freeholders. This made the right to petition a straightforward process and enabled a forum for open, collective debate though not necessarily agreement. While the town meeting was open to all

Bostonians, town law limited voting to freeholders and "other inhabitants," those who paid an annual estate tax equal to at least two-thirds of the poll tax. During the last twenty-plus years of the eighteenth century the number voting at town meetings varied greatly, but the regulations for voting were broad enough that a sizable portion of the male population was probably enfranchised.[158]

Repeated attempts to incorporate Boston point to dissatisfaction with the existing system on the part of some inhabitants. That these attempts, most notably in the mid-1780s, were successfully defeated demonstrates that the majority of voting inhabitants were content with the institution as it presently stood. Mechanics in particular ardently defended the town meeting, and incorporation would signal the end of the town meeting and direct annual election of the town's governing officers. Belief on their part that replacing the town meeting with a mayor, aldermen, and city council took power away from the inhabitants at large and placed it in the hands of a few successfully delayed Boston's incorporation until 1822.[159]

The possibility of a more efficient and modern government simply did not outweigh the desire of most to maintain the 150-year-old system of direct and immediate control of local affairs by the town's inhabitants and freeholders. During the years of economic rebuilding the town meeting time and again would prove to be a useful tool for collectively discussing the needs of the community and instructing the town's representatives to the state legislature for the purpose of seeing that its needs were adequately represented. This was the purpose of the instructions provided by the inhabitants to their representatives in a town meeting in May 1783. Their instructions made clear that legislation benefiting Boston as a trading town was essential to its survival and growth.

The Lamb Tavern in the South End. Widow Abigail Moore
was the innkeeper during the 1780s. (James H. Stark,
Antique Views of Ye Towne of Boston, Boston, 1901.)

The Green Dragon Tavern in the Central District.
(James H. Stark, *Antique Views of Ye Towne of Boston*, Boston, 1901.)

Tremont Street Mall looking north and Boston Common, 1800.
Painting by the daughter of General Henry Knox.
(James H. Stark, *Antique Views of Ye Towne of Boston*, Boston, 1901.)

Tremont Street Mall looking south and Boston Common, 1800. Visible are the
hay scales and the Haymarket Theater, a massive wooden structure erected in
1796. (James H. Stark, *Antique Views of Ye Towne of Boston*, Boston, 1901.)

Faneuil Hall, 1789, with the market area on the right.
(James H. Stark, *Antique Views of Ye Towne of Boston*, Boston, 1901.)

Charles River Bridge. (*Massachusetts Magazine*, 1789.)

State Street and a front view of the Old State House in 1801.
(Justin Winsor, ed., *The Memorial History of Boston including Suffolk County,
Massachusetts, 1630–1880*, Boston, 1882.)

Rear view of the Old State House looking down State Street from
Washington Street. (*Massachusetts Magazine*, 1793.)

4

Bostonians at Work

IN 1784 DANIEL MALCOLM, shopkeeper, had lived for at least four years in the North End, on the busy major thoroughfare of North Street. Malcolm owned a house, a horse, and a chaise, and the assessment on his property that year reflects that although not a wealthy man, he was solidly one of the middling sort in Boston. As with most Bostonians during the postwar years he was also at the mercy of a fickle economy. When Daniel married Nabby Brocas in 1791, the couple had been engaged for several years, having posted their intentions to marry in 1788. Perhaps they waited while Daniel acquired an adequate financial foundation to start a family. Over the course of the next eight years their family grew to include five children.[1]

Nabby, Daniel, and the children occupied only one end of the two-story wooden house on North Street, which comprised 768 square feet. The other end was used as Daniel's shop, which he shared with another shopkeeper, Samuel Martin. Also typical for a number of Bostonians during these years, Malcolm changed jobs or at least took on additional work as a laborer, perhaps to make ends meet if his business had fallen upon hard times. Considering the growing number of shopkeepers in Boston, did he find the business too competitive to make a sufficient living?[2]

As a laborer Malcolm was one of the 10 percent (or approximately 400) of male heads of household working in this occupational category around the turn of the century in Boston. Although an unskilled occupation, it is likely that Malcolm's job provided steady work, for as the town's economy gradually recovered, Bostonians began to build and remodel houses and erect public buildings and manufacturing houses. Perhaps he found work in one of the many shipyards that began hiring more men as Boston's economy rebounded, fueling the recovery of the maritime industry. Such employment provided the training and experience to move from unskilled to skilled worker. Malcolm's employment as a maritime laborer cannot be verified, but he is listed in the 1803 town directory as a shipwright, a skilled occupation.[3]

By 1821 Daniel Malcolm had lived for at least thirty-seven years in the North End, where with Nabby he had raised a family, established himself as a skilled artisan, and acquired a second North End property. Unlike a number of Bostonians, Malcolm remained in the same residence for a substantial part of his life. During the years following the American Revolution, the circumstances of some Boston residents necessitated moving from ward to ward to seek affordable housing and improve their circumstances. Still, the times demanded flexibility and adjustments in other ways. This might include completely changing one's occupation, temporarily if not permanently, or engaging in several different lines of work at once. In this sense, Daniel Malcolm was a typical late-eighteenth-century Bostonian.

As a legal inhabitant of Boston, Daniel Malcolm may well have been present at the May 13 town meeting in 1783. At that gathering he would have heard the moderator read the instructions for the representatives to the Massachusetts General Court stating their obligations to the port town. You will "always remember," the instructions declared, "that you represent a Trading Town . . . [and] you will not fail to exert yourselves in proposing and enforcing every Measure Adapted to cherish and extend our Trade." As important as Agriculture might be, trade remained paramount, especially if the town of Boston was to survive.[4] From the elite merchants who drove around in chaises and furnished their homes with English goods to the small shopkeepers who sold everything from cheap clothing, gingerbread, and garden seeds to hardware and locally made shoes, Boston was indeed a trading town. A commercial center, it was also a maritime center employing hundreds of men in the art of shipbuilding and employing sailors to man those vessels. Boston's lifeline depended not only on the larger Atlantic world but also on the extractive industries of Massachusetts and greater New England, which provided, among other products, the lumber to build ships and barrels and products to fill the hulls of Boston's vessels. Thus, between 1774 and 1786, when the economy of Massachusetts neared collapse as exports dropped by 75 percent and once flourishing trades like the logging industry suffered severe times, Boston was also caught in the vortex.[5] The larger crisis compounded the catastrophic consequences of the Port Act and the siege. In 1785, one observer noted the "numbers of failures which daily take place" in Boston and stated that "Under [the] circumstances it would be an act of insanity to think of contracting commercial connection."[6]

Thousands of Bostonians felt the reverberations of the economic crisis at hand. In 1786, as in the years preceding, individuals requesting abatement of local taxes repeatedly complained of "no business," as did Thomas Vernon, who had "no personal Estate of any kind" and had not seen a "vessel" at his wharf during the entire "year past." The trader Benjamin Jepson lost "his last & only vessel," leaving him without any "property . . . except a few state notes," which were taken when he was "sued for debts." Peter Doliver, also a trader, had not fared much better during the war years. His "Schooner [was] seized in the West Indies" and circumstances had "obliged him to give up his store." Subsequently he had "no business," either. The personal hardship and financial loss cut across all economic sectors of the town. The shipwright Jacob Rhodes, an artisan of property and middling status, informed the assessors that in the course of a year he had "only sheathed one ship." To add to his hardship he had ten children, a mother, and his brother's children to support, they having lost their father in "the late war."[7] In each of these cases, and in others, the assessors approved abatements. Inability to collect adequate taxes meant in turn that the town constantly struggled with inadequate funding to assist the poor, run the almshouse, pay salaries to schoolmasters, and meet the quotas requested by the state government for shoes, shirts, and beef for the army, among many other expenses.

Inhabitants of Boston argued in 1781 that building a healthy commercial economy that "rested upon the Staple Commodities" of their own nation was of paramount concern, for the wartime economy, which had rested upon such activities as supplying "Foreign Armies and Navies," would "inevitably fail" with war's end. In this light, Boston agreed with her "sister" maritime community, Marblehead, as to the necessity of instructing government representatives on the importance of considering fishing rights in any peace treaty drawn up with Great Britain.[8] The preservation of trade also proved critical, not only for Boston but for all parts of the Commonwealth. There were the "Mechanicks, necessarily employed in the building, rigging and fitting out . . . of Vessels" that enabled the trade and those who made "the Staves, Hoops" and barrels to carry the goods. By extension, there were those ancillary trades and occupations directly affected.[9]

Events and circumstances outside Boston also threatened to reduce the seaport town to a place of little importance in the commercial and maritime world. It was not a foregone conclusion in 1783 that Boston would survive the trials of the past decade. For those who had been around long enough to remember some of the woes the town had faced during the previous fifty years, current events may have seemed to be a continuum of troubles that had marked Boston throughout the century. Although the early decades of the eighteenth century proved promising for the town, the troubles that emerged by the late 1730s, including imperial wars, smallpox epidemics, serious fires, and frequent economic slumps, had created both demographic and economic stagnation.[10] For Boston, plagued for most of the century by these circumstances that retarded growth, the American Revolution initially appeared to be just one more inhibitory factor. But the Revolutionary years ultimately created new opportunities for Bostonians in the final two decades of the 1700s.

Following the siege of Boston and throughout the ensuing years, former inhabitants returned home and new faces arrived. Accordingly, Boston's population climbed to 10,000 in 1780, a figure still barely two-thirds of that recorded in the 1770 census. By 1790, the population reached an all-time high of slightly over 18,000, and by 1800 nearly 25,000 inhabitants lived in the seaport town.[11] Reflecting upon these developments in the 1780s, one contemporary commented to a friend, "When you come [to Boston] you will scarcely see any other than new faces . . . the change which in that respect has happened within the few years since the revolution is as remarkable as the revolution itself."[12] The population growth experienced by the community during the 1780s and 1790s was not steady. Rapid increase in the early 1780s, as the population regained its footing following the devastating years of the siege era, was followed by a brief slowdown near the end of the decade and another rise in the early 1790s. During the course of the twenty-five-year period 1775–1800, approximately one-half of Boston's growth was attributable to the migration of outsiders into the town.[13]

Some migrants during this last quarter-century were only so-journers, ultimately moving to other destinations. Consequently there existed a constant ebb and flow of men, women, and families. Examining a sample group of 1,057 heads of household from a broad cross-section of the population for the period from 1784 to 1794 demonstrates these patterns in greater detail.[14] By 1794, approximately 40 percent (427) of the sample group had departed from Boston, representing a high level of out-migration.[15] The persistency rate for the sample group was 60 percent (630). One-third of these 630 heads of household had resided in Boston for at least ten years, whereas two-thirds were predominantly newcomers who arrived in the decade after 1784, with a majority settling in town during the early 1790s.[16] The sample group demonstrates the ebb and flow of people into and out of the community and points to in-migration being higher than out-migration. Despite economic problems, as the largest urban area in New England, Boston became a magnet drawing substantial numbers of migrants and filling the streets and markets with new faces.[17]

The postwar population explosion increased the demand for services, which in turn provided even more opportunity and continued to draw people into the port town. By the late 1780s Boston's economic picture appeared more promising. The number of complaints concerning appalling economic conditions in the town began to decline.[18] Changing circumstances in the maritime and building trades revitalized work opportunities for shipwrights, caulkers, and all men working in the shipbuilding industry.[19] Between 1780 and 1790, the number of Bostonians working in ship-building and ancillary trades almost doubled. Various public works projects, manufacturing enterprises, and the construction of new houses created scores of new jobs.[20] This growth percolated to ancillary trades and other businesses. The number of chairmakers, cabinetmakers, wood-carvers, and upholsterers collectively quadrupled between 1780 and 1799. To supply and deliver these goods required improved commercial transportation and more shopkeepers and merchants.[21] Some men found it possible to expand their businesses, such as the truckmen George and Jonathan Blanchard, who by 1799 had six journeymen truckers in their employ, while Phillip and Phineas Wentworth hired at least three.[22] Grocers, bakers, butchers, and fishermen were needed to feed the growing population, and tailors and shoemakers to clothe them. Conspicuous consumption also drove economic growth.

A number of merchants and profiteers were equipped with the means to turn the tide in their favor, and they emerged from the 1770s and 1780s financially strong. During the war, privateering brought substantial wealth to some Bostonians, such as the merchants John Coffin Jones, Stephen Higginson, and Thomas Russell. The break with England and the consequent removal of the Navigation Acts opened European ports for American traders. Commercial opportunities with Russia, Sweden, Spain, and France in particular seemed limitless. By 1799 the financial status of Higginson, Jones, and other Boston merchants well placed to take advantage of the economic opportunities brought by the break with England placed them among Boston's leading elite. Following the war, Boston harbor filled with foreign ships, and wharves were "heaped high with foreign goods." During the last eight months of 1783, "twenty-eight French vessels, and almost the same number of English merchantmen, brought cargoes, worth almost half a million dollars, into Boston Harbor." Although most of the goods were luxury items, merchants quickly purchased them on credit, a risky venture considering the economic climate of the times. For a number of Bostonians, the "*habits* of *Luxury*" made importing a lucrative business and filled their coffers. Trade in luxury items brought other "families . . . distress." Through "unlimitted Credit," some contracted debts they found themselves unable to pay. Circumstances led a 1786 Boston town meeting to produce a "Circular Letter" to its sister communities in Massachusetts urging all to "lay aside the *destructive fashions* and *expensive superfluities* of the day,

[and] be *sober, temperate* and *industrious.*"[23] This admonition was apparently to no avail.

The voracious consumer appetite of those with means in postwar Boston fueled importation and resulted in a seemingly endless variety of goods available, including those from England the taste for which had not been dampened by the war. The "feverish activity of importing, along with earlier privateering successes" resulted in "the extensive use of luxuries" in Boston and other "maritime towns of Massachusetts."[24] Shop windows, auction houses, market stalls, and even peddlers offered a vast assortment of wares. John and William Molineaux, merchants in Ward 11 who operated a store on State Street, sold "A beautiful assortment of English Goods" including textiles ranging from broadcloth to silk and lace, "Madeira, Red-Port, . . . and Currants." A customer at one of William Greenleaf's auctions in Cornhill might acquire "guns, . . . iron hoes, . . . metal and mohair buttons, . . . men's fine thread Hose," and even a "silver Hilted Sword." Procter and Lowell's auction room, located at the corner of Wing's Lane, and Parkman & Hinckley's auction room "opposite the South Side [of] Faneuil-Hall Market" offered European goods consisting of shoes, clothing, fabric, household furnishings, and various items. The wholesalers Breck and Green sold everything from "China Cups and Saucers" and "Barcelona Handkerchiefs" to Spanish "Turpentine per Barrel [and] Cage Wire." Reflecting the times, payment could be made in any number of ways, including "Hard or Paper Money, French, Spanish or Dutch Bills of Exchange," "Continental Currency," and "furrs."[25]

Merchants such as these were the proprietors of many stores that stood in the well-located and desirable Central District, lined the busy wharves, or could be found along the increasingly fashionable thoroughfares such as Marlborough Street. Along with the rising class of professionals in banking, government, law, and manufacturing, these successful merchants were some of the wealthiest residents in the community. They were Boston's elite, and they owned fine furniture, fine clothing, and carriages. Merchant Samuel Breck, co-owner of Breck and Green, owned one sulkey, one phaeton, one chaise, and two chariots, while the privateer-turned-merchant Thomas Russell possessed one chaise, one phaeton, and one chariot. These men employed numerous individuals, black and white, as servants, and the town assessors described their homes as "Elegant" and "Handsome."[26]

As these individuals consolidated their wealth through business, social, and marriage connections, many also began to congregate in specific neighborhoods, changing the spatial demographics of Boston. Whereas before and during the American Revolution the residences of men of wealth were distributed throughout the town in the North, West, and South Ends, by the early 1790s, Boston's elite were living in more limited areas. During the course of the 1790s, Ward 7 and part of Ward 9, which together constituted the West End and part of the central business district, showed a substantial increase in the number of wealthy householders. Correspondingly, other wards lost such residents. This development was gradual, but the geographic concentration of the homes of the wealthy in specific areas of Boston represented a phenomenon divergent from previous patterns. A number of these men were new arrivals in town, being North Shore merchants and the local gentry from towns in the New England countryside who sought both the economic and political advantage made available in the wake of the Loyalist exodus. They would come to form the backbone of Federalist Boston.[27]

To listen to the diatribes of some contemporaries, one might conclude that late-eighteenth-century Boston was a world turned upside down. "Even [Boston's] . . . tavern keepers are gentlemen," complained one disgruntled resident.[28] Property now flowed into channels "where before it never was: often making "the *meaner people*, . . . almost the only men of power, riches, and influence." Another complained that "fellows who would have cleaned my shoes five years ago, have amassed fortunes, and are riding in chariots."[29] Such comments beg for investigation. Were they simply the jeremiads of the wealthy fearful of social leveling, or were average men experiencing significant improvement in their economic conditions? Although the fragmentary and irregular records make it difficult to determine the situation with absolute certainty for the years between 1784 and 1799, it is possible to draw certain preliminary conclusions.[30]

The patterns of tax assessment found in the Boston Taking Books strongly indicate an improvement in economic circumstances for a number of Bostonians, especially artisans, shopkeepers, tradesmen, small freeholders, and the like, who represented what contemporaries in the eighteenth century referred to as the "middling sort."[31] Broadly defined, these were neither the economic and social elite of society nor the unskilled or unemployed poor. Whereas approximately one-half of all heads of household in Boston were assessable in 1784, by 1799 those assessable approached 70 percent, with percentages even higher in certain individual wards.[32] At the close of the eighteenth century nearly one-third of Boston's heads of household owned real property valued at $100 or higher. Of those individuals 45 percent were artisans and 35 percent were small shopkeepers, boardinghouse keepers, mariners, and laborers. Merchants were the majority of the remaining 20 percent, with slightly less that 1 percent being physicians, attorneys, and government officials. In sum, approximately 80 percent of Bostonians owning realty were not of the merchant or professional class, consisting instead of a broad-based "middling" class that appears to have been somewhat fluid in its makeup.[33]

Relatively few houses elicited the response that William Clapp's did of one assessor. In 1799 the town official noted that the merchant owned "a superb house." The type of property held by the average Bostonian varied. Mary Billings owned a lot on Hanover

Street with "two tenements," both "620 square feet" three-story structures, of which she occupied one and leased the other to Zechariah Hicks, who ran a saddlery business on Cornhill. Enoch James, a blacksmith living in the North End, owned a store and blacksmith shop. The laborer Peter Spring owned a "small . . . neat" house in the South End, where he lived with his wife and seven children. The housewright Joseph Wade, a newcomer to town during the 1790s, owned half of a small two-story house in the West End, not far from the African-American laborer Samuel Bean, who owned half of a small "1 story" house. Bean was one of seventeen African-Americans residing in Boston during the late 1790s and recorded as property owners. These seventeen individuals, who represented 10 percent of those black Bostonians recorded by the assessors in the 1799 Taking Book, lived predominantly in the West and South Ends. The houses of middling Bostonians, both black and white, were usually smaller than those of the wealthy, and sometimes "old fashioned," as one assessor described the property owned by the constable Shubael Hews. Still, Boston's substantial middling group of property owners outnumbered both the elite and poor.[34]

This was not a society where wealth was evenly distributed. There were Bostonians who did not own property, and the two extremes of great wealth and dire poverty existed, as indicated by the problems the town faced in caring for the poor. Clearly, though, there was another component to the picture, that of an emerging broad-based middle-class sector. The growing demand for goods, the improving economy, and the opportunity available in Boston as suggested by a growing middle class worked as a pull factor in drawing a large number of artisans to the community.[35]

Skilled artisans, shopkeepers, and tradesmen of the broad middle ranks of eighteenth-century American society arrived in Boston seeking an opportunity to improve their economic lot after the hard years of the war. Tracking Boston's heads of household through the lean economic years of the war, its aftermath, and the recovery that followed sheds important insight into the life of the community and how the "plain people of Boston" survived the war and, in many instances, ultimately improved their lot. It is possible to identify close to 80 percent of Boston heads of household by their occupations during the 1780s and 1790s.[36]

Commerce and retailing constituted the largest single sector of Boston's workforce. By 1790, as Boston began to recover from economic depression, several occupational groups showed growth, including the maritime trades, the building trades, and the service sector.[37] Between 1780 and 1794 those employed in the distribution of goods, such as merchants, traders, shopkeepers, auctioneers, and hucksters, formed the largest segment of Boston's adult workforce when compared to any other single occupational category. Over the fifteen-year period from 1780 to 1795, the percentage of men and women in such enterprises decreased relative to the population, but this occupational sector still surpassed all others. In the community as a whole, merchants and traders represented less than 40 percent of those engaged in Boston's distributive sector. In actuality the shopkeeper or small retailer dominated in this economic endeavor, representing more than 60 percent. Shopkeepers and retailers had become one of the largest occupational categories, making Boston a reflection of its former mother country: a "nation of shopkeepers."

Neighborhood shops run by small retailers dotted the peninsula, their numbers including seasoned shopkeepers, men who had left other occupations, those engaged as both artisans and shopkeepers simultaneously, widows, single women, and newcomers to Boston. The group covered a broad economic range, from those assessed as "poor" to those owning property. Shops differed in size, including "1/2 small shop," "a small shop," and a "very small" shop.[38] A glimpse into patterns found in the lives of some of these individuals helps illuminate the experience of surviving the economically lean years of the 1780s and early 1790s. Such efforts required ingenuity, flexibility, determination, and perhaps a degree of luck.

Men, women, and families weathered the storm of the postwar years in a variety of ways. People moved around the peninsula. They changed occupations or took whatever work became available. In the economic climate of the 1780s possession of a skilled trade was not necessarily a guarantee of work. Artisans might try to double as retailers by setting up small shops in their homes, and those whose primary means of income derived from retailing sometimes shared shop space. Any number of choices might mean the difference between keeping or losing property, gaining the opportunity to purchase one's own residence, or simply providing food, clothing, and shelter for one's family. Thomas Popkins worked as both a blacksmith and whitesmith between 1780 and 1803. By the 1790s he also kept a shop where he may have sold tinware produced in his trade as a whitesmith. As a single man, Popkins had some flexibility. He lived and worked in several different locations and in the early 1790s appears to have left Boston for at least a year or two, perhaps seeking opportunity elsewhere. Popkins did not own his workshop, but he was assessed as a low-end property owner for his place of residence. Shared with other smiths, his shop, located on Rawson's Lane close to Boston Common in the South End, was owned by the well-to-do trader John Ballard.[39] Other townspeople of the middling rank remained in Boston, moved less often, but changed occupations more frequently. Henry Foye's experiences provide one example.

Henry Foye resided in Boston for at least eighteen years, during which time he changed occupations three times. He first enters the records in 1781, when the selectmen issued him an innholder's license for his house on Ann Street in Ward 5, in the North End. Three years later he no longer sold "strong drink" at his inn; instead, he ran a slop shop on Fish Street, not far from his original place of business. When townsmen agreed to fill the town dock in his neighborhood to create more market space, Henry Foye was one of seventy inhabitants donating funds to the project.[40] Both innkeeping and shopkeeping were occupations in which his wife Sarah, whom he had married in 1780, could readily participate, especially since in both instances Henry ran the business in their home. As their family came to include four daughters during the following decade, Sarah would have been able to work side by side with her husband while caring for the children. Then in the early 1790s the Foyes moved and Henry changed jobs. In 1794 the family relocated to the South End and he took a position as a "doorkeeper" with the town's new Federal Street Theater. This didn't last long, however, for within two years, Henry returned to his former occupation, and the family once again resided in the North End.[41] Perhaps the increased competition in the cheap clothing business had led to difficulties, or Henry may have believed that the new theater seemed to offer opportunities that didn't exist in his current occupation. The reasons behind Henry Foye's decisions remain unknown, but whatever the cause, employment in several different occupations was not an unusual pattern among Bostonians during the 1780s and early 1790s.

Whatever the merchandise, for the small shopkeeper business proved uneven at best. As the number of people involved in the distribution of goods grew, competition forced some men into other means of making a living. Turnover appeared generally high, with 50 percent of those listed as shopkeepers in 1794 having arrived in Boston since 1790. In the slop shop trade during the fifteen-year period between 1784 and 1799, only two out of twenty-five proprietors identified in the records remained in the business for more than four years, and one of those was Henry Foye.[42] Despite this turnover, the sale of cheap, ready-made clothing was a growing business. The number of such businesses tripled between 1784 and 1799, and this may well be a conservative figure. Competition came from those tailors who ran a "small shop in back end" or in "1 room" of their residence. Of those who specifically opened a slop shop, only one owner was actually a tailor. The remainder were primarily storekeepers, as well as some boardinghouse owners, a sea captain, and a tobacconist. Unable to make the clothing themselves, these individuals acquired their merchandise elsewhere, whether from the poorer tailors in town or women who took outside work such as sewing into their homes to make ends meet.[43]

Besides being a town of traders, shopkeepers, and those engaged in commerce, Boston was also a maritime community. The war and subsequent depression took a heavy toll on the shipbuilding industry, which "came to a standstill" for lack of markets. Before the Revolution "about one hundred and twenty-five vessels had been launched in Massachusetts" annually, with Boston claiming a substantial portion of that number. This plummeted to "forty-five vessels" in 1784, and "between 1785 and 1787, only fifteen to twenty were built annually" in all of Massachusetts.[44] Thus, one Bostonian expressed great "pleasure" when he read in a Boston newspaper in 1788 that "subscriptions were filling up to build 3 ships for the encouragement of our industrious mechanicks."[45] In the years before the war approximately "5 to 10 percent" of Boston's workforce labored "directly in shipbuilding."[46] Occupations related to shipbuilding included boatbuilder, caulker, mastmaker, oarmaker, rigger, ropemaker, sailmaker, ship carpenter, shipbuilder, ship chandler, ship joiner, shipward, shipwright, and head builder. Between 1780 and the early 1790s, these occupations represented only 4 to 5 percent of Boston's male heads of household, a reflection of the poor condition of the shipbuilding industry. The dismal state of Boston's shipbuilding industry was a major topic of discussion at town meetings in the 1780s. During the American Revolution, Boston had lost markets for export and for Boston-built ships. Events in the 1780s would put Boston back on the high seas, and the town's shipbuilders back in the yards.

In 1783 the first Boston ship headed for China sailed out of the harbor: a "little fifty-five-ton sloop *Harriet* of Hingham . . . with a cargo of ginseng." Merchants realized the difficulty of competing with the British for the Chinese market and the need to find a more accessible and salable product than ginseng. By the late 1780s they had found their commodity—furs from the Pacific Northwest coast. On August 9, 1790, a large crowd of Bostonians gathered on the wharves to give "three huzzas and a hearty welcome" to *Columbia* as she dropped anchor in Boston's inner harbor and fired "a federal salute of thirteen guns." Three years before, *Columbia* had set sail for Canton. Her return marked Boston's entry into the Northwest fur trade and hence the China trade. "By 1792 the trade route Boston–Northwest Coast–Canton–Boston was fairly established." The opening of the China trade played an important role in the market's turnaround during the 1790s.[47] The ensuing China trade and the new national government's tariff legislation that "aimed . . . at protecting and encouraging the American merchant marine and shipyards" signaled a bright future for maritime Boston. "Between 1789 and 1795, 1,152 vessels were either enrolled or registered at the Boston custom house; . . . 860 gave Boston as their home port."[48] These changing circumstances revitalized the maritime trades, eventually creating work for shipwrights, caulkers, and others in shipbuilding-related occupations.

In 1799 the majority of Boston's shipbuilders lived near the shipyards in the North End, although approximately 10 percent could be found in the South End and a handful in the West End.[49] Some shipyards stood in the South End, as did the one belonging to Thomas Page and former sea captain Seth Webber, although both men resided in the North End. Located at the bottom of Milk Street, their shipyard sat close to the Commercial Coffee House, a convenient location for procuring new business. When hard times hit the shipbuilding trades during the 1780s, Webber and Page managed to come through with their business intact.[50] During the difficult years, many men in the shipbuilding trades stayed with their occupation, unlike those in a number of other occupations. The Trueman family consisted of six male heads of household and their dependents, all of whom lived in the North End and worked in the shipyards. During the course of the 1780s and 1790s each of the men continued in his trade as caulker, although in 1780 John Trueman Sr. engaged in two occupations simultaneously, those of caulker and trader. Family members continued in the shipbuilding trades into the nineteenth century.[51]

Those unable to secure work in the shipbuilding industry might enter a related trade. For example, ship joiner John Lambert was by 1794 working in a cooper's shop. By 1796 he had opened his own business on Union Wharf and by 1799 he owned property in the South End. In the early nineteenth century Lambert could still be found working as a cooper at Union Wharf. By 1806 Thomas and William Lambert, also coopers and presumably relatives, had joined him.[52] Those in the shipbuilding industry and related trades became one of the more stable occupational groups between 1780 and 1799. Few of these artisans moved their residence, most managed to retain their existing property, and some even gained new property. Very few left Boston to seek work elsewhere, but they also had skills that could be plied in alternative ways, as in the case of John Lambert. By contrast, mariners fared poorly.[53]

Mariners faced particularly hard times during the postwar years as Boston's export business collapsed and the number of vessels embarking from Boston's harbor decreased rapidly. The assessors recorded a range of approximately one hundred to two hundred Bostonians working as mariners in the late eighteenth century, with the number reaching above two hundred by 1799.[54] These figures are possibly low, as sailors were likely to be omitted from the Taking Book if at sea. Seamen as a rule were considered unskilled laborers, excepting mates and captains, and most of them had little or no real estate holdings. "Sickly and poor" and "out of business" mariner Enoch Howes found the decade of the 1780s harsh. Still "out of business" in 1794, he turned to coopering two years later.[55] Whether or not this turned his fortunes around is unknown, for by 1799 Howes disappears from the Boston records. As relatively unskilled laborers, mariners generally had fewer choices when it came to searching for other sources of income. The occupation of mariner seldom provided much opportunity for occupational mobility or advancement, as Billy G. Smith demonstrated in his study of mariners in Philadelphia, where promotion from "seaman to mate to captain" was extremely rare. Ship captains came from the ranks of those who could afford to apprentice their sons to captains or merchants or send their sons as supercargoes. "The barriers between common seamen and ship's officers rarely were hurdled."[56]

During the war, the best opportunities were often found sailing on a privateer. Until the final two years of the war, when "the British tightened their blockade, captured a large part of [the] fleet, and drove the rest into port," privateering proved a very profitable undertaking for merchants and provided many jobs for mariners.[57] These opportunities would again present themselves with the outbreak of the Napoleonic Wars in 1793, when demand for seamen once again increased. Signing on with a privateer sometimes meant a share of this "legalized piracy" for the seamen. Raising a crew for such a venture could require placing an advertisement in the local paper. Samuel Nicholson bought an ad in the *Independent Chronicle* in May 1780, calling on all "brave Boys, to the Rendezvous in Fore Street, where you will find your jolly Companions, and receive greater Advantages than in any private ship whatever." Promises of "the best of Chances for making their Fortunes" and news of the work spreading through the North End's waterfront taverns no doubt gained Nicholson his "able-bodied Seamen."[58] Few men specifically gave their occupation as "privateering" to the 1780 assessors, though it is probable that individuals listed as sailors or seamen found work on such ships.

Some mariners simply left the seafaring life, as did Daniel Warner and Joseph Shed Jr. The circumstances of Daniel Warner can be traced. A privateer in 1780, Warner had by 1784 moved from the West End to the North End in Ward 2, although he owned no property. By 1784 he had left the sea, working simultaneously as a laborer and shopkeeper. By 1789 he was listed only as a laborer, and had acquired a property on Sheafe Street. Five years later, in 1794, Warner held the same occupation and property. Only two years later the *Boston Directory* listed him as a mason. In the sixteen years between 1780 and 1796, Warner had gradually improved his lot.[59] What property seaman Joseph Shed Jr. possessed in 1780 and 1784, when he had work "at sea," was gone by 1790 and he found himself "out of all employ." In 1794 he was still "poor." Shed finally gave up the sea life, and in 1796 he worked as a "victualler" in the South End, although in 1799 times were still difficult, as he had "no business." His father, a grocer in the South End since at least 1780, may have brought Joseph Jr. into his business by the early 1800s, for he was listed as a victualler in 1803. By 1806 his father's grocery business had become "Joseph Shed Father and Son."[60]

When former mariner Daniel Warner became a mason, he entered the third-largest occupational category in Boston, that of the building and woodworking trades. Over the course of the 1780s and 1790s, the total number of heads of household engaged in building and ancillary trades grew from 3 percent in 1780 to 5 percent in 1790, and remained stable throughout the decade as the economy began to stabilize. Since Boston's population increased from eighteen to twenty-five thousand during the 1790s, the number of skilled workers in the building trades had sharply increased. Before the Revolution Bostonians undertook few public or private building projects, and during the war the industry stagnated.[61] Between 1784 and 1794, however, housewrights built 315 new houses. By the summer of 1799 "new houses" and "half finished houses" sat scattered across the South End.[62] Public projects included the construction of a new almshouse, a workhouse, seawalls, wharves, and the Massachusetts State House on Beacon Hill. By the 1790s architect Charles Bulfinch's plans for Boston included not only magnificent public structures such as the State House and the impressive Federal Street Theater but also elegant private residences in both the West End and the South End. His design and supervision of these buildings represented the beginning of a keen interest on the part of certain Bostonians in postwar civic pride, which reflected itself in architectural accomplishments and in turn boosted the building trades.

New construction was not the only work that kept the skilled and the unskilled in the building trades busy. As the economy improved, property owners were able to invest money in their own residences and rental properties. Landlord William Donnison hired a number of artisans to repair various properties around town. This provided work for masons who laid brickwork, repaired "hearth[s] & Cellar Walls," and did some "White & Yellow-Washing." Carpenters and other artisans made window sashes, laid floors in cellars, shingled roofs, repaired privies and garrets, built barns, and painted chimneys. During the 1790s Donnison's properties provided work not only for white men in the building trades but also for black laborers.[63] The work of repairing, remodeling, and restoring was a mainstay of employment for artisans and laborers, keeping them busy throughout most of a year. A business relationship with a man like Donnison proved fruitful.

Church buildings offered another source of work for carpenters, masons, and other mechanics. Members of the New Brick Church in the North End appointed a committee in April 1785 to ascertain what repairs the meetinghouse needed. The committee had "to take with them such Trades-Men of Different occupation as may assist them in forming an Estimate of the Expence thereof." In August, the steeple required immediate attention. By December the congregation determined to whitewash the meetinghouse and undertake additional repairs. Following the desecration of its interior by British soldiers during the siege, Old South Church in Brattle Square required repair work. In the process of performing the repairs, additional jobs were undertaken between the years 1776 and 1792. While installing an organ in 1792, carpenters removed some columns, replaced others with smaller ones, and reduced the size of the gallery. In 1784 the First Church in Boston also underwent repairs and remodeling.[64] A steady working relationship with a substantial property owner like William Donnison, membership in a church or social organization, or any number of connections could provide ways of maintaining a steady flow of work, especially through the long winter months, when trade work traditionally slowed.

Newspaper advertising, especially in the *Boston Gazette*, proved a valuable resource for numerous artisans offering their services and products for the maintenance and decoration of the home. Thomas and Richard Bright, cabinet- and chairmakers located downtown at 44 Marlborough Street, were only two of the thirty-six men engaged in this business in 1794. As with the building trades, those mechanics employed in the woodworking and ancillary trades represented a growing sector in Boston between 1780 and 1799. The number of men in this occupational category, which besides cabinet- and chairmakers included turners, carvers, upholsterers, chaisemakers, and painters, grew at a steady rate. By the mid-1790s approximately 6 percent of the heads of household in Boston made their living in woodworking or a related trade. Painters increased in number from nine in 1780 to thirty in 1784, forty-six in 1794, and more than fifty by 1799. The scope of their business included a wide variety of work from painting business signs, carriages, furniture, and home interiors to limning, gold leaf work, and linen stamping. Other aspects of the woodworking trades also continued to grow and fare well. The number of coaches and chaises owned by financially well-to-do Bostonians steadily increased throughout the period, with some gentlemen and gentlewomen owning two or even three, as did former privateers and now prosperous merchants Samuel Breck and Thomas Russell. Chaisemaker Thomas Chapman, located across from John Ballard's livery stable, and Jeremiah Bulfinch, located near the Mill Bridge, also dealt in the sale of second-hand carriages. Bulfinch leased horses and chaises to the public and as another sideline "carried [letters] by Express to, any part of the Continent."[65] Once again ingenuity, entrepreneurialism, and flexibility marked the operations of numerous individuals.

Strategies such as temporarily changing or diversifying one's line of business proved a key to survival through the difficult years of the 1780s. Engaging in two or more related trades, shifting to a related occupation, or selling a few shop goods on the side was not an unusual occurrence in late-eighteenth-century Boston. Numerous advertisements placed by men like Jeremiah Bulfinch attest to the enterprising nature of Boston's tradesmen. At the Brights' cabinet and chair shop the consumer could also purchase "Floor, Stair, and Chaise Carpeting," and a various "assortment of *Upholsterer's Goods*." The proprietors also manufactured "Coach and Livery Lace" on the premises. Next door to Richard and Thomas Bright, at 43 Marlborough Street, Richard Salter offered "Genteel Boarding, and good Keeping for Horses," storage of gentlemen's chaises, and a "Choice of Lynn Shoes, and best Indigo." For those gentlemen doing business "at the General Court or State Treasury" Salter noted the excellence of his location.[66]

Cabinetmaker John Cogswell entered Boston's artisan community prior to the Revolution in the mid-1760s. Like many others facing financially hard times during the war years, he "subsisted by taking advantage of social, religious, fraternal, and political connections." By 1782, forced to seek his livelihood in another manner, Cogswell applied for and received from the selectmen a retailer's license. He then kept a shop on Middle Street in the North End's Ward 4, where he owned his residence. In 1780, Cogswell reported himself to the assessor as a trader and in 1784 as a huckster, although he did get some commissions. At some point during that four-year period he "made a serpentine bombe desk for Boston merchant Thomas Amory, Jr." By 1789 Cogswell no longer appeared in the records as a trader, but he returned to his occupation by training, that of "cabinetmaker." During the 1790s he became a "surveyor of boards and shingles" for the town, a position that he still held in 1806. During the early nineteenth century he also served as a "surveyor of mahogany." John Cogswell's expertise on fine woods and lumber made him an ideal candidate for the job. Throughout the difficult years at the end of the eighteenth century Cogswell managed to hang on to his North End property, and to return once again to his trade. When he died his estate was "valued at $4,218.65, a figure indicative of moderate success." Cogswell, like other previously unidentified furniture makers, made exquisite pieces for the Boston elite. Ultimately, as with numerous artisans, merchants, and unskilled workers, survival through the difficult years of the Revolutionary era depended upon ingenuity and the ability to diversify.[67]

Black Bostonians found many jobs closed to them and, as Adelaide Cromwell has stated, were economically "restricted from growth and development by conditions in the larger community."[68] During the economic depression of the 1780s, when competition developed for even the most undesirable jobs, black men and women faced particularly hard times. When enslaved African-Americans received their freedom in the early 1780s, they encountered a bleak job market. For lack of other employment, the newly emancipated often remained in their existing positions as servants.[69] However, even those forced to remain in domestic service sometimes found ways to improve their situation to one degree or another. Some chose to exercise their freedom by leaving Boston entirely, if only for short periods of time. Between 1784 and 1794 the town assessors noted more than 10 percent of black heads of household as either "gone," or absent in some other manner, such as "in the country."[70]

Boston's assessor recorded almost four hundred black heads of household between 1784 and 1799, by both first and last names. Of this number, the occupation is listed for 212, more than 50 percent.[71] Throughout most of the period, half of those worked as servants, with the number dropping down to slightly over 40 percent by 1799. Some of these men remained with the same employer throughout the fifteen-year period, suggesting that those who were slaves before 1783 may have remained in the same household. The hard economic times and slow job market of the 1780s provided no other choice. These men were not necessarily engaged exclusively in domestic service. As employees of shopkeepers, merchants, sugar bakers, distillers, wharfingers, hatters, and a barber among others, it is highly likely that some acquired skills in various trades, which may have allowed them to later become self-employed. Some individuals recorded as "servants" worked for the same employer, as did James Cammil, Peleg Crosby, Cato Inches, Richard Pollard, and Samuel Topney, who worked in the shop of merchant and bank director Peter Dalton. A workplace shared with fellow black men provided a situation conducive to support, collective action, and collective consciousness that an individual house servant working alone would not experience. As the percentage of African-Americans working as servants decreased, so did the number employed as laborers increase. By 1799 almost 40 percent fell into this occupational category. Some secured jobs as carters, chimney sweeps, sailors, waiters, tailors, shopkeepers, hairdressers, barbers, and ropemakers, although these were relatively few in number.[72] In 1799 four men worked as journeymen ropemakers. Applying for a tax abatement in 1786, Cato Inches, a sixty-year-old resident of the South End, informed the assessor for Ward 10 that he worked "at Gray's Ropewalk when he can get Business." He also told the assessor that he could not get his son "into a free school & thinks it hard to pay a Tax."[73] Prince Watts, the sponsor of Clarissa and Butter-field Scotland's son at the child's baptism, owned a soap-boiling business. By and large, occupations such as these were relatively rare opportunities for black heads of household in late-eighteenth-century Boston.[74]

One area of employment for free black men throughout the eighteenth century was that of seaman. Ten black Bostonians listed mariner, or seaman, as their occupation during the 1780s and 1790s, although it is likely that their numbers were higher. Black seamen faced a terrifying risk in going to sea, one not shared with their white counterparts: the possibility of being kidnaped and enslaved. In 1788 a petition was presented to the General Court of Massachusetts by "a great number of Blacks." Early that year a ship's captain from Connecticut lured three black laborers working in the harbor onto his ship "under pretense that his vessel was in distress" and then "put them in irons and carried them off from their wives and children, to be sold for slaves." This raised two critical issues: the existence of the slave trade in Massachusetts, and its danger to the "lives and liberties" of free black men and women. This issue found resolution with the passage of a law by the Massachusetts legislature "to prevent the slave trade" in that state. The second issue, closely related to the first, concerned work opportunities for African-Americans. The petition noted that "good seamen" were "obliged to stay at home through fear" and "loiter about the streets, for want of employ." If lawfully protected, these same men "might get a handsome livelihood for themselves" and their families, which under the present conditions they could not do.[75] As one historian has noted, for African-American men seafaring became "an occupation of opportunity." Maritime work "allowed widely dispersed black people a means of communication," paid wages, and "shaped their identities." Although the maritime world was not race blind, nonetheless opportunities existed for these sailors that were not always possible elsewhere. Seafaring continually presented itself as a job opportunity, when so few occupational options existed for free African-American men in the eighteenth century.[76]

Black men represented on average 12 percent of the fifty-two barbers and hairdressers working in Boston during the late 1790s. The occupation of barber often encompassed a variety of skills, including peruke-making and ladies' hairdressing.[77] John Lewis, a "French Negro" peruke-maker, had provided Bostonians with wigs since at least 1778, as evidenced by his run-in with the law that year. Lewis received a visit from Isaac Peirce, a representative of the selectmen, advising him to cease working on Sunday or face prosecution. An agreement had been signed by the town's peruke-makers and submitted to the selectmen acknowledging that they would not "carry on their Business in their Shops or in private Houses on the Lords Days as the practice appears . . . not only contrary to the Law of God and the Land, but to be highly offensive to the sober inhabitants." However, Lewis continued to work on Sunday, which brought him to the attention of the selectmen. Clearly the very act of certain Bostonians' employing Lewis on the Lord's Day indicated that some inhabitants did not find this "highly offensive." It did not appear to hurt his business either, for at the turn of the century he was still working as a successful hairdresser.[78]

Within a decade after the institution of slavery ended in Massachusetts, new occupational patterns began to emerge in Boston's black community. Racial prejudice on the part of white Bostonians may have kept African-Americans at the bottom of the job hierarchy, but the most pervasive problem, and one not necessarily separate from the issue of prejudice, was the lack of training in skilled jobs available to black men. Still, the freedom to have some choice in occupation had an impact on the black community as early as 1790. Although a significant percentage of black heads of household still worked as servants, a dramatic decrease in the number of men working in this capacity occurred. The next-largest employment category, that of laborer, was unskilled and unsteady work, yet it allowed 16 percent of these heads of household to become property owners by 1799, most of them in the South End and the rest in the West End. While few in number, these black laborers, shopkeepers, tradesmen, and entrepreneurs represent the beginnings of what would become in the nineteenth century an African-American middle class in Boston.[79] Part of this process included the ownership of homes and businesses. Between 1784 and 1799 town officials assessed forty-four black heads of household for the ownership of real property, the majority of which appears to have been acquired after 1790. Among those new black property owners were Peter Jessemen, who owned "a small new house" in Ward 7, the soap boiler Prince Watts, and Juba Hill, who kept a shop "owned by self." In 1794 at least five of Boston's seven black barbers owned real property. Within the service sector, the skilled trade of barber constituted one of the core occupations in the black middle-class community that emerged in the early decades of the nineteenth century.[80]

When circumstances necessitated securing employment, women also found themselves limited in their choice of occupations.[81] The American Revolution created a large number of widows, many of whom were reduced to living on poor relief or simply became part of the "wandering poor" strolling from community to community seeking assistance. It was not only the death of a husband that might leave a woman in dire straits. When men went off to fight in the Revolution, their wives sometimes had little means of support. In November 1777, churches in the southern part of town raised money for sixteen wives and widowed mothers living in their ward whose husbands and sons were "serving in the Continental Army."[82] Tax abatement records reflect the difficulties faced by women such as Captain Stephen Hill's widow, who was "left with 8 small children" in her care. In the maritime community of Boston, women found themselves alone for lengthy periods of time while their husbands went to sea. One wife informed the assessors that her husband had gone to France for at least twelve months, leaving "her with 3 small children to maintain."[83]

The American Revolution not only created widows, it also greatly reduced the pool of men available for marriage. Thus the war produced a large number of unmarried women who needed to find their own means of support in a world that offered them few choices and, with a few exceptions, usually kept them at the lower rungs of the economic ladder. Generally these occupations represented an extension of the responsibilities women traditionally held in relation to domestic production and managing a home and family. These single women might keep a small shop, run a boardinghouse, or manage a tavern or "victualing" house. For others, especially girls and younger women, domestic work, including housekeeping and childcare, provided employment. A woman might market her needlework skills as a seamstress. Boston's early manufacturing industry, such as the sailcloth factory in the South End, demanded spinners and weavers. Some trades such as mantua making required an apprenticeship, which cost money, but also provided a comfortable living and a position of higher status than some other areas of employment.[84]

When Joanna Jennison moved from "Liberty Square to Scarlett's Wharf Lane, North End," she so advised her customers in the local paper, telling them that she "continued to make Plumb-Cake, and other Cakes" as usual.[85] As a baker, Jennison drew upon skills taught to female children from an early age as preparation for marriage. Women might also turn to nursing both the young and the old as a means of income. Besides using the almshouse, the overseers of the poor sometimes placed those who were very ill in the care of private individuals who in turn received payment from the town treasury. Abigail Lynch nursed "Patrick Toamy, a poor blind Stranger," for which she and her husband received recompense, and "Violet Winslow, a Negro Woman" received two shillings per week "for nursing & supporting a Child, born of a Negro Woman who lived at the house of Captain Edmund Howes in Federal Street and was sent from thence to the Almshouse where she died."[86] Wet-nurses "with a good Breast of Milk" ran advertisements in the local papers to "take a Child to suckle." New mothers also sought wet-nurses for their babies, as did the woman who noted in her advertisement that "none other need apply" than those "with good character." Employers sought adult domestics with "sober" and "industrious" natures, but also girls of ten, eleven, twelve, or thirteen years to come into their home and care for young children or do light housework. Traditional gender-specific skills served in a variety of ways for white and black women in acquiring work.[87]

The largest occupational category for women, whether widowed or single, was shopkeeper. On average more than 50 percent of the licenses issued to women by the selectmen between 1776 and 1800 were for retail, and at the close of the American Revolution women constituted close to 30 percent of those legally licensed to run a retail establishment.[88] Viewed as a natural extension of female domestic duties, and easily incorporated into home life especially if a shop existed in one's house, shopkeeping was considered a respectable form of work for women. Widow Mercy Gleason, a North End resident, operated a small shop out of her home in Ward 3 for twenty-four years. Female shopkeepers carried a wide variety of goods, including "Cutlery, Hard Ware, Jewellery and Trinkets," groceries, assorted dry goods, and "English goods" among their wares. Rosanna Moore sold "buckles for Ladies and Gentlemen" and "Pewter and brass Wares."[89] To make ends meet, individuals might blend shopkeeping with other lines of work, as did Mary Freeman, who operated an inn and small retail shop in her house "near the Liberty Tree" in the South End. In the same area Mary Butler ran a "boarding house for gentlemen" and sold all sorts of "Garden Seeds," which she "imported from London." Shopkeeper Elizabeth Flynn also taught school, which could provide a woman with some income. Children under the age of seven frequently acquired their early education at "Womens Schools" before entering the reading and writing schools that constituted part of the town's public education system.[90] By 1799 at least twenty-five women served the community as "schoolmistresses." Some of these were the traditional "Womens" or dame schools for young children while others provided what was known as a female ornamental education. "Charlotte & Jane Caroline Sutherland" opened such a school, upon the approval of the selectmen, where they taught "Young Ladys embroidering work &c." The 1780s and 1790s show a steady increase in the number of female teachers in Boston, which points to later developments. In the nineteenth century the number of women working as teachers both with young children and in female academies would rise substantially throughout New England.[91]

As with the Sutherlands, it was not unusual for women to pool talent, capital, or both and work as joint proprietors. Pooling of capital, energy, and time might prove more lucrative or simply be the difference between survival and failure. Milliner Anne Love ran a shop on her own between 1776 and 1782, after which she went into business with another milliner, Mrs. Greeley. At their shop, located near the South Meeting House, the two offered a wide assortment of milliner's goods and made "ladies Hatts, Bonnets, Caps, Aprons, and Cloaks . . . in the newest fashion . . . upon the most reasonable terms." Mrs. La Barre, a French immigrant, produced in her millinery shop "work in the newest and most elegant taste."[92] Consumer demand for fashionable clothing kept milliners and mantua makers busy. Both milliners and mantua makers held high status in the female occupational hierarchy, with their skills matching that of any fine gentleman's tailor. Abigail Woodman apparently was Boston's only female tailor, or "staymaker and mantaylor." Perhaps she was unable to sustain an adequate living from her skills, for by 1803 she had joined the ranks of female shopkeepers and opened a toy shop.[93] As one historian notes, "mantua making required a lengthy apprenticeship, but girls who received such training in the art of fashionable dressmaking could hope for a more secure and affluent life" than women simply using basic sewing skills. These women made the fine clothes that adorned the backs of Boston's gentlewomen.[94]

For those unable "to pay the Tailors, Mantua-makers, and Milliners" for new clothes and finery, the ingenious widow Mary Causey, who operated a cake shop next to the White-Horse Tavern in the South End, opened a business "not much practiced" in Boston, that of selling used clothing. This entrepreneur bought, sold, and took in on commission "cast [off?] clothes, of men, women, and children." She pointed out in her newspaper advertisements that this gave those who wished it an "opportunity of clearing their houses of Cloathing, out grown, out of fashion, and useless to them" but also provided the less affluent the opportunity to dress in better-quality clothing than they could otherwise afford. With limited opportunities and choices as to the means of earning a livelihood, Mary Causey demonstrated a special stroke of ingenuity. As with the growing number of slop shops run by men such as Henry Foye, Widow Causey took advantage of consumer demand in the clothing business.[95] The only recorded female proprietor of a slop shop was Sarah Pelte, located on Fish Street, where Foye also ran his North End business.

All of the tailors in Boston during the 1780s and 1790s were male, except for the above-mentioned Abigail Woodman. As with the growing shoe trade, however, women undoubtedly participated in the clothing manufacturing business either as contributors to a family business or by taking in piecework to support themselves. Sewing skills were part of the Boston school curriculum for young girls so that they would have a future livelihood and not end up on public assistance in adult life. Piecework was one aspect of slop shop clothing production. Like shoemaking, home sewing also fast became a cottage industry that made possible the early phases of the industrial revolution in the nineteenth century, when consumer demand increased and New England's exports of cheap clothing and shoes to the South mushroomed. The increase in the number of tailors and shoemakers in Boston in the early 1790s suggests a market already demonstrating growth. As with Boston's early manufacturing plants, like the duck factory and card-making factory, women and children engaged in home sewing under conditions that damaged eyes, backs, and fingers.[96] The needle trades were simply seen as a natural extension of women's domestic work and training.

Boardinghouses, inns, taverns, and "victual" houses offered another livelihood for women. Sometimes women took boarders into their homes to help make ends meet. Mrs. Abigail Otis of William's Court offered "Genteel accommodations for Boarding Ladies and Gentlemen." Some boardinghouses offered rooms only for men, others only for "single women." With the population boom of the 1790s, greater numbers of Boston's women reported taking in boarders. However, judging by the number of women recorded by the town assessors in 1799 with "no boarders," this form of extra income was not steady. Husbands and wives might also take boarders into their homes. In the summer of 1779, Mildred Byles and her husband Elisha, who served the town as a surveyor of boards that year, took in a boarder, Benjamin Bagnal, and "let a chamber" to Susannah Wells, who had returned to Boston after "temporarily residing in Waltham." Wells had been an innkeeper from her home on Milk Street before departing at the time of the siege. Mildred also ran a "School for teaching Children Reading." The extra income received by the Byleses from her students and their boarders most likely proved useful. However, the 1784 assessor noted their condition as "poor." Surviving in post-Revolutionary Boston often meant the ability to acquire income through various means.[97]

Women also ran taverns with their spouses or, if widowed, continued the business after the husband's death. Taverns were sometimes no more than a few rooms in the owner's place of residence, but they might also constitute large, well-known establishments. Of 125 applications by women to the selectmen for business licenses in the 1770s and 1780s, twenty-five requested permission to operate taverns and inns. Immediately following the war women constituted 20 percent of the total number of those holding licences to operate inns and taverns in town. After her husband died, Margaret Johonnot continued operating their inn, a fairly valuable piece of property in the South End. When her husband died in the mid-1770s, Elizabeth Marston continued running his tavern, the Bunch of Grapes, but later changed to "retailing spirits" at her home near Wheelers Point. When Marston decided to retail liquor from her home, Agnes Lobdell took over the operation of the Bunch of Grapes. Lobdell made "many . . . alterations and additions" to the tavern and accommodated "Boarders and Lodgers."[98]

Desertion or the untimely death of a husband left some women with few options as to a livelihood. Running a public house (tavern) was one of these. Between 1776 and 1781 Elizabeth Fadre kept a public house under "the Sign of the Falmouth Packet and Pine Apple," moving her family and the location of her business twice. The first move appears to have been one of choice, but the second one, resulting from what Fadre thought were unfair dealings, was not. When the selectmen granted her an innholder's license in 1776, she kept her tavern at Dock Square, in the heart of the town's business district, not far from King Street, Long Wharf, and Merchant's Row. Five years later, by 1781, she had moved to a public house at the head of Long Wharf on State Street, an excellent location. Within a few months, however, Elizabeth found herself thrown out of this location when it was taken over by a male tenant. Furious at this injustice, she ran an advertisement in the local newspaper announcing her indignation and informing her loyal customers that she could now be found near Scarlet's Wharf at the familiar sign of the "Pine Apple and Packet," where she "hopes to get a Living yet for her Fatherless Children."[99] Four years later, in 1785,

she married sea captain and widower Nehemiah Skillings, a home-
owner from the North End with two children, a daughter Sarah,
age sixteen, and son Nehemiah, age eleven. It appeared as though
circumstances might well be looking up for Elizabeth Fadre. However, by the end of the decade she was once again a widow.[100] The
few short years of Elizabeth Fadre Skillings's life that appear in
the records illustrate some of the difficulties women living alone
experienced, and some of the ways they found to make ends meet.

For women like Elizabeth Fadre, changing attitudes toward female tavern keepers could prove devastating. "In the middle decades of the eighteenth century," writes historian David Conroy,
"widows had comprised approximately one-third of the license-
holders in Boston." This had decreased dramatically by 1796, and
by 1812 "of 56 tavernkeepers licensed . . . there were no women."[101]
The occupation of taverner was one of those niches in the job market that women had traditionally cut out for themselves, some no
doubt by choice and others by desperation. With opportunities so
limited even for skilled women, selling spirits could provide income
for a widow and her family. As attitudes and ideas regarding wom-
en's role in the family and the public and private spheres underwent
change in the early republic, it is not unlikely that female taverners
might become targets. This was not an occupation of "virtue," nor
was it one that fit within clearly defined boundaries between the
public and private spheres.

As concepts of the republican mother and the republican woman
slowly began to create opportunities for women in areas such as
education and teaching, some occupations previously available to
women closed. Perhaps middle-class women benefited, but the consequences for the uneducated or the widowed mother, who at one
time may have been able to secure a retail spirits license, could
prove disastrous. With the exception of widows of means and single
women with capital enough to comfortably maintain themselves as
feme sole traders, all women faced economic uncertainty because

they had inadequate training in the skills needed to compete in the larger job market. As they had done for centuries, women in late-eighteenth-century Boston continued to carve occupational niches for themselves in the public sphere.[102]

For some men and women who fell upon hard times, the best choice was to leave the port town, either temporarily or permanently. Advertisements appeared in the Boston newspapers recruiting tradesmen and individuals interested in farming to places in the hinterland in need of settlers. "A number of Tradesmen, such as Blacksmiths, House Carpenters, Joiners, Shoemakers, Tanners, Clothiers, Potters, Brickmakers, Masons, Leather Dressers, &c. [were needed] to settle" areas in upstate New Hampshire "about 62 miles from Portsmouth," read one notice in a Boston paper. Perhaps a young unemployed tradesman, or a laborer seeking a chance at something better, sat by his fire one December evening and from the local paper read to his wife: "This place is . . . the best situated for carrying on . . . trade. . . . [and] nature has accompanied it with so many advantageous circumstances, that a great trade must of course center there."[103] Did he take a chance? The disappearance of some young tradesmen from the late-eighteenth-century records suggests that some of those Bostonians who left during the great ebb and flow of migration that marked the Revolutionary era did indeed take that chance. Others, satisfied with the opportunities they had found and the gains they had made, determined to call Boston their home.

At 3 o'clock on the afternoon of Thursday, May 19, 1785, a town committee read to those Bostonians assembled at Faneuil Hall a draft of one more set of instructions to the "Gentlemen who Represent this Town in the General Court." After amending one of the paragraphs, those gathered at the meeting approved the document. The instructions consisted of various economic concerns of the townspeople, especially "the present reduced and declining State of many of our Manufactures" and the overcrowding of the harbor with foreign ships of commerce, particularly those of the British.[104] Like many Americans in the years following the Revolution, Bostonians became increasingly concerned about and supportive of domestic manufacturing. Two different types of manufacturing systems started to develop in Boston during the 1780s. One was the local production of decorative wall paper hangings and related products, which were relatively small-scale enterprises. The other was large-scale production and included newly constructed card factories, a glass factory, and a sailcloth factory.

The production of paper hangings and stained paper became an important local industry in Boston following the war. According to one source, by the turn of the nineteenth century, the quantity of these two items produced in the town provided enough not only for the Massachusetts market, but also for the other states.[105] Paper hangings had become available in the colonies in small quantities as early as 1737. By midcentury availability had increased, and in the 1760s domestic manufacture began. Paper hangings were not pasted on a wall as was wallpaper, which was developed later. They were "suspended against the wall or on wooden frames as tapestries." Prior to domestic production, whose growth increased beginning in the late 1780s, paper hangings were imported from France and England and were prohibitively expensive for all but the elite.[106] Domestic manufacture began to change that situation. By 1795, five men dealt in the paper hanging and paper staining business: Joseph Hovey, Thomas Clark, Ebenezer Clough, Josiah Bumstead, and Moses Grant.[107]

Joseph Hovey's "American Manufactory" may have been the first paper hanging and paper staining business in Boston following the American Revolution. Hovey worked as a paper stainer and painter in Boston as early as the 1780s, if not before. During the 1780s and 1790s he moved several times around the North End and Central District, at one point occupying a store on Winter Street that was later leased to a fellow artisan for two years, cabinetmaker

Simon Hall. By 1790 Joseph Hovey's American Manufactory could be found at 39 Cornhill "near the market," where it remained until his death in the mid-1790s. In his shop he produced "elegant Pannel Papers, suitable for wainscoting and stair cases—beautiful Flower Pots for chimney boards," and a wide assortment of other "elegant Paper-Hangings," which he claimed equal, if not superior to, "any manufactured in the Union." Because he manufactured all of his prints on-site, thus reducing costs, his merchandise sold 10 percent "cheaper than at any other place." To further facilitate sales, he took West India goods, English goods, and "country produce" in addition to cash for payment. No doubt those items that he could not use personally made useful trade items at other businesses, perhaps even to acquire some of the materials he needed for his trade. The shop's clientele was extensive and included not only Bostonians but persons from the surrounding countryside. Hovey's goods must have been of high quality and there clearly existed a market, both urban and outside Boston, for products to beautify and improve the home.[108] Joseph Hovey provides an excellent example of the type of small-scale manufacturing that developed in postwar Boston and demonstrates the kinds of businesses that Bostonians wanted their political representatives to encourage through supportive legislation.

By 1795, there were four other businesses in Boston dealing in the sale of paper hangings. Moses Grant, an upholsterer, sold imported French paper hangings as well as ones of domestic manufacture. Josiah Bumstead dealt in a wide assortment of goods for the home including furniture, mattresses, looking-glasses, fringes, and tassels; paper hangings represented just one item in his diverse stock. Only two owners, Thomas Clark and Ebenezer Clough, appear to have manufactured the product themselves. Thomas Clark retailed and wholesaled papers "of his own manufacture," but it seems he was primarily a shopkeeper, not an artisan as were Hovey and Clough. In 1795 Clough, the son of artisan brazier John, ran a

"Paper Staining Manufactory" in the North End. His 800-square-foot, two-story wooden "workhouse," which he had built a few years earlier, stood on a tenth of an acre in the North End along with an impressive 3,600-square-foot, three-story brick dwelling. Clough operated a retail and wholesale business that continued into the nineteenth century. His advertisement in 1795 for "three or four active Lads as Apprentices" for the manufactory indicates a busy and successful business.[109]

It was the encouragement that the new government gave to the development and growth of domestic manufacturing that rallied so many of Boston's mechanics to its support by the early 1790s, including men like Ebenezer Clough. In his report on manufactures in late 1791, Alexander Hamilton informed the House of Representatives that "[m]anufactories of paper" were "most adequate to national supply and that "paper-hanging" represented "a branch" in the American economy "in which respectable progress has been made."[110] By 1794 the Boston paper hanging manufacturers produced "twenty-four thousand pieces annually, for the demand of that part of the country." A portion of this domestic American production came from Ebenezer Clough's plant on Prince Street in the North End.[111]

During the late 1780s and the 1790s, a glass factory, five card factories (for cotton and wool), and a duck factory were built in Boston. Eager to encourage domestic industry, the Commonwealth of Massachusetts granted subsidies and special privileges to such enterprises. The Boston Glass House and the sailcloth factory are two cases in point. A "subsidy went to the manufacture of sailcloth, duck, and twine in Boston in 1788 and 1791" to encourage the industry and to encourage the growing of flax by hinterland farmers.[112] The Commonwealth granted the Glass House a fifteen-year monopoly on glass production and privileges such as freedom from state taxation. The first glass factory, which stood at the foot of Essex Street, was taken down when its design proved impractical, and it was replaced with a wood building lined with brick, "100 feet in length by 60 in width." The factory ran into further problems when it could not acquire enough employees. This in turn delayed the beginning of full-scale operations until late 1792. The "crown window-glass" produced in the establishment was "of a quality superior to any imported," and by 1798 the factory "produced about 900 sheets per week, worth $1.75 per sheet, or $76,000" per year.[113]

Wool card manufacturing had taken place in Boston prior to the Revolution but had since ceased. By 1788 production began again under the auspices of Giles Richards and several others. That year they opened a factory "near Windmill bridge," which produced "63,000 pair of cards" annually. Six years later, in 1794, Mark Richards & Co. started another card-making establishment not far from Faneuil Hall. By 1797 a third card factory existed in Boston, founded by Amos and William Whittemore. Boston also had "three smaller" card factories. "Four-fifths of the cards" produced in Massachusetts came from the two larger factories by Windmill Bridge and Faneuil Hall. The cards, of all different kinds, undersold those imported from England, and the companies shipped most of them to the southern states.[114]

The Duck Manufactory stood on Frog Lane in the South End. Built during 1788 and 1789, it reached two stories in height and measured 180 feet long. As with domestically produced cards, the sailcloth produced in the Boston Duck Manufactory undersold imported goods. In 1790 only fourteen men listed their occupation as factory worker, one as a "duck manufacturer" and twenty-two as cardmakers. By 1794 this had increased to thirteen "factory men," twenty-five "cardmen," and six males employed in the "DuckYard," four of whom were African-Americans. Other employees most likely included men from outside of Boston. The Duck Yard preferred young male weavers *"without families."* That the factory appears to have provided housing for some of its employees could explain the advertisement placed in the *Independent Chronicle* requesting only single men.

The "factory men" in 1790 and 1794 were all residents of Ward 12, indicating that they most likely worked at the sailcloth factory located there. A number of these men lived in individual rooms in a shared house that they owned. The cardmen, or cardmakers, lived predominantly in Ward 6, close to the card factories. A few lived in the North End. Unlike the other factory workers, all but a few of them in both 1790 and 1794 listed themselves as journeymen with Richard Giles, the owner of the first card factory built in Boston. They worked at least twelve hours a day at a machine, cutting and bending wire for cards. Although all of them did not own real property, those who did held property of greater value than that of the sailcloth factory workers. One source claims that sixty men worked in Giles's card factory. The number of cardmakers recorded by the assessors does not come close to this. Perhaps the young boys who worked there accounted for the forty-five males not listed in the 1794 Taking Book.[115] The card factories and duck factory did employ numerous children who worked under terrible conditions, presaging the plight of child labor in the Industrial Revolution. At the duck factory young girls worked from 8 A.M. to 6 P.M. in various menial and tedious tasks. Some had the job of standing with the flax around their waists as it fed onto the looms. Others spent their days turning the wheels of the twenty-eight looms. "[W]ith this assistance" the spinners "each . . . turn[ed] out 14 pounds of Thread per day," if they worked constantly. They were "paid by the piece." Male employees did the weaving.[116] Together the three larger card factories employed hundreds of children from poor families, not atypical of other contemporary manufacturing endeavors.

Despite the demand for English goods after the war, there was broad support in the new nation for freeing the country from dependency on foreign products. To become independent from European manufactures necessitated the development of American manufactures, but who should work the factories? Not men; they were in short supply immediately after the war. Furthermore, they were needed to improve agricultural production and become artisans and tradesmen. Women and children proved the logical solution. Many Americans in the young republic felt secure in their assumption that they could avoid the pitfalls of the horrors that had developed in Britain's factories and manufacturing towns, where children toiled in living conditions that bred disease, filth, and numerous vices. The young female employees in Boston's sailcloth factory were "daughters of poor families" and "girls of character," preventing the workplace from becoming a place of vice. To further improve the "morals" of young workers, a Sunday school was established on the premises. This was not a new idea. The concept was first put into practice in the factories in England and had been tried in Pennsylvania. Since manufacturing that employed children on this massive scale was new to Boston, the factory Sunday school was also previously untried. With the editorial support of the *Boston Gazette* and various Bostonians, the Duck Manufactory established the Sunday school in the spring of 1791 for those "young daughters of Industry employed in the Factory" who were unable to receive instruction on any other day.[117] By the nineteenth century these schools would become numerous throughout Boston and other American cities.

Legislation favoring domestic manufacturing and protecting American trade, and early attempts at building factories did not turn Boston into a manufacturing town overnight. Commerce and trade continued as the hub of the port town's existence well into the nineteenth century. As a port center with a growing commercial sector, the town of Boston was moving into a new period of growth and expansion. Artisans found a demand for their goods and services. The improving economy, population growth, and the conspicuous consumption of the nouveau riche fueled both demand and opportunity. Some argued that too much of the local economy depended on the importation of foreign goods while too little rested on the expansion of domestic production. On January 6, 1791, the editor of the *Independent Chronicle* greeted the new year and his customers with rousing reminders of "the pleasing situation of [the] Country." All Americans, he claimed, looked forward with hope. "The tradesmen and manufacturer, anticipates the happy period, when their several occupations will be promoted and encouraged, to the total extirpation of all foreign supplies."[118]

For some individuals, the development of domestic manufacturing meant not only an improved lot for the tradesman and artisan, but also the preservation of public and private virtue and the success of the town and even of the Republic. They argued that the importation of anything European brought harm to the American people, who had allegedly cast off the decadence of the Old World. Nevertheless when European vessels brimming with luxury goods and credit terms to accompany them arrived at Boston harbor, ready buyers purchased the goods. British goods came under particular attack. Partly this attitude was related to the alleged "evil" and "decadence" the use and influence of British goods would bring upon Americans, but it also reflected attitudes concerning the purchase of imported goods when domestic industries should be supported. As an editorial in a 1785 issue of the *Boston Gazette* warned townspeople: "Cease to import Goods from that imperious, insolent, debauched and intrigueing Kingdom of Great Britain. Abstain from British luxury, extravagance and dissipation or you are an undone people." This infiltration, he argued, was ultimately a plan to introduce "every kind of Dissipation and Luxury predominant in Europe" with an eye to "*overthrow*[ing] these American Republics." The "mad rage among us for *British manufactures and for British follies*," observed another in his address to "Brethren of America," would clearly destroy the new nation.[119]

Late one Friday afternoon four months after these articles appeared in the local newspaper, a gathering took place to consider the problem of "British Factors who were residing here and monopolizing to themselves the benefits of commerce." This was not simply an issue of foreign infiltrators. Bostonians brought English goods in by way of Nova Scotia, Amsterdam, and the West Indies. Regarding the importation of English goods prohibited by Congress, Jonathan Amory wrote to his brother in 1782, "I think they might be so managed that by Invoice and mixed with Holland goods that there would be but little difficulty. And English goods sell best." Public demand pushed the import trade along. And it was not only luxuries that undermined American manufactures. Jeremiah Allen advertised numerous English-made rope products for sale at his store, when Boston had its own ropewalks and ropemakers.[120]

For a number of concerned Bostonians two issues were at hand that they felt most urgently demanded attention. The first of these was the damage that imports did to Boston's own economy and tradesmen, and the second was the threat that luxury and dissipation laid at the town's front door. Each of these was inseparable from the other; both were one and the same monster. In a lengthy discourse on the destruction of America by "the supine Negligence" of virtue "which possesses" her people, "A Young American" explained to his readers the eminent danger. "Most certain it is that where Luxury and Extravagance are the prevailing Character of a People, . . . the final Issue must necessarily be unhappy," he wrote. What would eliminate the vices of luxury and excess destroying America? Domestic industry! For "*each Individual* [must] exert himself and encourage the Mechanick Arts, Manufacturers, Agriculture, in short, every thing that might tend to the Emolument of America." Then "Honour, Plenty and Happiness will be the Reward of our Industry," he concluded.[121] The combination of the uncertainties of war and its aftermath, economic upheaval, a relatively fast-growing and -changing population—all contributed to citizens touting both the opportunities that lay ahead and the dangers. Nowhere were these dangers more apparent than in the presence of vice, in its many forms, which threatened both individual and public virtue. Concerns as to European influence and its negative impact on Boston would repeatedly manifest themselves not only in relation to domestic industry but also in relation to social and cultural developments within the community during the closing years of the eighteenth century.

5

The Politics of Leisure

AT DAWN ON THE WINTER'S MORNING of February 8, 1788, church bells pealed throughout Boston. These were not fire alarms or funeral bells but a celebration of the ratification of the United States Constitution by the Massachusetts Convention. The bells rang all day and into the early evening as part of a three-day celebration consisting of speeches, discharges of cannon, "and other demonstrations of joy" that culminated in a magnificent parade in honor of the event.[1]

At nine in the morning on the day of Boston's ratification parade, townspeople began gathering around Faneuil Hall as mechanics and artisans readied themselves for the procession organized earlier in the week by the "The Committee of Tradesmen."[2] The "Grand Procession" was one of the largest public gatherings ever assembled in Boston. At least fifteen hundred persons participated, including more than one thousand of Boston's "mechanicks and artizans of every description," many husbandmen from "adjacent towns," close to one hundred seamen, and 250 merchants.[3] The "worthy" husbandmen of Roxbury headed the parade with a "Plough drawn by two horses, and two yokes of oxen." Dressed as "Sowers, with baskets, strewing grain," and "Reapers . . . Thrashers . . . Mowers . . . and Haymakers," accompanied by oxen, cattle, and horses, the mechanics paraded through the streets.[4]

Following the tribute to agriculture came the master mechanics and artisans of Boston representing more than forty trades. Seventy-five ropemakers marched to music, "their waists encircled with hemp" as they pulled "a cable-sled . . . decorated with colours." All the artisans carried their tools, decorated with ribbons of many colors. Eight "coach and chaise makers" carried "a Coach painted on paper," while twenty-six hatters decorated themselves with "Bows" and "Furs," and the "Tallow Chandlers" carried "a miniature Press."[5]

The town's shipbuilders offered Bostonians several large and festive displays including a replica of a "dock-yard" built upon a platform containing thirteen ships of various sizes, "the ship Federal Constitution" on "runners" pulled by "thirteen horses," and the ship "Confederation."[6] Five horses drew a cart containing the British flag and men armed "with muskets" who fired repeatedly at its "tattered remnants," reflecting the scorn held for the former mother country for hindering "commerce and obstruct[ing]" all "nautical proceedings."[7] Closing the procession marched the "Republican Volunteers."[8]

Beginning at Faneuil Hall the procession wove around the town, stopping at the residence of each of Boston's delegates to the state convention, where marchers gave "three huzzas" as they paraded by. On the march back to Faneuil Hall, where "refreshment was liberally provided," the huge procession passed the State House and offered a "salute of 13 guns." By this time their numbers had swelled so that Faneuil Hall, which held fifteen hundred people, could not contain everyone.[9]

Throughout the course of the day and into early evening, Boston's "hardy sons of Neptune" delighted the crowds with their antics and festive floats and flags. The seamen constantly played music as they accompanied thirteen horses pulling "the old ship Confederation" on a "sled." Brimming with "anticipation of [a] reviving and flourishing commerce," the sailors frequently let forth loud and excited "huzzas."[10]

At day's end amidst the ongoing clamor of the bells, the noise of the crowds, and the cheers of the parade, the sailors dragged the symbolic ship "Confederation," now "deemed unfit for further service," to Boston Common, where they burned it. Capturing the symbolism and power of the moment for Bostonians, one local paper described the "rising sun" that morning in all its great brilliance as "break[ing] forth, from the dusky horizon, with uncommon grandeur, partaking . . . of the joy [into] which an event so propitious immersed the souls of the people."[11]

Thus ended a three-day celebration for the town's citizens that accompanied the ratification of the United States Constitution by the Massachusetts Convention, which had convened in Boston between January 9 and February 7, 1788. The vote for ratification had been close, with 187 in favor and 168 opposed, pointing to the tension surrounding the event.[12] One day before the convention met, 380 of the town's "respectable *real* Tradesmen" who earned their living "from the sweat of their brow, and the labour of their hands" published in the *Massachusetts Gazette* their resolutions in support of the "proposed frame of government." Arguing that the Constitution promoted "industry and morality," they outlined the consequences if the convention did not ratify the document. For these tradesmen, or mechanics, rejection of the Constitution promised that "the small remains of commerce yet left us, will be annihilated," the "various trades and handicrafts" would "decay," the number of "poor will be increased," and "many of our worthy and skilful mechanicks" would be "compelled to seek employ and subsistence in strange lands."[13]

The parade and public celebrations on February 8, 1788, not only marked a momentous occasion for Bostonians but also made a clear statement as to the centrality of the Boston working man, reminding town and state leaders of the importance of the artisans' political support. Accordingly the artisans demonstrated to the convention delegates their satisfaction with a political job well done and the hope for a brighter future in domestic industry.[14] The festivities drew the community together, temporarily putting aside discord over town issues, debates between Federalists and Anti-Federalists, and strife from economic woes. They also marked the end, officially at least, of the upheaval that began in the 1760s.

Public events such as the ratification parade served to display patriotism, unite people in a common cause, or make a political statement. Accordingly they were often replete with rich symbolism as in October 1780, when a number of Bostonians paraded an elaborate stage through town upon which stood an effigy of Benedict Arnold. The general had two faces, "emblematical of his traitorous conduct," and in one hand held a mask and the other a letter "from Belzebub" telling him it was now time to hang himself, having completed his traitorous act. Behind Arnold, who was on his knees, stood a black-robed devil "shaking a purse of money at the General's left ear" and prodding him into hell with a pitchfork. On the front of the stage a "a large lanthorn of transparent paper" listed the treasonous crimes of the general. Either side of this depiction stood a gallows with two figures hanging as their reward for being traitors.[15]

When the "Definitive Treaty of Peace" was signed ending the War for Independence the town celebrated with processions and military parades, as they would in 1788. Local and state dignitaries gave speeches at the State House and Faneuil Hall where many townspeople gathered to sing anthems. Into the night Bostonians could still see the "bonfires on Dorchester heights and at Roxbury," which "made a most brilliant appearance."[16] In February of 1790 celebrations for George Washington's birthday included an evening "display of fire-works in State Street."[17]

Bostonians also gathered at the "Civic Festival" and feast honoring the founding of the French Republic. To recognize the birth of the "second Republic" citizens proceeded from the State House to Faneuil Hall accompanied by music and flags of both France and the United States. Not only did this draw local inhabitants but also "Republicans in the adjacent towns."[18] Celebrations for the Fourth of July were equally festive.

Parades and other high-spirited public gatherings provided the opportunity to put aside divisions and offered respite from daily toils. They were festive affairs but might also serve to make a political statement, unite the people, educate, or provide a moral message. Boston's mechanics made it clear in their resolutions in support of ratification of the Constitution that their concerns included the promotion of "industry and morality" and respectability before the world.[19] These concerns manifested themselves in a variety of ways, including the attacks during the 1780s and 1790s on the alleged moral degeneracy of the community as witnessed by the love of luxury, the importing of foreign goods, monopolizers in the marketplace, and problems with crime.

The expressions of concern as to the virtue of the community were serious in nature. Industry, the soul of the town's youth, the future of the community, its reputation, and even its survival rested upon Boston being a virtuous community. This applied not only to the marketplace, the system of public education, or the way Boston cared for its poor, but to the social activities of the town's residents. Accordingly, some Bostonians found evidence of moral degeneracy and an overall lack of virtue among residents not only in their love of luxury and their avarice in the marketplace but also in the growing affection for balls, card parties, gaming, theatrical entertainments, and clubs such as the elite "Sans Souci Club" for "the exclusive domain of the newly parading gentry."[20]

Compared to the years of self-sacrifice that revolutionary agitation had required before 1776, Boston seemed to be sinking into slothful ways, and Samuel Adams's concept of a "Christian Sparta" was fading fast. Imminent disaster lurked as the people were "prostituting all . . . [their] glory . . . for new modes of pleasure, ruinous in their expences, injurious to virtue, and totally detrimental to the well being of society."[21] The "social character" of the individual, the public virtue of the community, and even the success or failure of the republic rested upon individual actions and the collective behavior of the community at large. Nowhere was this more evident than in the frenzied and vitriolic debate that emerged in the early 1790s when one group of Bostonians sought to repeal the state and town laws that proscribed theatrical entertainments.

Town bylaws were clear as to what constituted immoral behavior. Gaming with "Dice, Cards, Pawpaws, Coppers . . . or any thing whatsoever" was strictly forbidden "in any of the Streets, Lanes, Alleys, . . . Market places . . . or Wharves." Such vice and immorality as theatrical entertainments was also clearly outlawed both in local and state legislation because of "the many and great mischiefs which arise from publick Stage-Plays, Interludes," and the like.[22] These "mischiefs" damaged morality, hindered industry, and destroyed frugality. The job of enforcement fell to the selectmen, but they in turn were bound by law to consider the petitions of inhabitants.

When John Templeman appeared before the selectmen in 1782 applying for "liberty to exhibit on the Slack Wire," they immediately refused him on legal grounds. Templeman did not give up. Three weeks later he appeared in their chambers again, this time with "several Petitions of the Inhabitants" requesting that the selectmen permit him to perform. As town law allowed that petitions presented by ten inhabitants or more be addressed in the town meeting, the matter was put in the warrant for March 11. Accordingly the next town meeting addressed the article concerning the use of Faneuil Hall for inhabitants "to be entertained with Mr.

Templeman's Exhibition." A lengthy debate ensued and the vote reflected a close division among inhabitants concerning the performance of this slack-wire artist. With an almost even number of votes both for and against Templeman's performance, "the meeting determined that" there existed "obvious doubt among citizens" and accordingly tabled the proposition. The petitioners withdrew their requests, and Templeman departed from Boston, no doubt in search of a more receptive audience to whom he might display his acrobatic talents.[23]

The case of John Templeman was not unique. Theatrical entertainments had long been outlawed by provincial as well as local law because they were deemed morally damaging and harmful to industry and frugality. Consequently, the majority of itinerant performers and theatrical troupes touring colonial settlements avoided Boston during the eighteenth century, although there were a few exceptions. One such performer was John Childs, "the flying man," who arrived in Boston in September 1757. Childs, using ropes for his acrobatics, had "flewn off of most of the highest steeples in Old england." He now chose to demonstrate his talent for the benefit of the people of Boston by flying "off of Dr. Cutler's Church." He accomplished his feat three times "to the satisfaction of a great Number of Spectators." The selectmen, however, were not pleased, for his performance was in violation of the provincial law. They forbade his "flying any more in the Town," since his "Performances led many People from their Business."[24] Ten years later, in 1767, when Mr. Moulton permitted an exhibit of "the City of Jerusalem in Wood work" at his tavern "at the sign of the White Horse," the selectmen immediately ordered it closed because the entertainment drew "considerable sums from the Inhabitants." The exhibitors were shown the way out of town and Mr. Moulton ordered never again to permit such exhibits in his establishment.[25] In November of 1785, town officers advised the persons giving puppet shows in the marketplace "that they immediately desist from such exhibitions, otherwise they may expect to be prosecuted." In each of these instances, the performances were judged by the selectmen as under-mining the frugality and industry of the townspeople.

Winter offered its own forms of entertainment that elicited the disapproval of the law. While children sledded down icy hills and threw snowballs at unsuspecting passersby, the holidays brought mummery and revelries into the streets despite bylaws to the con-trary.[26] During the Christmas season, roving groups of "Anticks," or amateur performers, deliberately attired in dirty, ragged clothes and wearing masks, descended upon the festivities held in the homes of the well to do. The custom included their performance of short skits followed by the chant "Ladies and gentlemen sitting by the fire/Put your hands in your pockets and give us our desire." Once remunerated for their entertainment they departed.[27] In mid-December 1784, the selectmen and justices deliberated over how to prevent "the Disorders that take place on Christmas & New Years Nights." One week later they placed advertisements in the newspa-pers warning against "Persons entering Houses & parading the Streets in disguise on Christmas & N[ew] Years Evening."[28]

Itinerant performers and resident amateur actors were not the only persons subject to the scrutiny of the law. Keepers of any type of public house found themselves before the selectmen for provid-ing entertainments, gaming, billiard tables, "and other Disorders in their Houses." In 1781, nine tavern keepers received "a Warning & caution" to obey the town laws after a number of inhabitants com-plained concerning these proprietors. When Daniel Jones applied for a "license as an Innholder" in 1781, the selectmen gave their approval only after "having his assurance that his utmost endeavors will not be wanting to prevent any breaches of the Law for regula-tion of Taverns." Strangers who attempted to set themselves up in a tavern, the market, or any public or private place for the purpose of "juggling," providing entertainment, reading palms, or "feigning . . . to have knowledge in physiognomy" could soon find themselves committed to the House of Correction.[29] Any duplicitous act that deceived the people was unacceptable, whether it was gambling, claiming to know the future, or performing stage plays that presented fiction as reality, taught that immoral acts were acceptable, and promoted the vices of "Luxury—loose morals, fashionableness, Europeanization, [and] false gentility."[30]

The growth of provincial culture earlier in the eighteenth century had brought theater to Virginia, South Carolina, New York, and Pennsylvania, although the theater in Philadelphia "survived in a climate of [Quaker] scorn."[31] The Puritan stronghold of New England displayed the fiercest disdain and distrust of theatrical entertainments, traceable back to the early seventeenth century with William Prynne's scathing 1633 rebuke *Histriomastix*.[32] Prynne, along with other Puritans, found plays "all to be concerned with adultery and fornication." They promoted "hypocricy and deceit . . . drunkenness, luxury, impudence, theft, [and] murder." Equally as dangerous, he argued, "most actors [were] papists."[33] In 1687 Increase Mather displayed his distaste for the theater in his *A Testimony Against Several Profane Superstitious Customs*. In declaring the theater as "dangerous to the souls of Men," Mather voiced the opinion of a majority of Bostonians.[34] Although Mather noted that "there is much discourse now of beginning Stage Plays in New England," no indication of any public performances during the seventeenth century appears to exist.[35]

In March 1750 the General Court of Massachusetts passed "An Act to Prevent Stage-Plays, and other Theatrical Entertainments," which caused "great mischiefs," wasted money, discouraged "industry and frugality," and increased "immorality, impiety, and a contempt of religion."[36] Persons permitting the use of a "house, room," or any other place for "theatrical entertainments" of any kind received a hefty £20-per-day fine for each day of violation, and if a group of more than twenty persons was involved, the spectators and actors paid a fine of £5 per day. Informers received one-half of the fines collected, while the other half went to the government.

This law did not prevent small, private, nonpaying gatherings of fewer than twenty individuals.[37] To evade the law, some Bostonians held private readings of plays, as evidenced by an advertisement for the *Provoked Husband* in a local newspaper.[38] Thus, while the London Company of Comedians, escaping the ramifications of the earlier British Licensing Act of 1737, brought "a repertoire of plays by Shakespeare, Rowe, Steele, and Garrick" to the southern and middle colonies, the players left New England off their circuit.[39] Following the American Revolution the Massachusetts legislature reinstated its proscriptive 1750 legislation.[40]

Before the early 1790s few advertisements for public entertainment appeared in Boston's newspapers. Those rare persons who did receive permission to provide some form of stage entertainment for residents offered so-called "moral lectures" and similar edifying presentations. In April 1789 a Mr. McPherson presented a "Lecture on Heads." This included his "celebrated" lecture and the exhibition of thirteen heads, such as "An American Soldier and Patriot, contrasted with *Alexander the Great*, A Cherokee Chief, and An Old Maid." McPherson assured the audience that the presentation was "interspersed" with "dissertations on Friendship-Gratitude-Generosity-Esteem-Publick Spirit, and common Sense." Asserting the moral worth of his show was an astute move in a town renowned for its hostility toward theatricals of any nature.[41] Concert Hall offered "musick, dancing and other polite entertainments" at various times, and the genteel might choose to attend the Friday afternoon public balls hosted by the local dancing instructor, Mr. Griffiths, "for the improvement of the scholars" attending his school. At these public balls or at Concert Hall, students could demonstrate their dancing skills learned under Griffiths, including "four different minuets—the newest cotillions and country dances."[42] Such activities taught grace and proper, polite behavior befitting the station of the genteel.

Late in 1789, in the winter, a troupe of "Rope Dancers and

Balance Masters" arrived in Boston and proceeded to give a performance. What followed transformed the cultural topography of Boston. The community's reaction to the performance was mixed, but it soon became evident that not everybody agreed with the proscriptive legislation that controlled entertainment in the town. One distressed citizen complained in a local newspaper about those who had invited the performers and in the process encouraged "every species of dissipation." These theatricals damaged the manners and morals of Boston's youth and took money that could be put to better use in the "Almshouse" and in helping "the poor in general." Besides issuing the familiar railings against the theater, he also noted that introducing these "romantic amusements of Europe" would make the republic "easy prey to" American "enemies" and thus ultimately lead to its downfall. The affronted citizen appealed especially to the clergy to help thwart this menace.[43] Soon letters of this nature became common in Boston's newspapers as town inhabitants engaged in a moral and political debate concerning the repeal of the ban against theater. In one short decade the end result would be not only circumvention of the proscriptive 1750 act, but two theaters for stage plays, an amphitheater, museums, and numerous forms of related entertainments for the men and women of Boston.

Determined to establish a theater in Boston, a group of townsmen prepared a petition in January 1790 for presentation to the Massachusetts General Court arguing that the showing of appropriate stage plays would act as a deterrent to the immorality and vice that infested Boston. While most Bostonians seemed to agree that "Vice" was "spreading with" incredible "Velocity" and some means was needed "to check its mad Career," the nature of exactly how to check it was in dispute. Neither side agreed with the other's solution because they viewed the theater from diametrically opposed positions.[44] In local newspapers opponents of stage plays saw vice, luxury, and the corruption of Europe clearly apparent in the theater. They expressed concern over the scarcity of money and how it might be put to better use than on theatrical entertainment, and bemoaned the danger of the theater to Boston's youth. Promoters of the theater, by contrast, saw it as a means of improving mankind. The theater in America, unlike in England, might operate as "a school of virtue."[45] Since stage plays taught "the duties of virtue, and morality" and brought forth "the finer feelings of the heart" they made "mankind more humane, just and virtuous" and served to educate the republic's citizens in right thought and behavior. Therefore they strengthened, not weakened, the republic.[46] Other benefits of stage plays were put forth besides those of imparting virtue and improving humankind. One Bostonian went so far as to claim that if Bostonians established a theater, "Vice of every Species" would "be taken of an Apoplex and die of a Consumption."[47] Supporters argued that the theater would provide a way for Boston's "industrious Tradesmen" to spend their "many leisure hours" and the "Overplus of their Day's Earnings."[48] This was most likely not a convincing argument for those rallying around the banner of industry, frugality, and thrift.

The petition of January 1790, and its failure, marked only the beginning in a series of attempts to convince the General Court of the need to repeal the theater ban. Between January 1790 and March 1793 heated words and appeals to reason appeared in print from both sides of the debate. Each time the pro-theater advocates proposed presenting another petition to the General Court, the opposing side launched a verbal war in the local newspapers. Six months later, in June 1790, the proprietors of the American Company, Hallam and Henry, took matters into their own hands. Encouraged by the "very many . . . citizens" in Massachusetts, they presented their own petition to the General Court asking permission to establish a theater.[49]

Experience in Philadelphia, New York, and elsewhere had polished Hallam and Henry's rhetorical skills in appealing to courts and councils. The lengthy new petition carefully and shrewdly de-

lineated regulations with which the Company would willingly comply and the benefits the Commonwealth might receive. Their suggestions included confining their performances to Boston, donating
a part of their profits to charitable causes in the town, and not performing any play without approval of a review committee selected
by the legislature. They further pointed out the benefits of the theater to the community, the way it brought people of all ranks together and improved the morals and manners of society "which
among a free people is the basis of government." The theater would
"improve the language of the citizens at large" and remove the
"provincialisms which are so disgusting to strangers." In case the
legislature needed further proof of the theater's value, Hallam and
Henry also pointed out how the theater improved "society, by pro-
moting national taste, genius and literature."[50] To address pecuni-
ary concerns, they pointed out that an influx of visitors would bring
money into the town, and that the theater "draws money out of the
pockets of the rich" and puts it "into the pockets of the poor" in
the form of wages paid to "the numbers of people employed in and
about a Theatre." Surely all of these benefits could not help but
"improve a sensible and free people."

Despite their cleverly crafted appeal to the legislature addressing the issues of morals, manners, virtue, thrift, and the well-being
of the republic, the two gentlemen again failed. After hearing their
petition on June 5, the House denied Hallam and Henry "permission to open a Theatre in the town of Boston." Ironically, next
to their June 12 publication of the rejected petition the *Columbian
Centinel* ran a lengthy article on "Idleness."[51] Meanwhile Bostonians continued to offer their viewpoints on the theater through
their local newspapers. One commentary claimed that "this source
of rational amusement and instruction" was gradually gaining acceptance.[52] Whether or not this was true, matters seemed fairly
calm during the summer and autumn months of 1790. Even "John
Brenon from Dublin" and his wife, "a native of Boston," demon-

strating "the curious and ingenious Art of Dancing on The Slack Wire, Balancing, &c." at the Green Dragon Tavern following an Air Balloon demonstration passed without any significant commentary.[53]

By the spring of 1791 Bostonians again turned their attention to the theater laws. For several months the *Columbian Centinel* ran a series of essays by "M. Gellert, in Defence of the Theatre." The articles systematically addressed the arguments against theater: that by example it leads to vanity, "deceitful dealings," encourages idleness, and causes men to waste their money. While refuting these arguments, Gellert explained the great benefit one might derive from the theater, most noticeably an understanding and acquisition of the virtuous behavior befitting a republican citizen. In case the noble argument did not convince, he included the practical. Idle people and spendthrifts would waste time and money whether theater existed or not, therefore surely it made greater sense to have them in the theater learning something constructive by example.[54]

The autumn of 1791 brought rising tensions. In October a group of Bostonians prepared another petition to submit to the Massachusetts House of Representatives for the repeal of the 1750 act. Aware that the subject was slated for discussion at the October 26 town meeting, citizens began another newspaper war with familiar arguments regarding virtue and vice. It was pointed out that Boston did not need to offer the "licentious performances" offered on the English stage. True, these were "highly dangerous to the rising generation," but a well-regulated theater was "of essential service to the community." To this end one writer proposed selecting a "standing committee" of clerical leaders from the Boston churches "to inspect each play," so as to prevent the public from seeing anything harmful to their character. Those theater companies wishing to perform in Boston would hesitate to perform plays that advanced "sentiments injurious to the interests of morality and religion" for fear of rejection.[55] As M. Gellert had previously argued, it was possible to use the stage as a teaching tool for the improvement of the republic, and having a board of censors would assure such a goal.[56] One editorialist remarked that the theater could "be made the School of Science, Patriotism, Conjugal Fidelity, and Honour."[57] The primary thrust of the debate continued to center around virtue, vice, education, and censorship, but another argument now surfaced, that of an individual's "natural . . . Rights." The "liberal principles" of the 1790s reflected man's ability "to pursue their own happiness," wrote one commentator, while the old laws formed under a monarchical government showed "a distrust of the people" and belonged to a time long past.[58] In the following months natural rights and ultimately the right to freedom of speech became central to the position of the theater advocates.

On October 26, 1791, Bostonians crowded into Faneuil Hall for what proved to be a "full meeting." The moderator of the town meeting read the petition regarding theatrical entertainments, and inhabitants gave their opinions "on the subject" in a "very lengthy and spirited debate."[59] An air of excitement filled the room as one person after another spoke. "Theatres [are] sinks of lewdness and debauchery," claimed Samuel Dashwood, an elderly shopkeeper and former sea captain from the South End of Boston. His "experience in foreign countries" verified this, he informed the crowd. Samuel Adams, a favorite of many of the town's mechanics and tradesmen, was barely audible above the shouts and hisses of the crowd as he spoke of the theater's vices. Attorney William Tudor immediately challenged him with a defense of the institution. Harrison Gray Otis provided the meeting with a "flowery Oration" in which he "strenuously opposed the petition" and the theater. The air was "electrical" with speeches and applause.[60] The oratory and discussions ran far longer than anyone expected, making it necessary to adjourn for a two-hour recess. No doubt a number of inhabitants continued their discussions and debates in the taverns and coffeehouses surrounding the busy Faneuil Hall area.

When the meeting reassembled the hall once again overflowed with citizens ready to take up the question of the petition. The debate generated many "ingenious and animated arguments," from new speakers and from those who had spoken earlier in the day. By seven that evening the citizens began to call for a vote on the fate of the petition. After hours of discussion, "a very large majority" decided in favor of presenting the petition before the General Court.[61] To this end the meeting appointed a committee of seven gentlemen to "draft instructions to the Representatives of the town to obtain a repeal of the aforesaid [1750] act." The committee would report to the townspeople at the next meeting, scheduled for the 9th of November.[62] One Boston newspaper reported that "morality, immorality [and] beneficial and pernicious effects of Theatrical Exhibitions" were by far the dominant issues in the debates. Whether or not the law in question "was an infringement on one of the natural and unalienable rights of the citizen" also raised voices.[63]

At ten o'clock on the morning of November 9, another large gathering packed Faneuil Hall to listen to the petition prepared by the committee. Attorney Perez Morton, head of the committee, read a rough draft of the petition, which noted that the law concerning stage plays "in its Present unlimited form operates as an undue restraint upon the liberty of the Citizen And as an infringement of his unalienable right." The "right to relax from the toils of Industry & the fatigues of Business" he read, by means of "any *rational & innocent amusement*" was "part of the happiness of Civil Society and one of the essential blessings confirmed to them by A free constitution and Government." The document further addressed the "Public and Private virtue" that might be gained from those stage plays that educated the public. The meeting voted to accept the petition and instructed that the town's representatives present it to the General Court.[64] Not everyone left the meeting impressed with the outcome. John Paul Martin, a North End tradesman, found the gathering extremely distressing. "The late Town-Meeting was no Town-Meeting" and "the vote . . . no vote," he later declared. Each of "the voters at that Meeting," he insisted "are, all of you, a set of ignorant, stupid, confused-headed Block-heads."[65]

Each of the opposing factions drew from Boston's elite, particularly the rising new class of young lawyers. Some of the town's leading citizens formed the committee of seven selected by the town meeting to prepare the petition. They included Perez Morton, barrister-at-law and a future director of the Union Bank; Thomas Crafts, attorney "practising at the Common Pleas" and acting justice; Captain James Prince; acting justice James Hughes; printer Joseph Russell; and Charles Bulfinch, future architect of the Federal Street Theater, the Tontine Crescent, and Beacon Hill homes in the West End.[66] Bulfinch derived considerable enjoyment from the theater and campaigned arduously for one in Boston. In April 1789, while in New York, he wrote to his parents that he, his wife, and their two sisters had seen five plays in their travels, three in Philadelphia and two in New York. Everyone in the party was "so charmed . . . that remarks upon the play and the different actors engross great part of our conversation." Bulfinch ended his letter by stating his belief that soon Boston would have a theater, as he had heard good news in that direction.[67] The members of the opposition also numbered among Boston's leading citizens. Their ranks included Lieutenant Governor Samuel Adams. Dr. William Eustis, and attorney Harrison Gray Otis. Writing from London, Otis commended his grandson for his part in opposing the 1791 petition during the October and November town meetings. "It affords me great pleasure," he wrote, "to hear of the Christian as well as political opposition you made . . . for the repeal of the Act against *plays*. If your Legislators have any regard for the morality of the people, they will not give the least countenance to the Stage."[68] Samuel Adams had stated in 1775 that citizens "may look up to Armies for our Defence, but Virtue is our best Security," and he remained steadfastly opposed to the theater.[69]

William Tudor went before the House on January 17, 1792, with the petition drawn up in the town meeting the previous October and November. When the House voted sixty-nine to thirty-seven against writing a bill to repeal the 1750 act, attorney John Gardiner called for a reconsideration of the vote. "Some attention was due to so respectable a town as Boston," he pointed out, and the House needed to consider that in their town meeting "three-quarters" of Boston's citizens "had voted for the repeal."[70] A second vote favored selecting a committee to consider the expediency of bringing in a bill to repeal the 1750 law. On January 20 the committee presented its report, Boston's representative William Tudor gave a "judicious speech" on repeal, and John Gardiner presented "a learned and elaborate essay."[71]

Gardiner's speech laid out a clear, well-constructed argument for repeal of the 1750 law and the advantages of a theater for Boston. First he addressed the economic benefits to the town, including increased business for "merchants, shopkeepers, tradesmen, mechanicks, and various crafts and professions" as a result of building, furnishing, and decorating the theater. He then argued that "theatrical Exhibitions were, by no means unlawful to Christians." The Apostles traveled widely in "the great cities of the Roman Empire which then abounded with theatres," but nowhere in the New Testament did they condemn the theater. Saint Paul even copied into his writing "several divine passages from the Greek poets and comick writers." Next, Gardiner "gave an historical and critical account of the rise, progress, and meredian perfection of the ancient Drama," followed by a discourse on the benefits of theater upon the manners, language, and knowledge of the audience. He concluded with a short history of the theater in England and Europe and reminded the members of the House that every commonwealth in the United States except Massachusetts had a theater, even "our adjoining sister State of Connecticut, ever remarkable for the strictest purity of manners." In closing John Gardiner "hoped that he had not tired the patience of the House."[72] Whether or not he did is unknown, but six days later, on January 26, 1792, the House sustained the committee's report that the repeal of the 1750 act was inexpedient. The legislature appeared immovable on the matter, and some Bostonians grew impatient in light of the fact that they were the only coastal city in the new nation without a theater.

When they opened their local newspapers in late 1791 and early 1792, Boston readers discovered that the "most amiable and respectable gentlemen of Philadelphia" had recently subscribed "one thousand dollars each" to build a new theater in their city. The news stories made a point of mentioning at some length that the Pennsylvania legislature had recently repealed the law banning theatricals because it "was inconsistent with unalienable Rights of the Citizen!" The *Columbian Centinel* queried, "Is the Legislature of Massachusetts less enlightened than that of Pennsylvania, or will it be less liberal?" Perhaps, the editor charged, Pennsylvania's legislators "understand something of the Rights of the Citizen."[73] With the Philadelphia theater completed later the following year, one proud Bostonian wrote "I . . . rest in the hope, that the publick-spirited citizens of Boston, will not suffer her sister metropolis to rival her in those edifices and institutions" that bring recognition from strangers, respectability, and wealth. To drive the point home, the author of the editorial included a lengthy description of the new theater recently announced in a Philadelphia paper.[74]

The salt in the wound for pro-theater advocates was the news that theaters now existed even in Portsmouth, New Hampshire, and Norwich, Connecticut. Why, asked a Bostonian, were "their neighbors" possessed of adequate virtue, discernment, and propriety that they may have "Stage Representations" while he and his fellow townsmen may not?[75] "Are we *so vicious and corrupt* a race, that we must have civil *Guardians and Conservators* of our morals?"[76]

Such "rational amusements" exist in every commonwealth except Massachusetts, "and who can boast an equal proportionate number of *Saints* as ourselves?" asked another.[77] A number of Bostonians became outraged when they read in their newspapers of the establishment of theaters in Rhode Island, Connecticut, New Hampshire, New York, and Pennsylvania, where not only did the law permit theater, but citizens also encouraged it. "Why, then," asked one correspondent, "are the citizens of *Massachusetts*—who live under the same government, and cheerfully bear an *equal weight* of the publick burthens, *singled* out, and prohibited amusement which their other fellow-citizens can freely enjoy?" These "*Croakers*" who forever "brood . . . over the eggs of misery" truly hadn't shown just reason for opposing the theater other than their own desire to "paint . . . human nature with the *sombre* pencil."[78] Portsmouth drew special attention from the *Centinel* perhaps because of its relatively close proximity to Boston. The paper informed readers of plays performed, accompanying music, and the cost of tickets for the nonsubscriber. Reviews of the plays carefully pointed out how productions "were given . . . in decent style."[79] Advocates increasingly began to assert their legal rights. One citizen, calling himself Atticus, expressed his "surprise that there should be found one advocate for a law, confessedly contrary to the Social Rights of Freemen."[80] Another claimed the "law to be virtually repealed by our bill of rights, . . . [even though] the General Court . . . refused to recognize the nullity of the law."[81]

What transpired between August 1792 and December 1792 was outright defiance of the 1750 act and town's bylaws, climaxing in the debate of 1793. In early August, London actor Charles Stuart Powell and Joseph Harper, formerly of the American Company, arrived in town. Whether they showed up simply hoping that the climate had changed in Boston or whether they were specifically invited by certain inhabitants is unknown. Powell and his troupe offered several "lectures" at Concert Hall including a "Moral and

Satirical Lecture on the Humane Heart," and "The Evening Brush, For rubbing off the Rust of Care," which included "Modern Spouters, Stage Candidates, Tragedy Taylors, Wooden Actors, Butchers in Heroics, Buffoons in Blank Verse, Bogglers and Blunderers, & c. &c." The troupe treated the audience to "humorous" dancing, "original songs," and orchestral music. Powell was blunt in his attitude toward his Boston critics: "When Vice or Folly swarm in any age,/Satire becomes the business of the Stage."[82]

Whether the troupe's performances "refine[d] the morals of the people" was questionable to one identifying himself as "Ploughjogger." Although convinced at the October and November 1791 town meetings that theater could educate and refine manners, he now found, after seeing Powell's production, that "the opposers of the Theatre were right in their conjectures." It seemed to him that the residents of Boston were as eager to attend "the paltry amusements of Rope Dancing and Tumbling, as they would the performances of Shakespeare or *Addison*." He failed to see what affinity "feats on the Tight Rope," or "Somersetts over a table," or the "nose of Susan Spitfire" shared with the "morality, and the love of liberty" that theater advocates claimed rested behind their support of the stage. The disconsolate "Ploughjogger" abandoned all hope for the theater in Boston. When he attended the town meetings the previous year, he had returned to his neighborhood and told his friends about the value of the theater as argued by its advocates. Now they laughed at him, saying that they no more approved of the theater reform than they had previously.[83]

In direct defiance of the 1750 act, Powell and Harper next rented a North End stable in "a muddy passageway" known as Board Alley. According to one inhabitant, with the "support from a class of citizens that *ought to know better*," they tore down the stable and began to erect a theater.[84] Since the legislature remained unmoved by the pleas of theater advocates, who constituted a sizable number of Bostonians, it appeared that some townsmen had made the decision to defy the 1750 law banning theater. Powell had put his beliefs on the line. A citizen's choice of entertainment was a personal decision, not that of the government. Although its offerings were titled "moral lectures," Ploughjogger was perhaps correct in his assessments of Powell's company. Activities at the Board Alley Exhibition Room appeared to be more biting satire than moral edification.

Two to three nights per week ladies and gentlemen of Boston who so chose were entertained at Board Alley by Monsieurs Placide and Martine, performing pantomimes and "Dancing the Slack Wire." Mr. Robert tumbled and M. Martine would "jump the Tramplin, and throw a Somerset over a Man on Horseback." Monsieur Placide sometimes danced "a Hornpipe on a Tight Rope, play[ed] a Violin in various attitudes, and jump[ed] over a cane backwards and forwards." By October the company's performances perhaps resembled somewhat more of what Ploughjogger hoped for. The "moral lectures," which were plays, became more frequent, and advertisements boasted well-known eighteenth-century stage plays, including *She Stoops to Conquer, Rosina, The School for Scandal, The Padlock, Inkle and Yarico, The Rivals*, and *George Barnwell*, among others. In December the company even staged Shakespeare's *Tragedy of King Richard III*. Whether or not the hornpipe performed after the Shakespearean tragedy added to the moment is unknown. For those who found tragedies not to their liking, the troupe later offered "Feats on the Tight Rope," Monsieur Placide dancing "with his Grandmother on the Tight Rope" and later "balanc[ing] a Peacock's Feather, different ways." Songs and dances followed. The Board Alley Exhibition Room offered varied entertainment to Boston's residents, and they flocked to see it. For some this was a novel experience. The illegal company in Board Alley managed to defy the authorities for four months.[85] More accurately, the authorities simply ignored the Board Alley presentations.

If officials ignored the Exhibition Room, the general public did not, and they proceeded to make their opinions regarding this addition to Boston well known.[86] An outbreak of smallpox in the late summer provided fodder for some of the anti-theater advocates.[87] Not only was there outright defiance of the law, wrote "A Friend to Humanity and Decency," but the money paid by the audience to attend performances at Board Alley "would be an ample support to hundreds of indigent families, who are now suffering under the distress of sickness." Parents were unable to care for children, fathers unable to work. "Is it not then a melancholy reflection amidst this general calamity, that many of our inhabitants are so *inconsiderate*, as to maintain a set of strangers at the enormous rate of 150 to 200 dollars an evening?" Responding to this sharp criticism, on August 30 Powell offered his evening show as a benefit to raise money for the poor who needed smallpox inoculations. "A Friend" wrote in the *Gazette* that Powell's gesture amounted to grandstanding, and the benefit performance was really just another opportunity for the company to "fleece them." "Friend" further opined that the "offer of a benefit night for the poor . . . [seemed] rather insulting; the inhabitants of Boston have never needed the aid of Rope-dancers for the purpose of assisting the poor." He failed to see the logic of breaking the law to provide charity. "Our money can be better appropriated to help our own needy inhabitants, than to encourage strangers to resort among us for the purpose of dissipation." The anonymous "Friend" closed with a plea for Bostonians to desist from further patronizing the Exhibition Room.[88] Despite his plea, Boston newspapers continued to carry advertisements for the performances. Playbills appeared on the streets of Boston each day. People thronged to the theater.[89]

Unlike earlier rounds in the debate, when the existence of a theater was a theoretical issue, one now operated in the very midst of the community. This proved troublesome, since the existence of the theater flew boldly in the face of the Commonwealth's laws. "Who gives Mr. Powell a right," a reader calling himself "Q" asked in a letter to the *Boston Gazette*, "to infringe on the Laws of the Commonwealth? What exclusive privilege has he more than others? If we suffer him, why not others? If we permit strangers to do it, why not our own inhabitants?" The issue, he argued, was not whether or not the law banning theater was just. That remained "a Legislative question" to be determined by the House. The concern of Boston's citizens, who chose to live in this "well regulated society," should be, he insisted, the "indignity offered to our Government" and the "impunity with which Mr. Powell breaks the law."[90]

As the Exhibition Room seemed in the eyes of some to nightly flaunt the laws and government of the Commonwealth, antagonism grew. The image Boston presented to other states and nations constituted a serious concern to certain inhabitants. What will happen to us if "we regard not the laws of our country," asked "A Friend to Humanity and Decency."[91] Those who wrote "pompous Paragraphs" in the newspapers claiming "the vast advantages arising from Theatres . . . must make this State appear ridiculous in the eyes" of the rest of the nation and Europe. It appeared as if the "honor" and "respectability, the happiness and rising glory" of the new nation "depended on Stage-Players, Rope-Dancers, Tumblers and Fiddlers," wrote the disgusted theater opponent "Q." The citizens of Boston were daily sacrificing the honor and pride of the Commonwealth for a few hours of entertainment.[92] This impassioned plea fell on deaf ears. Advocates now clearly stated that they believed the proscriptive theater legislation "to be virtually repealed by our bill of rights." Therefore the legislature needed to respect these rights and listen to the demands of the people. If the legislature nullified the 1750 law, then it could regulate the performance of theaters in Boston rather than contending with illegal sideshows, as was presently the case. This would benefit all involved.[93]

The illegal theater at Board Alley also angered Governor John Hancock, due not to any particular horror at the theater, but rather the flagrant disobedience of the Commonwealth's laws. Neither the

governor nor the authorities particularly wanted "to enforce an unpopular law." Hancock therefore chose to leave the problem to the
"vigilance and wisdom" of the Massachusetts legislature.[94] The theater had been in existence for approximately three months when he
finally addressed it, stating that he did not know whether "great
mischiefs," the loss of "industry and frugality," and "increased immorality, impiety and contempt of religion" arose from stage plays,
as stated in the 1750 law. He was certain, however, that since this
was Commonwealth legislation "surely it ought to claim the respect
and obedience of all persons who live or happen to be within the
Commonwealth." Hancock claimed that he did not know what
measures the authorities were taking to deal with this problem, but
government representatives were "the guardians of the Commonwealth's dignity and honor" and showing contempt for the law did
not demonstrate "vigilance and wisdom" to their "fellow citizens."[95]

Another month passed before the authorities took any action.
Meanwhile citizens of the town had begun circulating a petition
demanding that authorities close the illegal theater. The General
Court advised Governor Hancock to "call upon the Attorney-Gen-
eral, and the Magistrates of Suffolk county, to prosecute those who
acted in open violation of the law." Following this meeting the Attorney General filed a complaint with Justices Greenleaf and Barrett, "who issued their warrant."[96]

On Wednesday evening, December 5, 1792, Sheriff Allen arrived at Board Alley armed with the warrant to arrest Joseph
Harper, interrupting a performance of *The School for Scandal*.
Harper came onto the stage and told the audience that the sheriff
advised him that "unless the performances of the evening were immediately stopped, he should apprehend forthwith all the persons
of the company." The audience responded with an angry outburst
"at what they conceived to be a violent and untimely measure."[97]
Loud calls for the performance to continue came from the audi-

ence, and soon a riot broke out, apparently started by a small group of ruffians. Finally, the performers calmed the audience, requesting that they "peaceably retire." Joseph Harper offered to return their admission costs, but the audience refused to accept the money.[98] The next day, Harper appeared before the Court, which met in Faneuil Hall at the request of an overwhelming number of Bostonians. Harper's counsel contested the legality of the warrant and managed to "liberate" him "much to the satisfaction of a numerous and respectable audience."[99]

Following the raid on the Board Alley theater, the newspapers again filled with letters and editorials. Some tradesmen and mechanics raised the issue of the injustice in how authorities treated them compared to the treatment the rich received. Some believed that the closing of Board Alley was an attack against their kind, who, being excluded from "Concerts, Assemblies, or Card Parties," only had Board Alley to turn to for entertainment. One townsman, who identified himself as a mechanic, told how he took his wife twice to Board Alley and, neither of them having ever "before seen either plays acted, or persons dance on ropes," they had a delightful time. He and his wife were greatly upset when the sheriff closed down the theater in the middle of the show. Why was it, he wondered, that the authorities permitted other concerts and assemblies, which also directly violated the 1750 law prohibiting amusements? Nobody sent the sheriff to disrupt these gatherings that were equally a "breach of law," which he supposed was due to the fact "that our Rulers frequent these entertainments." This certainly was "not that species of liberty which I fought to establish," he affirmed to the reader. This was "tyranny, and ought not patiently to be submitted to." He included with his letter a copy of the 1787 act regulating taverns, which forbade "dancing or revelling" in such establishments. "Mr. Villa, who keeps Concert Hall is a licensed taverner," he pointed out. It seemed to this writer that the "most flagrant partiality" existed. Was it, he asked, because Board Alley welcomed anyone who could pay that those in power chose to shut it down?[100]

Believing that townsmen of the artisan, or mechanic's, class should not be attending the theater anyway, one inhabitant turned to the apocryphal in his letter to the local paper. The story told of Peggy, who had heard many stories about the "Moral Lectures" offered at Board Alley and kindly asked her husband if she might attend. Benjamin, "too good of a husband to give her a flat denial," consented, and he stayed "at home to take care of the family in her absence." Peggy seemed "so greatly improved in moral sentiment and social virtue" that Benjamin thought he might also benefit from attending these moral lectures. However, so that Peggy might go again he denied himself this opportunity. It was during her sixth visit to Board Alley that Sheriff Allen broke up the show. When Peggy returned home "earlier than usual: Benjamin, was singing to the Child in the Cradle." She recounted the events to him, at which Benjamin's heart rejoiced at the goodness of the governor for stopping these performances, and "if he were entitled to fifty votes, he would give them all for him at the next election." His wife had been spending "in one evening, more than half of what he earned by his day's work." No wonder "he was glad when the Moral Lectures were broken up."[101]

If nothing else could convince the people of Boston of the evils brought about by the theater then surely what it did to home, family, morality, and industry in the story of Peggy might. Peggy no longer fulfilled her proper role as wife and mother, and the theater was at fault. In case the reader missed the point, the author continued with numerous other alleged tragedies recounted to him by clergymen. When visiting the poor he found in one family "the children particularly, . . . dirty, ragged, crying for food, and quarreling with each other" only to discover the mother was attending theatrical entertainments. It was clear, argued the writer, that such activities as the theater were ill suited to "the families of tradesmen and labourers." It was this line of prejudicial reasoning that appeared to anger some of Boston's mechanics.[102]

Another opponent of the theater, seeing the moral character of mechanics as superior to that of the elite, argued that it was primarily the wealthy who chose to violate the theater law. He asked how these men would respond if his kind disobeyed the law and refused payment of taxes. Then decent townsmen would see if these "gentry [could] live in their splendor," he jeered.[103] Another noted how Boston's elite, those who can "*wallow* in gold, be clad in the richest silks, or roll in *silver* chariots drawn by Arabian Steeds," were not fit "to teach *Americans*" morals, despite their arguments to the contrary. "Who are these men that set themselves up to teach lessons of morality, and to dictate laws to a whole Commonwealth?" an indignant writer queried. It appeared to these individuals that the lawyers were in connivance with Harper. "I am led to suppose," one citizen sarcastically asserted, "that scent from the profits that have arisen from Board-Alley Theatre, has reached their noses."[104]

Identifying some of the leaders of the pro-theater movement gives validity to the attacks upon the wealthy. Members of the socioeconomic elite were in the vanguard of the fight for the theater. One case in point is the five men who assisted Powell and Harper in building the Board Alley playhouse. The "lawbreakers" included a prominent doctor, the owner of a large distillery, an auctioneer, and two substantial merchants. Three of these men had holdings in real property that placed them among the wealthiest 5 percent of Bostonians, and the other two were among the wealthiest 30 percent. Four held town offices, and one was a representative to the General Court. Perhaps the complaint that these five residents constituted "a class of citizens that *ought to know better*" in regard to breaking the law held a grain of truth.[105] At least forty-six other men who comprised the pro-theater contingent were primarily merchants and attorneys. A number served in various capacities in local and state government and were acquainted with each other through public office, business association, church, fraternal organizations, and private social life. At least four of Boston's nine selectmen in 1792 supported the theater. More than half of the forty-six men fell in the top 10 percent tax bracket, with the large majority in the top 5 percent. Furthermore, a number of these men would later become investors in the Federal Street Theater built in 1794.[106] In short, the claims made by the opposition regarding the leaders of the theater movement were not simply hyperbole.

On December 21, 1792, more than five hundred inhabitants crowded into Faneuil Hall for a town meeting to consider another petition for the repeal of the 1750 law.[107] The meeting appointed a committee to "Prepare a Petition and Remonstrance to the General Court" regarding the "The Act Prohibiting Stage Plays." Preparation of the document transpired so quickly that it suggests the document already existed. The strategy of the new petition differed from the previous two. It quoted extensively from the Declaration of Rights in the 1780 Massachusetts Constitution, emphasizing the unconstitutional nature of the prohibitory law. The Declaration, theater advocates asserted, secured "the Natural and *Unalienable* rights of the People" to seek and obtain "their own happiness." It was the legislature's duty to "Cherish the Interests of Literature, . . . and all Social Affections and Generous Sentiments among the People." It was therefore the legislature's responsibility to encourage any literature, including plays, that would fulfill those duties. The 1750 law also represented an "Indirect Attack on the *Liberty of the Press.*" Citizens had "the Right to Think, write and Print freely." This included the right to "read and repeat" to each other what is printed. The old 1750 law breached that right.[108] In closing, the petition asserted that this law was "neither consonant to the Spirit of Liberty, [n]or agreeable to the Liberal Principles" held within the Commonwealth's Constitution." In this petition theater advocates had essentially abandoned their moral argument in favor of a constitutional one. The 1792 petition passed "almost Unanimously." The instructions to the representatives on presenting the petition to the next legislature also passed with a near unanimous vote.[109]

On December 26, "the Committee appointed at the last Town-Meeting, waited on his Excellency [Governor Hancock], and presented the Address of the citizens." The address informed him that they again planned to "solicit the Legislature . . . for a repeal of the Law, which prohibits theatrical entertainments within the Commonwealth." They asked him to support their cause in the legislature.[110] His reply stated that the "honour and happiness of the town of Boston" were "dear" to him, and that he held a great interest in the welfare of his fellow citizens and in upholding "the Constitution and the Laws of our Republic." If the House of Representatives chose to lay before him a bill concerning theatrical entertainments he would "give it a candid examination, and approve or disapprove of it according to what I shall then conceive to be my duty to my constituents."[111] The committee received no commitment from the governor, but he did not reject their proposal.

Two months later, on Thursday, February 28, 1793, the House of Representatives "took up [the] Bill respecting Theatrical Entertainments." Debate on the subject "lasted nearly the whole day," both sides saying "all that possibly could be said in favour of, and against a Theatre." At the conclusion of the debate the House referred the issue to a committee comprised of seven men, who were to bring in a new bill.[112] The committee presented a bill on March 26 that permitted Boston "to have a Theatre erected, and Stage Plays performed under certain regulations and restrictions, &c." These restrictions included a stipulation that theaters operate only four months per year. After debating the old arguments pro and con one more time, the House voted in favor of the new bill, sixty-four to fifty-four. Then two days later, on Thursday, March 28, the secretary advised the Senate "that his Excellency" had "not signed the Bill respecting Theatrical Entertainments, but should make no objections to it." Governor Hancock's not signing the bill raised concerns for the representatives. Did the governor harbor thoughts of destroying the bill? Would it "become an Act if the Governour" failed to sign it? Letters in the Boston newspapers reflect that people were confused as to what was taking place. But John Hancock neither signed the bill nor appeared to "counteract the will of the majesty of the people" by rejecting it. In actuality the 1750 law would not be repealed until 1797, but based upon the vote of the legislature in April 1793, as far as the pro-theater contingent was concerned they had won their battle.[113]

By 1794 Bostonians had their first legal theater in the town's history, a stately neoclassical structure erected on Federal Street in the South End and designed by Charles Bulfinch. Although the Board Alley playhouse still operated, it finally closed in June 1793. Eight months later, on February 3, 1794, the Boston Theater— later called the Federal Street Theater—opened with the "truly republican Tragedy" of *Gustavus Vasa*, and various "orchestral pieces" including "Yankee Doodle [and] . . . General Washington's March."[114] The audience was boisterous as opening night began on a noble note with a dedication by the manager, Charles Stuart Powell, formerly of the Board Alley Exhibition Room.[115]

When the Federal Street Theater opened in 1794, the *Columbian Centinel* announced that the "Patrons of the *Drama*, at great expense, have erected an Edifice, which has been pronounced by the best architectural connoisseurs, the most elegant and convenient that the united efforts of the fine arts can produce."[116] The theater boasted two floors, the upper with "large arch windows" and the lower with "arches encircling the structure" and Corinthian columns embellishing the front facade. The interior was no less impressive with Corinthian columns supporting a ceiling of "large eliptick arches," gilded "mouldings, balustrades, and fret work . . . , crimson silk drapery" and "twelve elegant brass chandeliers." Above the ornamental columns on the stage, "a cornice and balustrade is carried" with "the arms of the Union of the State of Massachusetts, blended with tragick and comick attributes" and "a ribband" bearing the motto "All the World's a Stage." The building also contained an "elegant dancing room" that was "richly ornamented with Corinthian columns and pilasters . . . , chandeliers, and girandoles."[117]

Celebrated as the most magnificent architectural structure in Boston's history, the Federal Street Theater won the admiration of many. By contrast, the behavior of certain members of the audience did not. Proprietors soon found the need to run newspaper advertisements explaining to Bostonians that the orchestra musicians could not play every tune "called for" and that "throwing Apples [and] Stones . . . into the Orchestra" when their requests were not met was humiliating to the musicians, not to mention dangerous. One member of the audience threw a "Piece of Glass" into the Orchestra and "destroyed one of the Kettle-Drums." Since such actions endangered the orchestra, and the audience in the pit, the trustees offered a fifty-dollar reward for information leading to the perpetrator's arrest and conviction. Other requests were more routine. The theater proprietors asked that ladies sitting in the boxes with low seats "attend without hats, bonnets, feathers, or any other high head-dress" so as not to obstruct the view of those behind them. They had also prescribed detailed carriage parking instructions so as to comply with the town's bylaws and not obstruct traffic.[118]

One year after the completion of the Boston Theater, Ricket's Amphitheater opened, offering an alternative for the public's entertainment pleasure. Here Ricket offered his Equestrian Pantheon, or circus, which included "Mr. Ricket's throwing a Somerset over Five Horses with Persons on their Backs," or jumping through "A Blazing Sun, Never attempted by any one but himself." Props included "Roman column[s]" and monuments and an "Egyptian Pyramid."[119] Less flamboyant, but equally fascinating for many were

The First Boston Theater (Federal Street Theater), designed by Charles Bulfinch. (Justin Winsor, ed., *The Memorial History of Boston including Suffolk County, Massachusetts, 1630–1880*, Boston, 1882.)

Advertisement for a benefit at Board Alley Exhibition Room. (*Boston Gazette*, 21 January 1793.)

the scientific experiments demonstrated at the Green Lane Exhibition Room, which opened in 1795.[120] The following year Mr. Dearborn's Exhibition Room opened, and Mr. Bowen, who had exhibited an educational "Wax-Work" show at the American Coffee House in 1791, now returned to open Bowen's Columbian Museum "At the Head of the Mall" by Boston Common. Patrons could view wax models of "The President of the United States," and numerous "Heroes, Philosophers, Divines, Civilians, Financiers, Sages and Kings" in addition to an art exhibition.[121]

These forms of mass entertainment were open to anyone who could pay. The ordinary person could mingle with the gentry, the artisan with the patrician. The theater was a democratizing venue where citizens of the new republic could share the same entertainment experience in common. The emphasis upon education as a component in gaining acceptance of the new entertainments in Boston was a constant element in the advertisements appearing in the local newspapers. According to one reviewer Bowen's museum defied description and offered many educational benefits. Appealing to Boston's mechanics by emphasizing the virtue of industry, the reviewer noted that "the Mechanick of every profession, will receive additions to their inquisitive minds, which may help them on to greater usefulness in the line of their several occupations."[122]

The new theaters, museums, and exhibition rooms also continued the tradition of raising funds for charity. Before the arrival of these institutions, different clubs held benefits for needy individuals, such as that for "the relief of the Widow of the Rev. Mr. Gain," or the one for Oliver Barron, who "had the misfortune to freeze his feet to such a degree as to be under the necessity of having them cut off which . . . rendered him unable to support himself." Now such fund-raisers included instrumental music, lectures, readings, and sacred music, as in the *"Spiritual Concert"* performed "for the benefit of those among us who *have known better days.*" In January 1786, the Musical Society raised almost two hundred pounds "for

the purpose of affording relief to the debtors confined in [the] . . .
gaol."[123] A benefit concert for "Youth" during the winter of 1794
included both vocal and instrumental "Sacred Music" that concluded with "Handel's celebrated Hallelujah Chorus." Following
the example of the Boston Theater and the Concert Hall, Bowen's
museum offered the receipts from specific evenings to the funds
of the overseers of the poor "to be distributed among the most
needy."[124]

At times the charity of Boston's emerging entertainment industry extended beyond the town. Charles Powell, manager of the Boston Theater, donated more than $800 from receipts for "the benev-
olent purpose of relieving the unfortunate *American* captives in
Algiers" in the spring and early summer of 1794. Two years later
when a devastating fire consumed "upwards of three hundred
houses & stores" in Savannah, Georgia, leaving "the greater part of
its inhabitants . . . reduced to the utmost distress & many of them
to abject poverty," the mayor wrote to the Boston Selectmen asking
for assistance. The management of the Boston Theater donated
funds to Savannah on behalf of Boston, and it did likewise when fire
ravaged Portsmouth, New Hampshire.[125]

During the late spring of 1796 "a number of persons" began
"erecting" a second theater in Boston, the Haymarket located in
the South End, near Tremont and Boylston Streets. Concerned as
to the fire hazard the wood structure presented, fifteen area residents including merchants, manufacturers, and a tavern owner became alarmed. They petitioned the Board of Selectmen, requesting
that the builders be required to use "Brick or Stone." The board
included the matter in the warrant for the next town meeting, but
for reasons not clear in the records, the petitioners withdrew their
complaint.[126]

By late summer, 1796, the construction of the Haymarket was
well under way, with the framework in place by September. "Generous Wages" were paid to attract "Journey-men House-Carpen-

ters."[127] Even while the Haymarket was under construction, it became apparent that it would cater to the town's mechanics, unlike the Federal Street Theater, which drew the elite. As one mechanic informed the readers of a local newspaper, "I am highly pleased" to have "a new Theatre established upon a cheap and liberal plan, that we Tradesmen can go with our families and partake of a rational and pleasing amusement for a little money, and not be hunched by one, and the nose of another Aristocrat turned up at us, because we are Tradesmen." His words must have struck a chord, for a number of the town's artisans offered their labor to construct the building in payment for shares so that they might have "free admission to the theatre during the season." Clearly, some artisans found the Federal Street Theater "an imposition on the Town" and "a "School of Scandal" and "Aristocracy," with "the Slip Galleries" being "no better than brothels." For these Boston artisans, the issue was not the moral degeneracy of the theater itself, but of the "Aristocracy" who attended the Federal Street Theater. "A Theatre may be conducted on a very different plan from the present one," wrote a mechanic, "without licentiousness or immorality."[128]

Consisting of a number of mechanics, the shareholders of the Haymarket represented a different group of Bostonians than the patrons of the Federal Street Theater, who were the town's elite. The latter "spared no expense" to outdo their new competitor. The Haymarket, which opened in December 1796, was "an immense wooden pile, proudly overtopping every other building in the metropolis. It had three tiers of boxes, a gallery, [and a] pit." Unlike the Federal Street Theater's English theatrical company, the Haymarket's was American, a number of whom constituted some of the two dozen actors, comedians, musicians, scene painters, and theater laborers appearing in the 1799 assessor's records."[129] While the Federal Street Theater was a magnificent stone edifice designed in the neoclassical style, reminiscent of the grandeur of the old world, the Haymarket was plain in both its structure and interior appointments and therefore more reflective of the simplicity of style and plain virtue of the new republic.

The divisions that had existed within the community concerning the theater appeared again in 1798. On the chilly winter afternoon of February 2, the actors of the Federal Street Theater in Boston were occupied with the rehearsal of the pantomime *Don Juan*. Servants working backstage and in the dressing rooms somehow neglected to monitor the fires that warmed the rooms. Between three and four P.M., the theater caught fire. By the time someone discovered the flames, they had spread too far to be halted. When the designated alarm went out, the town's fire companies quickly arrived on the scene, followed immediately by those from "Charlestown, Roxbury, Dorchester, Cambridge and other adjacent towns." After nearly four hours, the "spirited zeal" and "indefatigable activity" of the firefighters and citizens ended the conflagration. Fortunately the speedy response and diligence of the fire companies prevented the close-standing wooden buildings crowded farther along the street from damage. Had their efforts not succeeded, the fire would have easily "carried destruction far and wide."[130]

That evening, onlookers stood gazing at the charred ruins of the Federal Street Theater. Little now remained of the forty-foot-high structure with its Corinthian columns and pilasters adorning the outside and the sumptuous ornamentation within.[131] However, within two weeks the theater owners had crews of laborers and craftsmen rebuilding the structure while the temporarily displaced acting company rented Mr. Dearborn's Exhibition Room in Theatre Alley, where they hoped that despite "the present embarrassing circumstances" Bostonians would award their "endeavours" with continued attendance at performances.[132] Using the original plans of Charles Bulfinch, the new Federal Street Theater rose from the ashes of the old within eight months.[133]

The fire drew theater opponents back to their pens and the

local newspapers, once again reflecting some of the sentiments expressed at the beginning of the 1790s. One witness to the "awful scene of the destruction" suggested that Bostonians next pull down the Haymarket Theater, which was both a fire hazard and a moral hazard. To this end, he offered financial assistance if the Massachusetts legislature would "wisely . . . prevent the building of any theatres, for the like future exhibitions."[134] Clearly, some still opposed theatrical entertainments and the serious threat they presented to public safety and virtue.

For over three years Bostonians had engaged in a spirited debate over the value of theatrical entertainments to their society and the legality of the proscriptive 1750 law. Two fundamental components comprised the 1791–1794 theater debate. Proving instrumental in the final appeal to the state legislature was the constitutional issue of individual rights. For the advocates of legalized theatrical entertainment, this centered on their "inalienable rights" developed from interpretation and application of the Declaration of Rights of the 1780 Massachusetts Constitution. The argument concerning individual rights may have been the final tie-breaker in the last contest, but the overarching issue throughout the entire period of disputation was the republican controversy over the nature of a virtuous community and how to create and sustain it. Reinforcing this was the revitalization of Puritan covenant theology during the Revolutionary era with its emphasis on an ordained mission, a regenerate population, and a virtuous society. The ongoing dialogue shared by Bostonians in their town meetings, newspapers, and other public forums shaped decisions regarding their civic institutions and public world as they struggled to rebuild their community in the wake of war.[135]

Epilogue

By 1796 John West's *Boston Directory* proudly noted that the town had "nineteen edifices of public worship," with most "ornamented with beautiful spires, with clocks and bells"; numbered eighty "wharves and quays"; and supported "Seven Free Schools" with almost one thousand "scholars." More than twenty societies held their meetings in Boston, including the "American Academy of Arts and Sciences," the "Massachusetts Historical Society," a library society, an immigrant aid society, and the "Boston Mechanic Association," in addition to "seven respectable Lodges of free and accepted Masons."[1] The town boasted the first of many elegant homes in the West End and the Tontine Crescent and Federal Street Theater in the South End, while the magnificent neoclassical Massachusetts State House would soon grace Beacon Hill.

Many elements contributed to making the final two decades of the eighteenth century a watershed in Boston's history. These years proved a pivotal period when Boston began its shift from an insular provincial town to a cosmopolitan community in the new nation. The forces shaping this transformation included the vicissitudes of war, the ensuing economic depression and recovery, population growth, and social and cultural upheaval. The American Revolution was the catalyst that set this process in motion, altering both individual lives and community institutions. During the twelve-month period from August 1787 to August 1788 "the expanding overseas shipments from Boston included fish valued at £66,000; rum, £50,000; whale and cod oil, £34,000; and furs, £10,000. Boards and staves, candles, leather and shoes, tea, coffee, and molasses were other commodities shipped in sizable quantities." This growth was further fueled by the adoption of "financial and foreign policies" by Congress in 1789 that would serve to "make Boston the leading port of the United States."[2] The Massachusetts State legislature passed laws designed to protect domestic industry and open new trade markets. Shipyards once again rang with the noise of artisans and laborers. The influx of new faces and a growing population generated demand and a growth in the service industry. All of this translated into job opportunities and for many individuals an improvement in their economic lot. Many who had the good fortune, ability, or perseverance to weather the 1770s and 1780s would find their situation improved by these changes.

As the dawn of the new century approached, the rejuvenated seaport town looked forward in anticipation of a more prosperous future. And well it should have. The town's economy was solid and growing. Boston's two local banks had combined capital assets in excess of $1.5 million, a vast sum of money for those times. The town's eighty or so wharves had in 1795 welcomed nearly eight hundred commercial vessels carrying cargoes bound for both local and distant merchants and traders. The town's domestic industry was healthy and growing, with thirty distilleries and two breweries producing spirits for an expanding market.[3] Ebenezer Clough's paper manufactory flourished as did the workshops of countless artisans. Former mariner Joseph Shed now ran a prospering grocery business with his father. The population was rapidly expanding, and the many local industries kept employment healthy and immigration attractive. These conditions were a far cry from twenty-five years earlier, when the town was demoralized by the siege and stripped of its vital workings, the economy in shambles, most of the people gone, many for good, and no road map for the future. Who that remained in Boston in late March 1776 would have envisioned that the war would go on another seven years? Who would have imagined that Boston's population would rebound so quickly, and grow to almost 25,000 inhabitants by 1800?

Bostonians exhibited a steadfast determination to push ahead and rebuild their community despite the numerous crises faced in the wake of the siege and the difficult years that followed. During the final two decades of the eighteenth century, the "new" Boston began to emerge. Cultural, social, and economic transformations transpired, but tradition also continued: the majority of Bostonians refused to relinquish their unique form of local government, the town meeting, and numerous Bostonians expressed concern about repeal of the 1750 anti-theater legislation. While 1800 proved a time of hope for some, such as the mechanics who had paraded through the town's streets more than a decade earlier, celebrating the state's ratification of the United States Constitution, it was also a time of uncertainty. Boston's poor—white, black, male, and female—struggled to make ends meet and even to survive. The elderly Mildred Byles waited out her declining years as a widow. After her husband Elisha's death, did she still take boarders or run a school for young children in order to get by? As poor as she and Elisha had been, it is improbable that Mildred found much, if any, economic security.

Outside of marriage, opportunities for women still proved extremely limited, and after the American Revolution with the loss of so many young men, even that avenue to security proved more elusive than before. By the early nineteenth century the one new occupation that would increasingly open up to women, teaching, clearly became an avenue of employment for a number of Boston widows and spinsters. Women ran spelling and reading schools in their own homes for children under the age of seven, and those possessing sufficient knowledge opened private schools to educate young ladies on the genteel subjects of music, language, embroidery, and ornamental arts considered appropriate for a refined young lady. Women also continued in the trades of sempstress, mantua maker, and tailoress, but competition from factory-related out-work would increasingly undermine their private enterprises. Women found that tavern licenses were increasingly difficult to acquire. Tavern keeper Elizabeth Fadre, twice married and twice widowed, disappeared from the records by the mid-1790s. Despite searches through records for her whereabouts, her trail seems to disappear into the web of history.

While the town's African-American men and women, forced by circumstance, forged a community within a community in Boston's West End, they continued to experience the ugliness and pain of discrimination. Inequality was evident in restrictive legislation that appeared in 1786 attempting to govern relationships between whites and blacks. Proscriptive Massachusetts law prohibited the joining in marriage of "any white person with any Negro, Indian or Mulatto, under penalty of fifty pounds; and all such marriages" were "absolutely null and void."[4] Two years later, in 1788, the state legislature passed another law entitled "An act for supressing and punishing Rogues, Vagabonds, common Beggars, and other idle, disorderly, and lewd Persons." This was not immediately enforced in Boston, but surfaced twelve years later. Specific provisions in the Act relating to "Africans and Negroes" were used by the Boston Selectmen in 1800 to direct those blacks not citizens of Massachusetts to depart "under penalty of being apprehended and whipped" or imprisoned in a house of correction. A notice to this effect, complete with a list of names, appeared in a September 16, 1800, edition of the *Massachusetts Mercury*. Along with 240 other individuals, the selectmen included Butterfield and Clarissa Scotland.[5] After more than a decade of making Boston their home, in the face of much adversity, the Scotlands now found themselves driven away. Those Bostonians who remained would continue to build a strong and thriving black community in Boston that would be instrumental in leading the fight to abolish slavery in the United States and demand civil rights.

The increased geographic mobility of Americans as a result of the disruptions of war brought many new faces into Boston. One consequence of this was the merging of new blood into Boston's elite. Another was the influx of large numbers of men and women down on their luck and faced with incredible hardships, as reflected by the expanding records of the Boston Overseers of the Poor. But the dynamic was more complex than the rich getting richer and the poor getting poorer. Increased economic opportunities combined with a new spirit of individualism fostered a growing middle class of mechanics, tradesmen, and shopkeepers.

By the late eighteenth century Bostonians began to significantly reshape their built environment and physical landscape. Expansion into the South End brought improved main thoroughfares, tree-lined streets, and the building of many new homes. The once desolate southern tip of the peninsula extending into the Neck gradually offered more than the town gallows, collapsing fortifications, and a few taverns. During the late 1790s Trimountain, located on the west side of the Shawmut, fell prey to the pick, shovel, and wheelbarrow, and the decades-long process of leveling the area ensued. By 1806 a metamorphosis of the Boston waterfront transpired. India Wharf, designed by Bulfinch and consisting of warehouses, stores, and countinghouses, "was considered the foremost waterfront development in the United States."[6] Not only was the area around Long Wharf transformed, but similar smaller projects had begun to appear in the North End by the close of the century.[7] Those institutions and industries deemed "less desirable" were relocated at the fringes of the peninsula, such as the new almshouse built in 1795 at Barton's Point, one of the most desolate areas of town. As the community crawled across the small peninsula it would eventually claim fields, cow pastures, and the low-lying marshlands around a large portion of the town's perimeter.

Population growth, an influx of outsiders, economic development, and the desire on the part of some to shed the town's provincialism fueled these changes. But this expansion and development also brought urban problems that led citizens to call for reforms establishing stricter building codes, creating a modern police force, and establishing traffic regulations, among other demands. Practicality and necessity were the principal motivators behind this push. There was, however, concern on the part of Boston's new elite that their community not be a mere shadow to the sister cities of Philadelphia and New York. Pride of place was not new among Bostonians. In 1774, John Adams had written, "Philadelphia with all its Trade, and Wealth, and Regularity is not Boston." Likewise, he noted, "The Morals of our People are much better, their Manners are more polite, and agreeable . . . our Spirit is greater, our Laws are wiser, our Religion is superior, our Education is better." For Adams nothing, except perhaps his home in Braintree, came close to the superiority of Boston.[8] Twenty years later John Adams's words rang true for the town's new boosters.

As the curtain closed on the stage of the eighteenth century many Bostonians faced an uncertain future. Many newcomers had no memories to enmesh them in the town's past. Others only begrudgingly let go of what Boston had been as they looked to what they believed Boston should become. By the late 1790s the commentaries filling the pages of Boston's newspapers reflected widespread divergent opinions as to how the town should grow and what the best answers were to its increased urban problems. The complexity of the issue often weighed heavily as Boston entered a new era.

Rather than being a period of only political significance in the city's history, the first two decades after the American Revolution, a time filled with drama and dynamism, demonstrate a city expanding on many fronts with a definite, if cautious, eye toward the future. Boston's Puritan forefathers would scarcely have recognized their city as the dawn of a new century approached.

Notes

PROLOGUE

1. The story of the Scotland family is compiled from data found in Taking Books, church records, and records of the Boston Overseers of the Poor. Butterfield Scotland first appears in the 1788 Taking Book, Ward 4. He and his family are listed as natives of Philadelphia in the warning-out records. For further information on the practice of warning out, see chap. 3. Boston Taking Books. 1784 and 1788, Boston Public Library/Rare Books Department, Courtesy of the Trustees, Boston (hereafter cited as Boston Taking Books); Warning Out Book, 1791–1792, Boston Overseers of the Poor, records, Massachusetts Historical Society, Boston [MHS]. On migration during the Revolutionary era see Jackson Turner Main, *The Social Structure of Revolutionary America* (Princeton, N.J.: Princeton University Press, 1965), 193; for slavery and the free black community in Philadelphia see Gary B. Nash, *Forging Freedom: The Formation of Philadelphia's Black Community, 1720–1840* (Cambridge, Mass.: Harvard University Press, 1991).

2. Boston Taking Book 1788.

3. Boston Taking Books 1790, 1791; Warning Out Book, 1791–1792.

4. Andrew Oliver and James Bishop Peabody, eds., *The Records of Trinity Church, Boston, 1728–1830*, Colonial Society of Massachusetts Collections, vol. 56 (Boston: Colonial Society of Massachusetts, 1982), 641, 643, 645, 648, 740, 806.

5. Boston Taking Books, 1792, 1794, 1799; Warning Out Book, 1791–1792; Petition to the Gentlemen the Selectmen of the Town of Boston, The Petition for a Number of Black Families Citizens of the Town of Boston, 4 October 1796, Boston Town Papers (loose papers), July–December 1796, Boston Public Library/Rare Books Department, Courtesy of the Trustees, Boston [BPL/RBD] (hereafter cited as Boston Town Papers).

6. Annie Haven Thwing, *The Crooked and Narrow Streets of the Town of Boston, 1630–1822* (Boston: Marshall Jones Co., 1920), 22.

7. For the era leading up to the war years two excellent studies that discuss multiple urban areas are Carl Bridenbaugh, *Cities in Revolt: Urban Life in America, 1743–1776* (New York: Alfred A. Knopf, 1955) and Gary B. Nash, *The Urban Crucible: Social change, Political Consciousness, and the Origins of the American Revolution* (Cambridge, Mass.: Harvard University Press, 1979). See also Gary Nash, "The Social Evolution of Preindustrial American Cities 1700–1820, Reflections and New Directions," *Journal of Urban History* 13, no. 2 (February 1987): 15–145. A broad study of port towns in the eighteenth century is Jacob M. Price, "Economic Function and the Growth of American Port Towns in the Eighteenth Century," *Perspectives in American History* 8 (1974): 123–186. There are a number of specialized studies of the two largest northern cities, Philadelphia and New York. A sampling of these, related to topics discussed in this book, includes Billy G. Smith's examination of Philadelphia's "lower sort," John Alexander's study of the poverty in Philadelphia, Karin Wulf's study of women in Philadelphia, Shane White's work on slaves and free African-Americans in New York City between 1770 and 1810, and the essays of Carl Abbott and Elizabeth Blackmar concerning New York neighborhoods. Billy G. Smith, *The "Lower Sort": Philadelphia's Laboring People, 1750–1800* (Ithaca, N.Y.: Cornell University Press, 1990); John Alexander, *Render Them Submissive: Responses to Poverty in Philadelphia, 1760–1800* (Amherst: University of Massachusetts Press, 1980); Karin A. Wulf, *Not All Wives: Women of Colonial Philadelphia* (Ithaca, N.Y.: Cornell University Press, 2000); Shane White, *Somewhat More Independent: The End of Slavery in New York City, 1770–1810* (Athens: University of Georgia Press, 1991); Carl Abbott, "The Neighborhoods of New York, 1760–1775," *New York History* 55: 35–74; Elizabeth Blackmar, "Re-Walking the 'Walking City': Housing and Property Relations in New York City, 1780–1840," *Radical History Review* 21: 131–48.

8. Boston Taking Book, 1794.

9. Allan Kulikoff, "The Progress of Inequality in Revolutionary Boston," *William and Mary Quarterly*, 3rd ser., 18, no. 3 (July 1971): 375–411; Lisa B. Lubow, "From Carpenter to Capitalist: The Business of Building in Postrevolutionary Boston," in *Entrepreneurs: The Boston Business Community, 1700–1850*, Conrad Edick Wright and Katheryn P. Viens, eds. (Boston: Massachusetts Historical Society, 1997), 181–209; John W. Tyler, "Persistence and Change within the Boston Business Community, 1775–1790," in Wright and Viens, *Entrepreneurs*, 99–100, n. 8; Main, *Social Structure*, 38–39. Some of my analysis of the Taking Books as it appears in this volume was previously published in Jacqueline Barbara Carr, "A Change 'as Remarkable as the Revolution Itself': Boston's Demographics, 1780–1800," *New England Quarterly* 73, no. 4 (December 2000): 583–602. See also Jacqueline Carr-Frobose, "A Cultural History of Boston in the Revolutionary Era, 1775–1795" (Ph.D. diss., University of California, Berkeley, 1998).

10. Boston Taking Books, 1784, 1790, 1794.

11. Peter R. Knights, *The Plain People of Boston, 1830–1860: A Study in City Growth*, The Urban Life in America Series, ed. Richard C. Wade (New York: Oxford University Press, 1971).

CHAPTER ONE

1. The first British troops arrived in Boston during October 1768. They were quartered in the center of town on Boston Common and in various privately owned warehouses scattered throughout the community. Townspeople could not avoid their presence. For further information see G. B. Warden, *Boston, 1689–1776* (Boston: Little, Brown & Co., 1970), 189, 198–199, 213–214, 291–293.

2. The Boston Port Act was part of a larger package of British legislation, the Coercive Acts or, as the colonists termed them, the "intolerable acts." The British government, believing that it had worked hard to accommodate the colonists over the course of the preceding decade, now aimed the Coercive Acts at suppressing disorder and rebellion in the colonies. Boston, believed to be the center of the troubles, was a central focus in achieving this goal.

3. Boston Town Records, 13 May 1774, 18 May 1774, 30 May 1774, in Boston Record Commissioners, *Reports of the Record Commissioners of the City of Boston* (hereafter cited as *Record Commissioners*), 31 vols. (Boston, 1876–1904) 18: 173–176; *Boston Gazette* 16 May 1774.

4. John Andrews, Boston, to William Barrell, 12 June 1774, in "Letters of John Andrews, Esq. Of Boston, 1772–1776," comp. and ed. Winthrop Sargent, *Massachusetts Historical Society Proceedings* 8 (July 1865): 329.

5. Samuel Salisbury, Boston, to Stephen Salisbury, Worcester, 30 September 1774, in Charles L. Nichols, "Samuel Salisbury—A Boston Merchant in the Revolution," *Proceedings of the American Antiquarian Society* (April 1925): 55, 56; John Rowe, diary, 15 June 1774, in *Letters and Diary of John Rowe, 1759–1762, 1764–1779*, ed. Anne Rowe Cunningham (Boston: W. B. Clarke & Co., 1903), 275.

6. *Massachusetts Gazette* (Boston) 7 July 1774; John Andrews, Boston, to William Barrell, Portsmouth [?], 12 June 1774, in "Letters of John Andrews," 329.

7. John Andrews, Boston, to William Barrell, Portsmouth [?], 12 June 1774, in "Letters of John Andrews," 330; John Rowe, diary, 12 June 1774, in *Letters and Diary*, 275.

8. John Rowe, diary, 14 July 1774, in *Letters and Diary*, 278.

9. John Andrews, Boston, to William Barrell, Portsmouth [?], 12 June 1774, in "Letters of John Andrews," 329.

10. The observation as to the decline in merchants' advertising in the *Boston Gazette* is based upon an assessment of the newspaper between May 2, 1774, and October 31, 1774. In mid-July scarcely more than one page of advertisements

appeared in the *Boston Gazette*, and by September the number of merchants and shopkeepers placing advertisements dropped to eleven. *Boston Gazette* 3 October 1774.

11. *Boston Gazette* 10 October 1774, 31 October 1774, 27 March 1775; John Andrews, Boston, to William Barrell, Portsmouth [?], 1 August 1774, in "Letters of John Andrews," 336.

12. John Andrews, Boston, to William Barrell, Portsmouth [?], 1 August 1774, 10 August 1774, in "Letters of John Andrews," 334, 339.

13. Boston Town Records, 26 July 1774, 9 August 1774, 30 August 1774, in *Record Commissioners* 18: 183, 187; John Andrews, Boston, to William Barrell, Portsmouth [?], 2 August 1774, in "Letters of John Andrews," 337; *Boston Gazette* 2 May 1774, 12 December 1774.

14. Boston Town Records, 26 July 1774, 9 August 1774, 30 August 1774, in *Record Commissioners* 18: 183, 187; *Boston Gazette* 2 May 1774; 12 December 1774; John Andrews, Boston, to William Barrell, Portsmouth [?], 2 August 1774, in "Letters of John Andrews," 337.

15. Boston Town Records, 4 July 1774, in *Record Commissioners* 18: 178–179. In June Boston received reports from various sources that its "Sister Colonies" would offer assistance. The first donation seems to have been on July 4 from the town of Windham. Boston Town Records, 28 June 1774, in *Record Commissioners* 18: 178.

16. John Andrews, Boston, to William Barrell, Portsmouth [?], 2 August 1774, in "Letters of John Andrews," 336; *Essex Gazette* (Salem) 26 July to 2 August 1774.

17. *Boston Gazette* 12 December 1774, 19 December 1774, 16 January 1775, 6 February 1775, 20 February 1775, 6 March 1775; Boston Town Records, 19 July 1774, in *Record Commissioners* 18: 181. Members of the committee changed from time to time and appear to have been primarily artisans and merchants.

18. *Essex Gazette* 26 July to 2 August 1774.

19. John Andrews, Boston, to William Barrell, Philadelphia [?], 26 November 1774, 30 November 1774, 12 December 1774, 16 December 1774, 19 December 1774, 9 January 1775, in "Letters of John Andrews," 387, 388, 391, 393.

20. John Barker, diary, 16 December 1774, in John Barker, *The British in Boston: Being the Diary of Lieutenant John Barker of the King's own Regiment from November 15, 1774 to May 31, 1776* (Cambridge, Mass.: Harvard University Press, 1924), 10, 11–12; John Andrews, Boston, to William Barrell, Philadelphia [?], 30 November 1774, 12 December 1774, 16 December 1774, 19 December 1774, in "Letters of John Andrews," 388, 390, 391.

21. John Andrews, Boston, to William Barrell, Philadelphia [?], 26 November 1774, 9 January 1775, in "Letters of John Andrews," 387, 393.

22. Boston Town Records, 25 October 1774, 3 November 1774, in *Record*

Commissioners 18: 193, 194; John Rowe, diary, 21 January 1775, 24 January 1775, in *Letters and Diary*, 289.

23. John Barker, diary, 15 November 1774, in *British in Boston*, 3, 4; Hugh Earl Percy, Boston, to the Rev. Thomas Percy, England, 25 November 1774, in Hugh Earl Percy, Duke of Northumberland, *Letters of Hugh Earl Percy from Boston and New York, 1774–1776*, ed. Charles Knowles Bolton (Boston: Charles E. Goodspeed, 1902), 44.

24. John Andrews, Boston, to William Barrell, Philadelphia, 1 August 1774, in "Letters of John Andrews," 333–334.

25. John Andrews, Boston, to William Barrell, Philadelphia, 22 January 1775, 23 January 1775, in "Letters of John Andrews," 396. British lieutenant John Barker recorded a slightly different account of events than Andrews. He claimed that officers were frequently insulted. John Barker, diary, 21 January 1775, in *British in Boston*, 22; *Essex Gazette* 17–24 January 1775.

26. John Barker, diary, 15 November 1774, in *British in Boston*, 4.

27. John Rowe, diary, 9 March 1775, in *Letters and Diary*, 290.

28. Anne Hulton, Boston, to unknown recipient, March 1774 [?], in Anne Hulton, *Letters of a Loyalist Lady: Being the Letters of Anne Hulton, Sister of Henry Hulton, Commissioner of Customs at Boston, 1767–1776* (Cambridge, Mass.: Harvard University Press, 1927), 73.

29. Worthington Chauncey Ford et al., eds., *Journals of the Continental Congress, 1774–1789* (Washington, D.C.: Government Printing Office, 1904–1937), 1: 58, 59–60.

30. John Andrews, Boston, to William Barrell, Philadelphia, 11 April 1775, in "Letters of John Andrews," 402.

31. John Rowe, diary, 19 April 1775, in *Letters and Diary*, 292.

32. *The Journals of each Provincial Congress of Massachusetts in 1774 and 1775, and of the Committee of Safety* (Boston: Dutton Wentworth, 1838), 518–519.

33. Ezra Stiles, diary, 21 April 1775, in Richard Frothingham Jr., *History of the Siege of Boston and of the Battles of Lexington, Concord, and Bunker Hill* (1849; repr., Boston: Little, Brown & Co., 1903), 91. Citations are to the reprint. Figures vary on the number of militiamen gathered outside Boston. Frothingham also gives the figure of sixteen thousand militiamen, *Siege of Boston*, 101. In a letter from Boston to a Portsmouth resident dated April 23, 1775, the writer states "thirty Thousand Men in arms in Roxbury and Cambridge." *New Hampshire Gazette* (Portsmouth) 28 April 1775. However, this number seems somewhat high considering that in April the militia outside Boston included only men from New England. Congress did not raise the Continental Army until June 14, at which time they added recruitments from Maryland, Virginia, and Pennsylvania to the New England forces camped outside of Boston. Robert Middlekauff, *The Glorious Cause: The American Revolution, 1763–1789* (New York: Oxford University Press, 1982), 281.

34. Proceedings of the Town of Boston, Cambridge, 22 April 1775, in Frothingham, *Siege of Boston*, 94; *New Hampshire Gazette* 5 May 1775.

35. *New York Journal* 6 July 1775.

36. Frothingham, *Siege of Boston*, 94, 237; Warden, *Boston, 1689–1776*, 319; *New Hampshire Gazette* 5 April 1775, 28 April 1775; John Andrews, Boston, to William Barrell, Philadelphia, 24 April, 1775, in "Letters of John Andrews," 405; *New Hampshire Gazette* 5 May 1775.

37. Frothingham, *Siege of Boston*, 237. John Rowe applied for a pass on April 28. He was denied. John Rowe, diary, 28 April 1775, in *Letters and Diary*, 294.

38. From "petition for a pass" for Henry Prentiss, May 1775, Henry Prentiss, Charlestown, to Oliver Wendell, Newburyport, 12 May 1775, in "Extracts From Letters Written At The Time of the Occupation of Boston by the British, 1775–6," ed. William P. Upham, in *Historical Collections of the Essex Institute* 13 (July 1876): 178, 181.

39. Rev. Edward E. Hale, "The Siege of Boston," in *The Memorial History of Boston including Suffolk County, Massachusetts, 1630–1680*, ed. Justin Winsor, 4 vols. (Boston: James R. Osgood & Co., 1881), 3:77; Philip Cash, *Medical Men at The Siege of Boston, April 1775–April 1776: Problems of the Massachusetts and Continental Armies*, Memoirs of the American Philosophical Society (Philadelphia: American Philosophical Society, 1973), 61.

40. Samuel Salisbury, Boston, to Stephen Salisbury, Worcester, 3 May 1775, 5 [6?] May 1775, 6 June 1775; Samuel Barrett, Boston, to Stephen Salisbury, Worcester, 3 May 1775, in "Samuel Salisbury," 57.

41. James Lovell, Boston, to Oliver Wendell, Newburyport, [?] May 1775; H. Prentiss, Charlestown, to Oliver Wendell, Newburyport, 9 May 1775, 12 May 1775, in Upham, "Extracts from Letters," 176, 177, 181, 184, 185–189.

42. John Nicoll, Boston, to Nathan Appleton, Salem, 26 May 1775, in Upham, "Extracts from Letters," 183–184.

43. "By the first of August [1775] there were thirteen thousand troops in Boston but only 6,753 civilians remaining out of the prewar population of over 16,000." Warden, *Boston, 1689–1776*, 319; John Andrews, Boston, to William Barrell, Philadelphia, 19 April 1775, in "Letters of John Andrews," 405; John Rowe, diary, 20 April 1775, in *Letters and Diary*, 292. See also chap. 1 of David Hackett Fischer, *Paul Revere's Ride* (New York: Oxford University Press, 1994).

44. Simon Tufts, Boston, to Oliver Wendell, Newburyport, May 1775; James Lovell, Boston, to Oliver Wendell, Newburyport, 5 May 1775, in Upham, "Extracts from Letters," 165.

45. Bushnell and Willoughby also rode "once a Week . . . to the Camps at Roxbury and Cambridge." *Connecticut Gazette* (New London) 9 June 1775.

46. John Adams, Philadelphia, to Abigail Adams, Braintree, 2 May 1775, Abigail Adams, Braintree, to John Adams, Philadelphia, 4 May 1775, in *The Book of*

Abigail and John: Selected Letters of the Adams Family, 1762–1784, ed. L. H. Butterfield, Marc Friedlander, and Mary-Jo Kline (Cambridge, Mass.: Harvard University Press, 1975), 82–83.

47. Simon Tufts, Boston, to Oliver Wendell, Newburyport, May 1775, in Upham, "Extracts from Letters," 165. See also *Connecticut Gazette* 9 June 1775.

48. James Lovell, Boston, to Oliver Wendell, Newburyport, 3 May 1775, in Upham, "Extracts from Letters," 172.

49. John Andrews to William Barrell, 6 May 1775, in "Letters of John Andrews," 408.

50. Frothingham, *Siege of Boston*, 94–95.

51. John Andrews, Boston, to William Barrell, Philadelphia, 24 April 1775, May 6, 1775, in "Letters of John Andrews," 405–406.

52. Andrew Eliot to [addressee unknown but probably Thomas B. Hollis], 31 May 1775, Andrew Eliot Papers, MHS.

53. John Rowe, diary, 30 April 1775, in *Letters and Diary*, 294; Eccl 7:14 (AV).

54. John Scollay, Boston, to Oliver Wendell [unknown destination], 16 May 1775, in Upham, "Extracts from Letters," 156.

55. Andrew Eliot to [addressee unknown, but probably Thomas B. Hollis], 31 May 1775, Eliot Papers.

56. Hale, "Siege of Boston," 77. The two hundred tradesmen and merchants formed a military corps: "the command of Timothy Ruggles, of Hardwick,—the same who presided at Philadelphia at the First Continental Congress ten years before." Hale goes on to say, "As the winter wore on, the Loyalists in Boston were formed into military organizations for guard duty and the like: the Loyal American Associators, Brigadier-General Timothy Ruggles, commandant; Loyal Irish Volunteers, James Forrest, captain; Royal Fencible Americans, Colonel Gorham." Hale, 77. See also Frothingham, *Siege of Boston*, 95–96.

57. Frothingham, *Siege of Boston*, 234–235.

58. *New York Journal* 14 September 1775; Anne Hulton to [addressee unknown], April 1775 [editor notes letter undated but a penciled date entered, presumably later], in *Letters of a Loyalist*, 79. Loyalist Anne Hulton writes in her letter of April 1775, "but the General has put a Stop to any more removing, & here remains in Town about 9000 Souls (besides the Servants of the Crown) These are the greatest Security, the General declared that if a Gun is fired within the Town the inhabitants shall fall a Sacrifice"; Hale, "Siege of Boston," 78; Frothingham, *Siege of Boston*, 96.

59. *Boston Gazette* 31 July 1775; 18 August 1775; *New York Journal* 14 September 1775. In late May, General Howe arrived in Boston with "ten companies of light infantry, ten of grenadiers, four regiments, and parts of a fifth—about 1500 men in all." Middlekauff, *Glorious Cause*, 287. Middlekauff provides a detailed discussion of the arrival and movements of British troops in Boston in the late spring of 1775 in chap. 13.

60. Anne Hulton, *Letters of a Loyalist*, 79.

61. *New York Journal* 14 September 1775; John Andrews to William Barrell, 6 May 1775, 1 June 1775, 11 April 1776, in "Letters of John Andrews," 406, 408, 411. Bad meat sold for 8 pence per pound and a "quarter of lamb . . . weighing only three or three and a half pounds" sold for a dollar. One report quoted the price of a sheep, "and them exceedingly poor," at eight dollars and eggs at twenty shillings per dozen. It is somewhat difficult to compare prices of food because prices are given in dollars and pounds. By comparison to the price of bad meat at 8 pence per pound in May 1775, beef, mutton, and pork had gone up to 1 shilling, 6 pence per pound by November, i.e., more than doubled in price. In 1774 beef could be purchased for only 2 pence per pound. Timothy Newell, 16 November 1774, "A Journal Kept During the Time that Boston was Shut Up in 1775–6," *Collections of the Massachusetts Historical Society*, 4th ser., 1 (1852): 270; Thomas Sullivan, in S. Sydney Bradford, ed., "The Common British Soldier—From the Journal of Thomas Sullivan, 49th Regiment of Foot," *Maryland Historical Magazine* 62 (September 1967), 241; *Constitutional Gazette* (New York) 9 September 1775.

62. *New York Journal* 25 May 1775; *New Hampshire Gazette* 19 May 1775. This letter never made it home to the soldier's parents. According to the *Gazette*, it was intercepted. Frothingham, *Siege of Boston*, 235.

63. Orders from General Howe, Headquarters, Boston, 22 July 1775, in William Howe, *General Sir William Howe's Orderly Book at Charlestown, Boston and Halifax, June 17, 1775 to 26 May 1776*, ed. Benjamin Franklin Stevens, Kennikat American Bicentennial Series (London: Benjamin Franklin Stevens, 1890; repr. London: Kennikat Press, 1970), 50.

64. *New Hampshire Gazette* 19 May 1775; Hale, "Siege of Boston," 80.

65. *New York Journal* 20 July 1775; General Gage to Lord Dartmouth, 20 August 1775, in Frothingham, *Siege of Boston*, 236.

66. *Providence Gazette* 3 June 1775.

67. *Connecticut Gazette* 14 February 1776.

68. *New York Journal* 20 July 1775.

69. *New York Journal* 20 July 1775; E. Alfred Jones, *The Loyalists of Massachusetts: Their Memorial Petitions and Claims* (London: Saint Catherine Press, 1930), 196–197.

70. Thomas Gage, *The Correspondence of General Thomas Gage with the Secretaries of State, and with the War Office and the Treasury, 1763–1775*, ed. Clarence Edwin Carter, 2 vols. (New Haven, Conn.: Yale University Press, 1933), 2: 678, 679.

71. *Connecticut Gazette* 14 February 1776.

72. Cash, *Medical Men*, 37, 53, 109, 113, 115; Howe, orders, 18 November 1775, 22 November 1775, 28 November 1775, 1 December 1775, in *Orderly Book*

144, 148, 155, 156; *Boston Gazette* 28 August 1775; *Constitutional Gazette* 9 September 1775.

73. Cash, *Medical Men*, 45–46; Howe, orders, 29 June 1775, *Orderly Book*, 25; *Constitutional Gazette* 2 September 1775.

74. Cash, *Medical Men*, 95, 107; *New York Journal* 10 August 1775.

75. *New York Journal* 7 December 1775; George Washington to Joseph Reed, Camp, 27 November 1775; Colonel Moylan to Joseph Reed, Cambridge, 5 December 1775, in William B. Reed, *Life and Correspondence of Joseph Reed: Military Secretary of Washington at Cambridge*, 2 vols. (Philadelphia: Lindsay and Blakiston, 1847) 1: 129–130, 134; Cash, *Medical Men*, 111.

76. Cash, *Medical Men*, 111, 112.

77. For further discussion on the smallpox epidemic see Elizabeth A. Fenn, *Pox Americana: The Great Smallpox Epidemic of 1775–1782* (New York: Hill and Wang, 2001), 14–15, 46–55, 89–90, 264–265.

78. *New York Journal* 14 September 1775. Few had the blind optimism of Samuel Paine, who wrote to his brother William, in London, on October 2, "such is the abundance of Provisions & Prizes daily taken & arriving here, that Boston Instead of being Starved, is like this Winter to be the Emporium of America for Plenty & Pleasure." In the same letter, Paine makes claims for the strength and good health of the town and the "good spirits" of the army. All of these claims make such a sharp contrast to numerous other accounts of the strife in Boston that the reader is left wondering if Paine's letters were deliberately optimistic for the sake of family. Samuel Paine, "Letter of Samuel Paine Upon Affairs At Boston In October, 1775," *New England Historical and Genealogical Register* 30 (July 1876): 371.

79. William Carter, "Letter," *A Genuine Detail of the Several Engagements, Positions, and Movements of the Royal and American Armies* (Boston, n.p.: 1938), 18.

80. Frothingham, *Siege of Boston*, 246–247; Cash, *Medical Men*, 115–116.

81. *New Hampshire Gazette* 15 August 1775; *New York Journal* 17 August 1775; Howe, orders, 13 August 1775, in *Orderly Book*, 68.

82. *New York Journal* 28 December 1775; George Washington to Joseph Reed, 23 January 1776, in Reed, *Life and Correspondence*, 147. Washington writes, "They are pulling down the houses in Boston as fast as possible."

83. *Connecticut Gazette* 6 January 1776; Newell, 16 October 1775, in "Journal Kept During the Time," 270.

84. Howe, orders, 13 December 1775, in *Orderly Book*, 169.

85. James Thacher, *Military Journal During the American Revolutionary War, From 1775–1783* (Boston: Richardson and Lord, 1823), 37; Paine, "Letter of Samuel Paine," 371.

86. Thacher, *Military Journal*, 37; Paine, "Letter of Samuel Paine," 371; Carter, "Letter," 13.

87. Carter, "Letter," 9.

88. Abigail Adams to John Adams, 25 September 1775, in Butterfield et al., *Book of Abigail and John*, 107.

89. *New York Journal* 14 September 1775; *Boston Gazette* 3 July 1775; 17 July 1775.

90. Howe, orders, 7 July 1775, in *Orderly Book*, 36.

91. Howe, orders, 13 August 1775, 3 January 1776, in *Orderly Book*, 69, 187–188. On the British soldier and military discipline see Sylvia R. Frey, *The British Soldier in America: A Social History of Military Life in the Revolutionary Period* (Austin: University of Texas Press, 1981). See also Caroline Cox, *A Proper Sense of Honor: Service and Sacrifice in George Washington's Army* (Chapel Hill: University of North Carolina Press, forthcoming 2004).

92. John Leach, "A Journal Kept By John Leach, During His Confinement By The British, in Boston Gaol, in 1775," *New England Historical and Genealogical Review* 14 (July 1865): 261–262.

93. *Boston Gazette* 17 July 1775.

94. *New York Journal* 25 May 1775; 6 July 1775; 14 September 1775; 28 September 1775; *Boston Gazette* 3 July 1775; 17 July 1775.

95. *New York Journal* 14 December 1775.

96. *New York Journal* 25 May 1775; 2 June 1775; *Connecticut Journal* (New Haven) 31 May 1775; *New Hampshire Gazette* 2 June 1775.

97. Unendorsed letter sent from the town of Salem, 18 May 1775, in Upham, "Extracts from Letters," 182.

98. Howe, orders, 18 November 1775, *Orderly Book*, 142–143; *Constitutional Gazette* 27 December 1775.

99. John Leach, 18 July 1775, in "Journal," 257.

100. Peter Edes, 19 June 1775, in *A Diary of Peter Edes, The Oldest Printer in the United States, Written During His Confinement in Boston, by the British* (Bangor, Maine: Samuel S. Smith, Printer, 1837), 7–8.

101. Peter Edes, 21 July 1775, in *Diary*, 12.

102. John Leach, 19 July 1775, in "Journal," 257; Timothy Newell records on July 14 that "Master James Lovell, Master Leach, John—Hunt, have been imprisoned for some time past—all they know why it is so is they are charged with free speaking on the public measures." Timothy Newell, 14 July 1775, in "Journal Kept During The Time," 264.

103. John Leach, 14 August 1775, 17 August 1775, 25 September 1775, in "Journal," 258, 262.

104. Ibid., 2 July 1775 to 17 July 1775, 256–257; Peter Edes, 2 July 1775, in *Diary*, 10.

105. John Leach, 14 August 1775, 17 August 1775, 25 September 1775, in "Journal," 258, 262.

106. Timothy Newell, 10 October 1775, in "Journal Kept During The Time," 268.

107. Abigail Adams to John Adams, July 16, 1775, in Butterfield et al., *Book of Abigail and John*, 101.

108. Eldad Taylor, "Evacuation of Boston, 1776, By An Eye Witness," *New England Historical and Genealogical Review* 8 (July 1854): 231.

109. Abigail Adams, 2 March 1776, 3 March 1776, in Frothingham, *History of the Siege*, 305–306.

110. Timothy Newell, 4 March 1776, in "Journal Kept During The Time," 272; Abigail Adams, 3 March 1776, in Frothingham, *History of the Siege*, 305–306.

111. George Washington to Joseph Reed, 3 March 1776, in Reed, *Life and Correspondence*, 166–167; Frothingham, *Siege of Boston*, 295–296; John Barker, diary, *British in Boston*, 69.

112. Timothy Newell, 5 March 1776, in "Journal Kept During The Time," 272. For a detailed description of General Washington's plans see Middlekauff, *Glorious Cause*, 308–311.

113. Frothingham, *Siege of Boston*, 301.

114. A letter to the Commanding Officer at Roxbury, 8 March 1776, in *Collections of the Massachusetts Historical Society*, 4th ser., 1 (1852): 272–273.

115. John Andrews to William Barrell, April 11, 1776, in "Letters of John Andrews," 409–410.

116. Howe, orders, 14 March 1776, *Orderly Book*, 237; *New England Chronicle* (Cambridge) 25 April 1776.

117. Printed proclamation of General Howe and British letters in the Massachusetts State House, in Frothingham, *Siege of Boston*, 306–307; John Andrews, Boston, to William Barrell, 11 April 1776, "Letters of John Andrews," 411.

118. James H. Stark, *The Loyalists of Massachusetts and The Other Side of The American Revolution* (Boston: W. B. Clarke Co., 1910; repr. Bowie, Md.: Heritage Books, 1988), 133–136.

119. Banishment Act of the State of Massachusetts, in Stark, *Loyalists of Massachusetts*, 134–135, 137; Wallace Brown, *The King's Friends: The Composition and Motives of the American Loyalist Claimants* (Providence, R.I.: Brown University Press, 1965), 19, 23, 26, 27.

120. Helen R. Pinkney, *Christopher Gore, Federalist of Massachusetts, 1758–1827* (Waltham, Mass.: Gore Place Society, 1969), 13.

121. Banishment Act of the State of Massachusetts, in Stark, *Loyalists of Massachusetts*, 137.

122. Thacher, *Military Journal*, 50; Dorothy Dudley, *Theatrum Majorum* (Cambridge, 1876), 60, in Colonial Society of Massachusetts, *Music in Colonial Massachusetts, 1630–1820*. vol. 1, *Music in Public Places* (Boston: Colonial Society of Massachusetts, 1980), 96 (proceedings of conference held May 17–18, 1973);

New York Journal 28 March 1775. Washington required that all persons entering Boston first have his permission due to concerns that the British had left a "pestilential trap" in the town in the form of smallpox. He had received information to this effect from "a person just out of Boston." Fenn, *Pox Americana*, 90.

123. Thacher, *Military Journal*, 50.

124. Abigail Adams to John Adams, 16[?] March 1776, in Butterfield et al., *Book of Abigail and John*, 120–121.

125. George Washington to Joseph Reed, 19 March 1776, Reed, *Life and Correspondence*, 176–177; *New York Journal* 23 November 1775, 28 March 1776; Taylor, "Evacuation of Boston," 231; Timothy Newell, 14 September 1775, 13 October 1775, 27 October 1775, 16 November 1775, 16 January 1776, 13 February 1776, 15 March 1776, in "Journal Kept During The Time," 268–269, 270, 271, 275–276; Warden, *Boston, 1689–1776*, 325, 332; Middlekauff, *Glorious Cause*, 540–541. James Thacher describes caltrops as an "implement [which] consists of an iron ball armed with four sharp points about one inch in length, so formed that which way soever it may fall one point still lies upwards to pierce the feet of horses or men, and are admirably well calculated to obstruct the march of an enemy." They were commonly called crows' feet. Thacher, *Military Journal*, 51.

126. Eldad Taylor, Boston, to his wife 18 March 1776, in "Evacuation of Boston," 231.

127. *New York Journal* 28 March 1776; *New England Chronicle* 25 April 1776; Eldad Taylor, Boston, to his wife 18 March 1776, in "Evacuation of Boston," 231–232.

128. *New Hampshire Gazette* 21 April 1775, 9 June 1775; *Providence Gazette* 27 May 1775, 3 June 1775, 1 July 1775.

129. *Connecticut Gazette* 23 June 1775, 21 July 1775; *Connecticut Courant* (Hartford) 15 May 1775, 4 September 1775; *Connecticut Journal* 14 June 1775, 18 October 1775; *New York Journal* 14 October 1775.

130. *New Hampshire Gazette* 21 April 1775; *Providence Gazette* 22 April 1775; *Connecticut Courant* 5 June 1775.

131. Abigail Adams to John Adams 24 May 1775, 16 June 1775, 12 July 1775, in Butterfield et al., *Book of Abigail and John*, 85–86, 87–89.

132. Boston Taking Books, 1780, 1784, 1790, John West, *The Boston Directory Containing the Names of the Inhabitants, their Occupations, Places of Business, and Dwelling-Houses* (Boston: Manning and Loring, 1796), in *Record Commissioners* 10: 239, 262.

133. Brown, *King's Friends*, 19, 23, 26, 27, 30, 32–33; Stark, *Loyalists of Massachusetts*, 133–135, 137–140, 275–280. See also Mary Beth Norton, *The British-Americans: The Loyalist Exiles in England, 1774–1789* (Boston: Little, Brown & Co., 1972).

CHAPTER TWO

1. John Rowe, diary, 19 March 1776, in *Letters and Diary*, 304; William Bant, Boston, to John Hancock, Philadelphia, 19 October 1776, BPL/RBD.

2. Abigail Adams to John Adams, 31 March 1776, in Butterfield et al., *Book of Abigail and John*, 119.

3. Boston Town Records, 8 November 1776, 18 November 1776, in *Record Commissioners* 18: 253–254, 256–257.

4. Henry Wansey, "The Three Chief American Cities in 1794," from *An Excursion to the United States of North America in the Summer of 1794* (Salisbury, 1796), 18–35, 57–66, 96–119, in *American Social History So Recorded by British Travelers*, comp. and ed. Allan Nevins (New York: Henry Holt & Co., 1923), 45, 49.

5. J. P. Brissot de Warville, letter, 30 July 1788, in Nathaniel Shurtleff, *Topographical and Historical Description in 1794* (Boston: A. Williams & Co., 1871), 84; Wansey, "Three Chief American Cities," 45, 49.

6. *Boston Gazette* 31 January 1781.

7. Barbara Vaughn to Miss K. W. Livingston, 26 September 1785, Matthew Ridley Papers, MHS.

8. Walter Muir Whitehill, *Boston: A Topographical History*, 2nd ed. (Cambridge, Mass.: Belknap Press/Harvard University Press, 1968), 8, 17.

9. Whitehill, *Topographical History*, 22; John Marston et al. to selectmen, 28 April 1797, Boston Town Papers.

10. West, *Boston Directory* (1796), in *Record Commissioners* 10: 217. The account of Boston used in the 1796 directory was extracted by the publisher from "the Rev. Dr. Morse's Gazetteer of America"; Shurtleff, *Topographical and Historical Description*, 36.

11. Shurtleff, *Topographical and Historical Description*, 138, 139; Boston Taking Books, 1784, 1790, 1794.

12. Shurtleff, *Topographical and Historical Description*, 127.

13. Boston Selectmen, minutes, 8 February 1715, in *Record Commissioners* 11: 240–241; Boston Town Records, 9 March 1735, in *Record Commissioners* 12: 131–133.

14. The exact length of the isthmus was one mile, thirty-nine yards. Thomas Pemberton, "A Topographical and Historical Description of Boston, 1794," *Collections of the Massachusetts Historical Society*, 1st ser., 3 (1794): 242; *Description of the Town and Harbour of Boston, Communicated to the Publisher, by a Gentleman from America*, broadside (London, 1775), BPL/RBD.

15. Barbara Vaughn, Boston, to Miss Livingston, 26 September 1785, Matthew Ridley Papers.

16. Ibid.

17. Whitehill, *Topographical History*, 26.

18. Boston Town Records, 14 May 1765, in *Record Commissioners* 16: 148; *Description of the Town*; Edwin L. Bynner, "Topography and Landmarks of the Provincial Period," in Winsor, *Memorial History* 2: 496.

19. Boston Town Records, 11 May 1762, *Record Commissioners* 16: 76; Bynner, "Topography and Landmarks," 503, n.2; Shurtleff, *Topographical and Historical Description*, 140.

20. Mifflin, *Plan of the British Fortifications on Boston Neck*, heliotype, in Winsor, *Memorial History* 3: 81.

21. Boston Town Records, 10 May 1763, in *Record Commissioners* 16: 93.

22. Ibid., 30 August 1774, in *Record Commissioners* 18: 189.

23. Boston Selectmen, minutes, 14 May 1777, in *Record Commissioners* 25: 38; Boston Selectmen, minutes, 27 March 1780, in *Record Commissioners* 25: 116.

24. Boston Town Records, 23 March 1767, in *Record Commissioners* 16: 208.

25. Boston Selectmen, minutes, 10 January 1781, 15 January 1781, in *Record Commissioners* 25: 137–138.

26. Ibid., 4 June 1777, in *Record Commissioners* 25: 39.

27. Ibid., 31 May 1784, in *Record Commissioners* 25: 245.

28. *The By-Laws and Town-Orders of The Town of Boston, Made and passed at Several Meetings in 1785 and 1786 and Duly approved by the Court of Sessions* (Boston: Edmund Freedman Printing Office, 1786), 49–50, Early American Imprints, 1st ser., no. 19515.

29. Boston Selectmen, minutes, 7 August 1782, 25 February 1783, 16 April 1783, 17 September 1783, 24 September 1783, 1 October 1783, 16 August 1786, in *Record Commissioners* 25: 189, 206, 211, 224, 225, 322; Boston Town Records, 13 May 1774, in *Record Commissioners* 18: 171; Boston Selectmen, minutes, 31 August 1789, 29 August 1791, in *Record Commissioners* 27: 100–101, 158; Boston Taking Book, 1790.

30. Wansey, "Three Chief American Cities," 49.

31. Whitehill, *Topographical History*, 35.

32. Barbara Vaughn, Boston, to K. W. Livingston, New York, 26 September 1785, Matthew Ridley Papers.

33. Pemberton, "Topographical and Historical Description," 243.

34. Boston Selectmen, minutes, 16 June 1784, 12 July 1786, in *Record Commissioners* 25: 246, 315.

35. Ibid., 4 June 1777, 13 July 1779, 25 February 1783, 11 August 1784, 1 June 1785, in *Record Commissioners* 25: 40, 96, 206, 249, 270.

36. *Tremont Street Mall, Looking North*, painting by a daughter of General Knox, Boston Public Library, reproduced in James H. Stark, *Antique Views of Ye Towne of Boston* (Boston: Morse-Purce Co., 1907), 155.

37. Whitehill, *Topographical History*, 60.

38. Shurtleff, *Topographical and Historical Description*, 143.

39. Boston Town Records, 4 July 1788, in *Record Commissioners* 31: 178–179.
40. Ibid.
41. Pemberton, "Topographical and Historical Description," 242–243.
42. Whitehill, *Topographical History*, 34–35.
43. Boston Taking Book, 1784. In 1784 there were forty-eight barns in Ward 10, fifty-two barns in Ward 11, and seventy-two barns in Ward 12, totaling 172.
44. *Independent Chronicle* (Boston) 17 January 1788; Boston Taking Book, 1784.
45. *Boston Gazette* 24 April 1793; Ann Smith Lainhart, ed. *First Boston City Directory (1789), Including Extensive Annotations by John Haven Dexter (1791–1876)* (Boston: New England Historic Genealogical Society, 1989), 78; Boston Taking Books, 1790, 1794; Stewart H. Holbrook, *The Old Post Road: The Story of the Boston Post Road.* American Trails Series, ed. A. B. Guthrie Jr. (New York: McGraw-Hill Book Co., 1962), 26. Pease was awarded the first mail contract in the United States, a Boston to New York line. The company went on to gain the Boston to Portsmouth and Boston to Concord, New Hampshire, mail contract. Pease also designed the first "government mail stage." Holbrook, *Old Post Road*, 28–31.
46. Boston Taking Books, 1784, 1790, 1794; Lainhart, *First Boston City Directory*, 55, 73; Boston Selectmen, minutes, 28 August 1782, in *Record Commissioners* 25: 191; Boston Selectmen, minutes, 25 April 1787, 30 November 1791, in *Record Commissioners* 27: 15, 165.
47. Boston Taking Books, 1784, 1790, 1794. Close to 60 percent of Boston's African-American population lived in the South End during the 1780s and 1790s. Fort Hill in Ward 10 was popular with both poor blacks and whites.
48. Boston, c. 1775, in *Atlas of Early American History*, ed. Cappon & Petchenik.
49. The 1798 U.S. Direct Tax lists the proprietors of Boston's wharves. Some wharves had multiple owners. Seven men owned Woodward's Wharf, but leased the four stores and one cooper's shop to tenants. Other wharves had single owners, such as David Spear's wharf, also consisting of stores and a cooper's shop. Alexander Giles owned Long Wharf. The 1798 tax lists forty-eight privately owned wharves. The United States Direct Tax of 1798, in *Record Commissioners* 22: 60, 61, 75, 536. A wharfinger is an owner or manager of a wharf.
50. Pemberton, "Topographical and Historical Description," 248.
51. United States Direct Tax, 1798, in *Record Commissioners* 22, 61; Boston Selectmen, minutes, 29 August 1781, in *Record Commissioners* 25: 155; *Boston Gazette* 25 September 1780, 24 September 1781.
52. To raise funds for repair, the proprietors continued an existing lottery. They had formulated this plan of four thousand tickets at two dollars apiece, with various prizes going to the winners, to raise the necessary money for repairs when damage occurred to the wharf from neglect during the late 1770s. *Boston Gazette*

31 January 1789, 25 September 1780, 13 May 1782; Boston Selectmen, minutes, 18 October 1780, in *Record Commissioners* 25: 132.

53. *Boston Gazette* 30 April 1781; Pemberton, "Topographical and Historical Description," 248; Joseph Hadfield, *An Englishman in America 1785: Being the Diary of Joseph Hadfield*, ed. Douglas S. Robertson (Toronto: Hunter-Rose Co., 1933), 187.

54. Boston Selectmen, minutes, 7 November 1776, 28 August 1782, 18 May 1786, in *Record Commissioners* 25: 330, 190, 303.

55. Wansey, "Three Chief American Cities," 46. Although Wansey does not state the name of the tavern, he gives the name of the proprietor as Colonel Coleman. Colonel Dudley Coleman applied for and received a license "as an Inholder at the Bunch of Grapes Tavern in State Street" in 1790; Boston Selectmen, minutes, 21 April 1790, in *Record Commissioners* 25: 116; *Independent Chronicle* 19 May 1788.

56. *New England Chronicle* 2 May 1776; *Columbian Centinel* (Boston) 9 October 1790.

57. *Independent Chronicle* 6 June 1782, 11 July 1782, 12 January 1795; Lainhart, *First Boston City Directory*, 49; Boston Taking Books, 1784, 1790, 1794.

58. Pemberton, "Topographical and Historical Description," 248.

59. *Boston Gazette* 1 January 1798.

60. "S.W. View of the Old State House," reproduced from *Massachusetts Magazine*, 1793, in Stark, *Antique Views*, 82; Pemberton, "Topographical and Historical Description," 249.

61. *Boston Gazette* 23 October 1780, 6 November 1780.

62. Pemberton, "Topographical and Historical Description," 248.

63. *Independent Chronicle* 7 April 1791; "[T]he Whipping Post be removed from current location," Court of Sessions, April Term 1786, Material from the Adlow Papers (Ms.Adl.JD1–25), BPL/RBD; "Whenever a Gallows may be necessary," Court of Sessions, April Term 1786, Adlow Papers; *Recollections of Samuel Breck*, in Horace E. Scudder, "Life in Boston in the Revolutionary Period," in Winsor, *Memorial History* 3: 172.

64. John Rowe, diary, 29 October 1778, in *Letters and Diary*, 319; Stark, *Antique Views*, 105.

65. Boston Selectmen, minutes, 19 March 1777, 2 April 1777, 21 September 1785, in *Record Commissioners* 25: 33, 280.

66. Pemberton, "Topographical and Historical Description," 254.

67. Ibid.

68. Boston Selectmen, minutes, 17 March 1784, in *Record Commissioners* 25: 238.

69. Ibid., 28 July 1783, 14 June 1786, in *Record Commissioners* 25: 218, 309.

70. Boston Town Records, 1 February 1775, in *Record Commissioners* 23: 212.

71. Pemberton, "Topographical and Historical Description," 246.

72. Boston Town Records, 25 March 1783, in *Record Commissioners* 26: 301–304.

73. *Boston Gazette* 15 May 1780, 1 October 1780, 12 January 1784.

74. Boston Selectmen, minutes, 2 September 1776, 28 August 1780, 21 January 1784, in *Record Commissioners* 25: 9, 128–129, 235; Boston Taking Books, 1780, 1784.

75. Boston Selectmen, minutes, 2 September 1776, 28 August 1780, in *Record Commissioners* 25: 9, 128.

76. *Boston Gazette* 8 May 1780. There are numerous descriptions of Boston housing structures in the 1784, 1790, 1794, and 1799 Taking Books and the United States Direct Tax of 1798, in *Record Commissioners*, 22. These descriptions vary but include building materials, windows, size, number of rooms, and, in the case of the Taking Books, sometimes the use of those rooms.

77. *Independent Chronicle* 30 June 1785.

78. Boston Selectmen, minutes, 5 March 1787, 14 October 1789, in *Record Commissioners* 27: 7–8, 104; Pemberton, "Topographical and Historical Description," 247; Map of Boston, c. 1775, in *Atlas of Early American History*; *A Plan of Boston from actual Survey by Osgood Carleton, 1796* (Boston: John West, 1796), in *Record Commissioners* 10: 303.

79. Map of Boston, c. 1775, in *Atlas of Early American History*; Lord George Gremain, *A Plan of Boston in New England with its Environs* (London, c. 1775); Charles Bouldry, *A Plan of the Town of Boston and the Charlestown Peninsula in New England, 1775* (Boston, 1969).

80. Boston Selectmen, minutes, 30 August 1779, in *Record Commissioners* 25: 100.

81. Joseph Hadfield, diary, 17 September 1785, in *Englishman in America*, 194.

82. Boston Selectmen, minutes, 26 April 1786, in *Record Commissioners* 25: 300; Boston Town Records, 3 May 1786, in *Record Commissioners* 31: 118.

83. Pemberton, "Topographical and Historical Description," 245.

84. Whitehill, *Topographical History*, 112.

85. *Columbian Centinel* 4 March 1795, 28 September 1796.

86. Boston Taking Book, 1794; United States Direct Tax, 1798 in *Record Commissioners* 22: 1–26, 127–8, 130–31; *Boston Gazette* 19 April 1794.

87. Shurtleff, *Topographical and Historical Description*, 138.

88. *Columbian Centinel* 10 September 1796, 24 September 1796.

89. Compiled from the 1784 Taking Book.

90. Bynner, "Topography and Landmarks," 522.

91. Shurtleff, *Topographical and Historical Description*, 139; *Independent Chronicle* 14 October 1790.

92. Whitehill, *Topographical History*, 52; Dell Upton, "The City as Material Culture," in Anne Elizabeth Yentsch and Mary C. Beaudry, eds., *The Art and Mystery of Historical Archaeology: Essays in Honor of James Deetz* (Boca Raton, Fla.: CRC Press, 1992), 54, 56–57; Boston Taking Books, 1790, 1794, 1799.

93. Whitehill, *Topographical History*, 60–62.

94. Wansey, "Three Chief American Cities," 45–46.

95. *Boston Gazette* 1 January 1798.

96. Whitehill, *Topographical History*, 60–62.

97. Based on an analysis of five Taking Books (1780, 1784, 1790, 1794, 1799) the average number of households for each ward over the twenty-year period between 1780 and 1800 was as follows: Ward 1, 147; Ward 2, 242; Ward 3, 222; Ward 4, 206; Ward 5, 243; Ward 6, 247; Ward 7, 305; Ward 8, 273; Ward 9, 228; Ward 10, 353; Ward 11, 273; Ward 12, 646. The actual number of heads of household in 1780 and 1790 for each ward was as follows: Ward 1 had 77 heads of household in 1780 and 190 in 1799; Ward 2 increased from 132 in 1780 to 315 in 1799; Ward 3 increased from 162 in 1780 to 252 in 1799; Ward 4 from 153 to 239; Ward 5 from 177 to 268; Ward 6 from 149 to 221; Ward 7 from 161 to 541; Ward 8 from 192 to 242; Ward 9 from 181 to 280; Ward 10 from 252 to 464; Ward 11 from 194 to 396; Ward 12 from 382 to 1,029. In 1784 every ward showed an increase in the number of heads of household. In 1790 Wards 1 through 9 decreased slightly, but Wards 10, 11, and 12 continued to grow. In 1794 and 1799, once again every ward demonstrated growth. Data compiled from the Boston Taking Books, 1780, 1784, 1790, 1794, 1799. For additional information and charts see Jacqueline Carr-Frobose, "A Cultural History of Boston in the Revolutionary Era, 1775–1795" (Ph.D. diss., University of California, Berkeley, 1998), 145.

98. The occupational categories selected include: truckmen (106), bakers (136), barbers/hairdressers (105), tailors (193), shoemakers (81), blacksmiths (103), housewrights (184), and laborers (319). Data compiled from the Boston Taking Books, 1784, 1790, 1794. For additional information and charts see Carr-Frobose, "Cultural History of Boston," 149.

99. Boston Taking Books, 1784, 1794, 1799.

100. Some historians have concluded that eighteenth-century urban land use was ordered in such a way that the city's wealthy occupied the center of town while the outward areas were progressively poorer. See Carl Abbott, "The Neighborhoods of New York, 1760–1775," in *New York History* 55 (1974): 35–54. Allan Kulikoff suggested for Boston the same pattern Abbott argues for New York, one of specific land use patterns determined by economic status and economic function. See Allan Kulikoff, "The Progress of Inequality in Revolutionary Boston," *William and Mary Quarterly*, 3rd ser., 28 (1971): 349–399. Analysis of my database compiled from five Taking Books (1780, 1784, 1790, 1794, 1799) as discussed in this chapter does not bear out this pattern for Boston. The description that Sam

Bass Warner Jr. provides of Philadelphia is more similar to the pattern of spatial use found in Boston. He notes, "The settlement pattern of the town combined two opposing social tendencies. The clustering of marine trades and merchants next to the Delaware suggested the beginnings of the specialized industrial quarters then characteristic of European cities. On the other hand, the rummage of classes and occupations found in many Philadelphia blocks continued the old tradition of mixed work and residence characteristic of American and English country towns." Ropewalks sat in the outer regions of the Shawmut Peninsula on the far side of Boston Common and on the far western edge of Ward 7. Shipyards were located at the docks on the north and east sides of the peninsula. Other than this, the businesses, manufactures, and residences of Bostonians comprised a mixed-use environment. Sam Bass Warner Jr., *The Private City: Philadelphia in Three Periods of Its Growth* (Philadelphia: University of Pennsylvania Press, 1968), 11.

101. Boston Taking Book, 1799; United States Direct Tax, 1798, in *Record Commissioners*, 22: 2–3.

102. Boston Taking Book, 1799.

103. The figures are as follows: North End, 1,151 heads of household to 680 "dwelling-houses and tenements"; West End, 297 heads of household to 170 "dwelling-houses and tenements"; South End, 1,817 heads of household to 1,250 "dwelling houses." Boston Taking Book, 1784; Shurtleff, *Topographical and Historical Description*, 138, 139.

104. Robert V. Wells, "Population and Family in Early America," in *The Blackwell Encyclopedia of the American Revolution*, ed., Jack P. Greene and J. R. Pole (Cambridge: Basil Blackwell, 1991), 49.

105. Boston Taking Books, 1790, 1794.

106. Ibid., 1784, 1794, 1799.

107. Ibid., 1784, 1790, 1794.

108. Ibid., 1780, 1784, 1790, 1795, 1799; Lainhart, *First Boston City Directory*, 33.

109. Lemuel Shattuck, *Report to the Committee of the City Council Appointed to Obtain the Census of Boston for the Year 1845* (Boston: John H. Eastburn, 1846; repr., New York: Arno Press, 1976), 3–5, 26; Boston Taking Books, 1784, 1790, 1794; Lainhart, *First Boston City Directory*, 33; *Independent Chronicle* 22 March 1781, 21 March 1782, 28 May 1789.

110. By cross-referencing the Taking Books with the 1790 Census certain observations may be made about the black community in Boston between 1780 and late 1799. Over the nineteen years from 1780 to 1799, 407 black heads of household appear in the Taking Books by first and last name; an additional 110 black heads of household are listed by forename only, making them harder to track. Of the 227 black heads of household listed in the 1790 federal census, one hundred are listed by first and last names. Comparing these one hundred individu-

als with names in the Taking Books revealed forty-nine names that did not appear in the Taking Books. These forty-nine heads of household may then be added to the 407 from the Taking Books, establishing a list of 456 black heads of household. The irregularity of these records, in terms of individuals not appearing in the Taking Books who do appear in the Census, suggests the problems inherent in identifying and studying not only African-Americans, but also women and poor white males during the period under consideration. Of the 456 heads of household who can be identified for the 1780 to 1799 period by first and last name, the size of only a few is available. These were as follows: John Comb's household consisted of four people; Cyrus Gardner's consisted of three persons; Thomas Nickols's, six; Cato Small's, two; and Oliver Nash's of four persons including his wife of seven years, Dinah Dean. It is highly likely that black family size was smaller than that of white families due to a higher level of poverty and the resulting problems of malnutrition, disease, and a high rate of infant death. Assessors' comments are especially valuable in determining living conditions for both black and white Bostonians. *First Census of the United States, 1790, Massachusetts* (Washington, D.C.: Government Printing Office, 1908; repr., *Heads of Families at the First Census of the United States Taken in the Year 1790, Massachusetts*. Department of Commerce and Labor, Bureau of the Census, Bountiful, Utah: Accelerated Indexing Systems, 1978); Taking Books, 1790, 1794, 1799.

111. During the American Revolution African-Americans presented various petitions to the Massachusetts state legislature regarding emancipation. One such document was a "Petition of Slaves in Boston" presented to the General Court on January 6, 1773. The seven African-American men who presented the "Second Petition of Massachusetts Slaves" on March 18, 1777, included two Bostonians, Lancaster Hill and Prince Hall. On June 9, 1777, the legislature responded to the various petitions with "An Act for preventing the practice of holding persons in Slavery." Nothing came of the bill, but "as the efforts towards the formation of a State Constitution gradually strengthened and took shape, the subject of slavery and the status of the negro came up again and again." After extensive debate and various proposals regarding slavery and citizenship for blacks, mulattoes, and Indians, the new state constitution failed to address these issues. In the years that followed, however, the Massachusetts Bill of Rights stating that "all men are born free and equal" would become the instrument through which litigation ended slavery in Massachusetts. The General Court never passed a law specifically abolishing slavery in Massachusetts, but a court ruling by Chief Justice William Cushing in the case of the slave Quock Walker rendered the institution unconstitutional in 1783. William C. Nell, *The Colored Patriots of the American Revolution* (Boston: Robert F. Wallcut, 1855; repr., New York: Arno Press, 1968, from a copy in the Moorland-Spingarn Collection, Howard University), 47–48, 58–59; Boston Taking Books, 1780, 1784; George H. Moore, *Notes on the History of Slavery in Massa-*

chusetts (New York: D. Appleton & Co., 1866), 180–185, 226–228; Leon Litwack, *North of Slavery: The Negro in the Free States, 1790–1860* (Chicago: University of Chicago Press), 10–11; Boston *Gazette* 5 October 1781, 19 November 1781; *Independent Chronicle* 14 February 1788. See also Elaine MacEacheren, "Emancipation of Slavery in Massachusetts: A Reexamination 1770–1790." in *Journal of Negro History* 55, no. 4 (October 1970): 289–306; Robert M. Spector, "The Quock Walker Cases (1781–83): Slavery, Its Abolition, and Negro Citizenship in Early Massachusetts," *Journal of Negro History* 53, no. 1 (January 1968): 12–32; Emily Blanck, "Seventeen Eighty-Three: The Turning Point in the Law of Slavery and Freedom in Massachusetts," *New England Quarterly* 75, no. 1 (March 2003): 24–51; William O'Brien, S. J., "Did the Jennison Case Outlaw Slavery in Massachusetts?" in *William and Mary Quarterly*, 3rd ser., 17, no. 2 (April 1960): 219–242.

112. Boston Taking Books, 1784, 1790, 1794.

113. Ibid., 1780, 1784, 1790, 1794, 1799.

114. Beginning in 1790 the black population in Massachusetts grew in absolute numbers but decreased as a percentage of the aggregate (white, black, and Indian) population. This larger pattern within the state was also evident in Boston, where blacks comprise 8 percent of the town's population in 1781 but only 4 percent in 1800, although the actual number had increased from 848 persons to 1,174. Boston Taking Books, 1784, 1790, 1794; Shattuck, *Report to the Committee*, 4–5; George A. Levesque, *Black Boston: African American Life and Culture in Urban America, 1750–1860* (New York: Garland Publishing, 1994), 25, 33. Studies of the formation and development of Boston's black community between 1800 and 1850 include James E. Horton and Lois E. Horton, *Black Bostonians: Family Life and Community Struggle in the Antebellum North* (New York: Holmes & Meier Publishers, 1979); Lorenzo Johnston Greene, *The Negro in Colonial New England* (New York: Atheneum, 1968); Litwack, *North of Slavery*; Adelaide M. Cromwell, *The Other Brahmins: Boston's Black Upper Class, 1750–1950* (Fayetteville: University of Arkansas Press, 1994); and Levesque, *Black Boston*.

115. In contrast to my conclusions regarding the South End based upon data compiled from the Taking Books, previous historians have proposed that the West End was the primary area of residence for African-Americas during the 1790s, with the North End also sustaining a sizable number of individuals. Adelaide Cromwell argues that before the large scale migration to Ward 7 began in approximately 1820, blacks were "limited to the outermost parts of the North End . . . known as New Guinea." Cromwell, *Other Brahmins*, 27, 43; the conclusion drawn by Horton and Horton that the North End was "the largest black neighborhood in the city" before 1830 concurs with this point. Horton and Horton, *Black Bostonians*, 5; George Levesque asserts that the movement to the West End "was well underway" by 1790 with a majority of black Bostonians living there "as early as 1800— [and] certainly by 1810." This, he argues, was the precondition necessary for the

formation of a cohesive community and its "communal institutions." George Levesque, *Black Boston*, 33–34.

116. Levesque, *Black Boston*, 33; Boston Taking Books, 1784, 1790, 1794.

117. Boston Taking Books, 1790, 1794, 1799.

118. Ibid., 1799.

119. Prince Hall, "Extract from a Charge delivered to the African Lodge, June 24th, 1797, at Menotomy, Massachusetts," in Benjamin Brawley, ed., *Early Negro American Writers* (Chapel Hill, 1935), 99, quoted by Litwack in *North of Slavery*, 17.

120. Boston Selectmen, minutes, 7 September 1791, 25 September 1792, in *Record Commissioners* 27: 159, 189.

121. Donald Martin Jacobs, "A History of the Boston Negro from the Revolution to the Civil War" (Ph.D. diss., Boston University, 1968), 42.

122. Boston Selectmen, minutes, 11 February 1789, 25 February 1789, 14 July 1789, 2 September 1789, in *Record Commissioners* 27: 82, 83, 95, 101.

123. Jacobs, "History of the Boston Negro," 43.

124. Whitehill, *Topographical History*, 71; Robert Hayden, *The African Meeting House in Boston: A Celebration of History* (Boston: Museum of Afro American History, 1987), 5; Horton and Horton, *Black Bostonians*, 3.

125. United States Direct Tax, 1798, in *Record Commissioners* 22: 101.

126. Boston Taking Books, 1784, 1790, 1794.

127. *By-Laws and Town-Orders*, 10–11.

128. Boston Selectmen, minutes, 29 September 1784, in *Record Commissioners* 25: 252–253.

129. Ibid., 15 June 1791 in *Record Commissioners* 27: 153.

130. Boston Town Records, 1 September 1794, in *Record Commissioners* 31: 368–371.

131. Carole Shammas discusses the density patterns of Boston, New York, and Philadelphia in "The Space Problem in Early United States Cities." In 1790 the average number of persons per square mile in Boston was approximately 15,000. Compared to Philadelphia and New York at approximately 40,000 and 32,000 respectively, Boston's residential patterns do not appear dense unless placed in the context that most Americans (95 percent) lived in rural areas and not large towns or cities. Carole Shammas, "The Space Problem in Early United States Cities," *William and Mary Quarterly*, 3rd ser., 57, no. 3 (July 2000): 506, 509.

132. *Columbian Centinel* 10 September 1796, 24 September 1796; Boston Selectmen, minutes, 20 March 1782, 1 January 1783, 30 July 1783, in *Record Commissioners* 25: 170, 203, 218–219; Pemberton, "Topographical and Historical Description," 249.

133. Pemberton, "Topographical and Historical Description," 251–252; Boston Town Records, 26 May 1766, in *Record Commissioners* 16: 184.

134. Boston Town Records, 24 March 1794, 23 March 1795, 13 May 1795, 21 May 1795, 25 May 1795, in *Record Commissioners* 31: 356, 392, 395, 397, 398, 399–400; *Independent Chronicle* 9 November 1795.

135. *Columbian Centinel* 5 August 1797.

136. Ibid., 24 September 1796.

137. *Boston Gazette* 2 May 1796; Petition of Edward Brinley et al. to the Inhabitants of Boston, 20 June 1796, Boston Town Papers; Petition to Selectmen [regarding] . . . shops or stores in Union & other streets in the vicinity of the Market, August 1793, Boston Town Papers.

138. *Columbian Centinel* 28 September 1796.

139. Boston Town Records, 2 November 1795, 6 November 1795, 13 May 1796, in *Record Commissioners* 31: 411, 412, 432; Physicians of Boston to Selectmen of Boston, 4 November 1795, Boston Town Papers, July to December 1795; *Columbian Centinel* 28 September 1796.

140. *Columbian Centinel* 10 September 1796.

141. Ibid., 10 September 1796.

142. Ibid., 24 September 1796.

143. Ibid., 10 September 1796; Dell Upton, "City as Material Culture," 53–54.

144. Pemberton, "Topographical and Historical Description," 250, 255–256; West, *Boston Directory* (1796), in *Record Commissioners* 10: 217–218; Wansey, "Three Chief American Cities." On the contributions of Charles Bulfinch to the Boston landscape see also chap. 3, "The Boston of Bulfinch," in Whitehill, *Topographical History*, 47–72.

145. In the later decades of the eighteenth century some individuals viewed the city as a sign of progress, rather than the den of iniquity painted by agrarianists. Philosophical ideas emerging from Europe were an instrumental part of these changing attitudes. James Machor emphasizes the significance, for example, of Condorcet's treatise that "argued that all societies naturally moved upward through a series of stages from primitive hunting and gathering, through herding, to agriculture." Therefore, progress equaled man's improvement of nature, and the more man improved upon nature the more civilized he became. Such ideas boded well for the city. "If cosmopolitan trading cities were the most advanced forms of civilization, . . . they were man's best and most 'natural' type of society." However, this created a paradox. What happened to "agrarian evangelism" and man's reverence for the rural environment, which was considered superior, if now cities were to be considered the most "natural" type of society? Machor suggests that "attempts at reconciliation did occur" between "agrarian philosophy and the new concepts of civilization and progress," which he identifies as the "urban middle landscape," or the idea of the "pastoral city." James L. Machor, *Pastoral Cities:*

Urban Ideals and the Symbolic Landscape of America (Madison, Wis.: University of Wisconsin Press, 1987), 84–85.

146. *Boston Gazette* 1 February 1796; 8 February 1796.

CHAPTER THREE

1. Boston Town Records, 29 March 1776, in *Record Commissioners* 18: 227.

2. Ibid., 226–227

3. Boston Selectmen, minutes, 12 May 1776, in *Record Commissioners* 25: 1.

4. To assist families of "Non-Commissioned Officers & Soldiers . . . engaged in the Continental Services" on behalf "of this Town" the community agreed to take up regular collections from "Churches and Congregations." Boston Town Records, 28 October 1777, in *Record Commissioners* 18: 291. For a detailed discussion of the economic consequences of the American Revolution in New England see Oscar Handlin and Mary F. Handlin, "Revolutionary Economic Policy in Massachusetts," in *William and Mary Quarterly*, 3rd ser., vol. 4, no. 1 (January 1947), 3–26.

5. Darret B. Rutman, *Winthrop's Boston: A Portrait of a Puritan Town, 1630–1649* (Chapel Hill: University of North Carolina Press, 1965; W. W. Norton & Co., 1972), 59.

6. Other elected offices were enginemen, clerks of the market, surveyors of wood, haywards, sealers of leather, informers of deer, assay masters, the town treasurer and various ad hoc committee positions. For example, they selected seven selectmen (nine beginning in 1777), sixteen firewards, twelve overseers of the poor, twelve constables, five surveyors of boards and shingles, four sealers of leather, and four hogreeves. After 1785 the number of hogreeves dropped to three, the sealers of leather increased to five. The surveyors of boards and shingles doubled to ten men by 1786 and then increased to twelve men in 1788. More than likely the increasing number of surveyors required by the town speaks to the gradual recovery of the economy, which had a concurrent impact on the building trades and in the shipyards. Boston Town Records, 1770–1795, in *Record Commissioners*, vols. 18, 26, 31.

7. Boston Town Records, 12 March 1781, in *Record Commissioners* 26: 173–174; *By-Laws and Town-Orders*, 133.

8. This analysis is based upon twenty-five years of data compiled from the yearly election of officers in March and replacements selected throughout the year in the instance of death or resignation from office as noted in the Boston Town Records. Boston Town Records, 1770–1795, in *Record Commissioners*, vols. 18, 26, 31; Boston Taking Books, 1780, 1784, 1790, 1794, 1799; *Boston City Directory, 1789* (Boston: John Nerman), in *Record Commissioners* 10; West, *Boston Directory* (1796). A detailed breakdown of this data accompanied by tables may be found in chap. 5

of Carr-Frobose, "Cultural History of Boston." On town office–holding patterns in eighteenth-century New England see also Edward M. Cook Jr., *The Fathers of the Towns: Leadership and Community Structure in Eighteenth-Century New England*, Johns Hopkins Studies in Historical and Political Science, no. 2 (Baltimore: Johns Hopkins University Press, 1976).

9. Data compiled from the yearly election of officers in March and replacements selected throughout the year in the instance of death or resignation from office as noted in the Boston Town Records. Boston Town Records, 1770–1795, in *Record Commissioners*, vols. 18, 26, 31; Boston Taking Books, 1780, 1784, 1790, 1794, 1799. A detailed breakdown of this data accompanied by tables may be found in chap. 5 of Carr-Frobose, "Cultural History of Boston."

10. Boston Selectmen, minutes, 3 February 1790; 16 February 1790, in *Record Commissioners* 27: 111. There is no record to explain what the complaint was against the police officer or reveal its outcome.

11. Ibid., 24 November 1784; 29 November 1784, 5 May 1785, 10 October 1785, in *Record Commissioners* 25: 255, 268, 282.

12. Ibid., 4 May 1785, in *Record Commissioners* 25: 268; Boston Taking Books, 1790.

13. Boston Selectmen, minutes, 19 March 1781, in *Record Commissioners* 25: 141; Ibid., 17 November 1790, in *Record Commissioners* 27: 137.

14. Ibid., 26 March 1787, in *Record Commissioners* 27: 10.

15. Ibid., 23 May 1792, in *Record Commissioners* 27: 177.

16. Ibid., 17 November 1784, in *Record Commissioners* 25: 255.

17. Ibid., 29 September 1784, in *Record Commissioners* 26: 253.

18. Ibid., 16 June 1786, 27 September 1786, 4 October 1786, 18 October 1786, in *Record Commissioners* 25: 310, 327, 329.

19. Ibid., 22 December 1784, in *Record Commissioners* 25: 257.

20. *By-Laws and Town-Orders*; Boston Selectmen, minutes, 19 May 1786, in *Record Commissioners* 25: 303.

21. Boston Selectmen, minutes, 19 May 1786, in *Record Commissioners* 25: 303.

22. Robert Pope To the Selectmen, State of the Town Clocks, December 1785, Thomas Christy Account, September 6 1783, Town of Boston to Enoch May, August 25 1785, Boston Town Papers.

23. Miscellaneous charges submitted to the Board of Selectmen, Shubael Hews, April 1796 to March 1797, Homer Lewis, April 1796 to March 1797, Boston Town Papers.

24. Miscellaneous charges submitted to the Board of Selectmen, Thomas Dakin, 24 February 1797 to 11 June 1797, Elisha Ticknor to Board of Selectmen, June 1794, Boston Town Papers.

25. William Cooper, Town Clerk, At A Meeting of the Selectmen, 28 January 1793, Boston Town Papers.

26. Boston Taking Books, 1780, 1784, 1786, 1790.

27. Boston Town Records, 24 May 1793, in *Record Commissioners* 31: 335.

28. Shurtleff, *Topographical and Historical Description*, 131.

29. Ibid., 131–132.

30. John Rowe, diary, 28 December 1778, 29 December 1778, 13 January 1779, 16 January 1779, 24 February 1779, in *Letters and Diary*, 325–326; Hazard to Belknap, *Collections of the Massachusetts Historical Society* 2, no. 5, 47, quoted in Horace E. Scudder, "Life in Boston in the Revolutionary Period," in Winsor, *Memorial History* 3: 171.

31. Rutman, *Winthrop's Boston*, 196.

32. *Massachusetts Colonial Records* 1: 196, 241, in Josiah Henry Benton, *Warning Out in New England, 1656–1817* (Boston: W. B. Clarke, 1911; repr. Freeport, N.Y.: Books for Libraries Press, 1970), 46.

33. *Records of Massachusetts Bay, 1650* 22–24 June, in Benton, *Warning Out*, 47.

34. Samuel Freeman, Esq., *The Town Officer: or the Power and Duty of Selectmen . . . and other town Officers: As Contained in the Laws of the Commonwealth of Massachusetts.* (Boston: J. T. Buckingham, 1806, 7th ed.), 226–227.

35. Boston Selectmen, minutes, 30 April 1788, in *Record Commissioners* 27: 54; Freeman, *Town Officer*, 227.

36. Freeman, *Town Officer*, 227.

37. Ibid., 227–228.

38. I would like to thank Cornelia H. Dayton for drawing my attention to the research that she and Sharon Salinger have undertaken on warning out for the years 1765–1767. They point to a number of youths coming to Boston from nearby communities in search of temporary work and others arriving in the port town to begin sea journeys. Cornelia H. Dayton and Sharon Salinger, "Mapping Migration into Pre-Revolutionary Boston: An Analysis of Robert Love's Warning Book," paper presented at the McNeil Center for Early American Studies, University of Pennsylvania, September 10, 1999. On in-migration, its causes, and warning out in pre-Revolutionary Boston see also Nash, *Urban Crucible*, 22, 123, 185–187, 253.

39. Freeman, *Town Officer*, 223–224, 228.

40. Ibid., 224–226.

41. Boston Selectmen, minutes, 20 November 1782, in *Record Commissioners* 25: 199.

42. Warning Out Book, 1791–1792, Boston Overseers of the Poor, records, MHS (hereafter cited as Warning Out Book).

43. Warning Out Book.

44. Benton, *Warning Out*, 18, 25, 46–49, 51–52, 116; the selectmen ordered that the new directions relative to "Paupers" be "put into a Frame & to be kept

constantly hanging on the Selectmen's Room, and the Room inhabited by the keeper of the Alms-house and Work-house." Boston Town Records, 15 March 1796, in *Record Commissioners* 31: 424. Douglas Lamar Jones states that "The 1794 poor law specifically ended the warning-out system, substituting a detailed procedure for the return of paupers who might fall onto the poor relief rolls. The element of control of both poor transients and of town expenses for welfare was preserved in the 1794 law. But at the same time the law required each town to provide care and immediate poor relief for all persons, regardless of their legal residence, for a period up to three months. The burden of responsibility of care for the poor finally came to rest on the towns as paupers were recognized as part of everyday life. The towns were given two courses of action in case they had to provide for a transient pauper: one, they could sue the pauper's town of legal residence in a civil action to recover their costs; and two, the towns could sue for costs on a complaint in the court of common pleas, subject to a two-years statute of limitations after the case arose. While transients were still subject to removal, they gained both short-term poor relief as well as procedural protections such as an appeal to the court of common pleas." Douglas Lamar Jones, "The Transformation of the Law of Poverty in Eighteenth Century Massachusetts," in *Law in Colonial Massachusetts, 1630–1800* (Boston: Colonial Society of Massachusetts, distr. University Press of Virginia, 1984), 190–191. (Proceedings of a conference held November 6–7, 1981, by the Colonial Society of Massachusetts.)

45. *New Hampshire Gazette* 21 April 1775; *Providence Gazette* 22 April 1775; *Connecticut Courant* 5 June 1775.

46. Boston Town Records, 8 November 1776, in *Record Commissioners* 18: 251.

47. Isaac Hobbs, Town Clerk, Weston, to the Selectmen of Boston, 1 May 1790, Boston Town Papers, January–June 1790.

48. Ebenezer Hall, chairman, by order of the Selectmen, letter, Medford, 9 August 1790, Boston Town Papers.

49. Benton, *Warning Out*, 18, 25; Rutman, *Winthrop's Boston*, 196; *By-Laws and Town-Orders*, 108.

50. Boston Taking Book, 1784; Boston Selectmen, minutes, 14 February 1787, in *Record Commissioners* 27: 5; Boston Selectmen, minutes, 27 November 1782, in *Record Commissioners* 25: 200.

51. Boston Town Records, 26 November 1787, in *Record Commissioners* 27: 39.

52. Boston Selectmen, minutes, 27 November 1778, in *Record Commissioners* 25: 79.

53. The assessment of the weightiness of this fine is based upon the cost of fish, meat, and bread listed in the Boston Town Records and newspapers during the 1770s and early 1780s.

54. *By-Laws and Town-Orders*, 108–109.

55. Warning Out Book.

56. Ibid. Boston Selectmen, minutes, 28 June 1786, in *Record Commissioners* 25: 312.

57. In "The Transformation of the Law of Poverty in Eighteenth-Century Massachusetts," Douglas Lamar Jones states that "the law of poverty in eighteenth-century Massachusetts represented a tension between the material needs of the destitute and the needs of the larger society to control the costs of relief as well as the movements of the poor themselves." He goes on to say, "welfare and control were intrinsically related parts of the administration and enforcement of the poor laws. Ultimately, . . . the poor laws embraced both the needs of the poor and the economic and social interests of the townspeople who provided public relief." Jones, "Transformation of the Law," 155–156. For an informative work on warning out in Rhode Island see Ruth Wallis Herndon, *Unwelcome Americans: Living on the Margin in Early New England* (Philadelphia: University of Pennsylvania Press, 2001).

58. Boston Selectmen, minutes, 3 April 1777, 9 April 1777, 28 June 1786, in *Record Commissioners* 25: 34, 312.

59. Register of admissions to the almshouse, 3 April 1777, Boston Overseers of the Poor, records, MHS; Boston Selectmen, minutes, 30 April 1777, in *Record Commissioners* 25: 36.

60. Register of admissions to the almshouse, 27[?] March 1789, Boston Overseers of the Poor, records, MHS; State of Massachusetts Bay to the Town of Boston, Cost of Boarding in Alms Houses, 1 January 1779 [for 1778], Boston Town Papers, 1779.

61. Register of admissions to the almshouse, 5 June 1777, 20 July 1780, Boston Overseers of the Poor Records, records, MHS.

62. Petition to selectmen: Condition of Almshouse, Boston, 2 July 1793, Boston Town Papers, May–August 1793.

63. *Columbian Centinel* 4 March 1795.

64. A Meeting of the Freeholders and other Inhabitants of the Town of Boston [report by the Overseers of the Poor], April 1781, Boston Town Papers, 1781; register of admissions to the almshouse, 5 February 1777, 30 April 1777, Boston Overseers of the Poor, records, MHS; Boston Town Records, 10 April 1781, in *Record Commissioners* 26: 189, 191; Boston Town Records, 14 May 1784, in *Record Commissioners* 31: 31; Boston Selectmen, minutes, 24 September 1776, 5 February 1777, 14 January 1789, in *Record Commissioners* 25: 11, 28; Boston Selectmen, minutes, 14 January 1789, in *Record Commissioners* 27: 79.

65. Boston Town Records, 10 April 1781, 1 April 1782, in *Record Commissioners* 26: 191, 242.

66. Register of admissions to the almshouse, 6 October 1788, 6 February 1789, 11 January 1790, Boston Overseers of the Poor, records, MHS.

67. Children bound out 1756–1790, Boston Overseers of the Poor, records, MHS; Boston Taking Books, 1784, 1794, 1799; Lainhart, *First Boston City Directory*, 25; *Boston Directory* (Boston: John West, 1803), 72; *Boston Directory* (Boston: Edward Cotton, 1806), 72; *Boston Taxpayers in 1821* (Boston: True and Greene, 1822; repr. Camden, Maine: Picton Press, 1988, ed. Lewis Bunker Rohrbach), 100.

68. Record of money granted at monthly meetings, 4 April 1738–1 March 1769, Boston Overseers of the Poor, records, MHS. There are three such undated contracts in this file, but they appear to be from 1769.

69. Boston Selectmen, minutes, 22 January 1765, in *Record Commissioners* 20: 128.

70. Ibid., 3 February 1775, 15 March 1775, in *Record Commissioners* 23: 243–244, 246. All but twelve women received at least £1 in the February 1775 distribution of the Brooker trust. A two-pound, four-ounce loaf of brown bread or a three-pound, four-ounce loaf of rye bread could be purchased for 4 pence. As a comparison, in 1772 maintaining an individual at the almshouse for one week, where care was as cost-efficient as possible, cost 8 shillings, 8 pence, thus making outside relief more cost-effective from the perspective of the overseers of the poor and selectmen, especially during hard times. Boston Selectmen, minutes, 9 October 1772, in *Record Commissioners* 24: 143.

71. Boston Selectmen, minutes, 2 July 1777, 1 September 1777, 7 December 1777, 13 January 1778, 21 January 1778, 22 February 1779, 4 October 1779, 8 January 1784, 19 April 1786, 7 November 1786, 22 November 1786, in *Record Commissioners* 25: 43, 48, 54, 55, 56–57, 86–87, 102, 232, 299, 330, 331; *By-Laws and Town Orders*, 24, 36.

72. Boston Town Records, 13 March 1786, in *Record Commissioners* 31: 97–98.

73. Boston Town Records, 28 June 1781, in *Record Commissioners* 26: 205. On private contributions during the pre-Revolutionary era see also Nash, *Urban Crucible*, 186. Nash states, "As town expenditures for poor relief rose, so did private contributions" that were "centered in the churches." This pattern continues during the war and postwar years. The Boston Town Records clearly point to the reliance on private contributions for poor relief when the town treasury was seriously depleted or overdrawn.

74. For a discussion on eighteenth-century society and attitudes toward poverty and charity, see chap. 1 and 2 in David J. Rothman, *The Discovery of the Asylum: Social Order and Disorder in the New Republic* (Boston: Little, Brown & Co., 1971).

75. Boston Selectmen, minutes, 20 May 1776, 17 July 1776, in *Record Commissioners* 25: 2, 3; Boston Town Records, 8 November 1776, in *Record Commissioners* 18: 252. The town made periodic salary adjustment to allow for the high cost of living. See, for example, Boston Town Records, 15 December 1777, in *Record Commissioners* 18: 294.

76. Ushers were assistant teachers. James Carter served as an usher at North Writing School between 1761 and 1768 and then at Queen Street Writing School until 1773, when he was appointed master of the school. James Tileston began as an usher at North Writing School in 1754 until he was appointed as master in 1761. Samuel Holbrook worked as an usher at the South Writing School, also known as "Writing School in the Common" between 1745 and 1753, when he moved to the Queen Street Writing School for sixteen years before returning to South Writing as a master in 1769. Samuel Hunt began his service as a master to South Grammar in 1768, and Abiah Holbrook served as a master to South Writing between 1743 and 1769 after having worked as an usher at North Writing for approximately one year. He became an usher at Queen Street Writing School in 1773 "on the recommendation of Samuel Holbrook and James Carter." John Lovell served as usher and then master at South Grammar School for more than forty years beginning in the late 1720s and remained until the school closed in April 1775. He evacuated with the British in 1776 and died in Halifax two years later. His son James Lovell served as an usher in the same school starting in 1760. After the siege James Carter, James Tileston, and Samuel Holbrook all returned as masters to the same schools, but Samuel Hunt moved to South Grammar. Abiah Holbrook and James Lovell returned as ushers. By 1785 only Tileston, Carter, and Hunt remained. Robert Francis Seybolt, *Public Schoolmasters of Colonial Boston* (Cambridge, Mass.: Harvard University Press, 1939), 8–9, 12, 14–19.

77. John Tileston wrote to the Board of Selectmen in May 1777 that "since his Return to the Town" the number of schoolchildren in his care had increased to the point that he needed assistance. Three months earlier another schoolmaster wrote that the "number of Schollars have increased to more than 150 . . . to great a Duty for him alone to perform." He noted "his present sickness is in a great measure to be attributed to his close attention to the Instruction of the Youth." He likewise requested an usher. Similarly, "As the Schollars of the Grammar School have been the year past so numerous as to render it impossible for a Master to pay the Attention to Individuals, that they stand in need of, and the Number is daily increasing," schoolmaster Samuel Hunt requested an usher on July 21, 1777. John Tileston to the Selectmen of Boston, May 1777, Unknown author to the Selectmen of Boston, 1 March 1777, Samuel Hunt to The Selectmen of the Town of Boston, 21 July 1777, Boston Town Papers, 1777–1832; Boston Town Records, 7 July 1777, in *Record Commissioners* 18: 287; Boston Town Records, 23 May 1775, in *Record Commissioners* 31: 79.

78. *Boston Gazette* 31 July 1780.

79. Boston Town Records, 4 April 1780, in *Record Commissioners* 26: 123–124.

80. Although the law remained on the books, it is not clear from the records whether or not this practice was still taking place in the late eighteenth century in Boston. In various town meeting discussions and newspaper articles, concerns

about uneducated children and children not attending school clearly existed in the years following the Revolution. Shurtleff, *Topographical and Historical Description*, 127–129, 131–132.

81. To the Gentlemen the Selectmen of the Town of Boston, The Petition of a Number of Black Families citizens of the Town of Boston, 4 October 1796, Boston Town Papers, July–December 1796; To the Selectmen of Boston, Elisha Sylvester precepter, a natural inhabitant of the Commonwealth of Nassau, 16 May 1798, Boston Town Papers; Boston Selectmen, minutes, 15 May 1798, in *Record Commissioners* 27: 328.

82. Boston Town Records, 5 April 1784, in *Record Commissioners* 31: 18.

83. Samuel Adams to Jeremy Belknap, Boston, 30 March 1795, in *Collections of the Massachusetts Historical Society*, 1st ser., 4: 83. Boston Town Records, 5 April 1784, in *Record Commissioners* 31: 16.

84. Boston Town Records, 16 October 1789, in *Record Commissioners* 31: 208–209.

85. The System of Public Education Adopted by the Town of Boston 15 October 1789 [with amendments in December], System of Public Education (H.189.148), BPL/RBD.

86. *Independent Chronicle* 5 April 1790, 15 July 1790; *Boston Centinel* 14 July 1790.

87. Boston Town Records, 5 April 1784, in *Record Commissioners* 31: 16–17.

88. *Boston Gazette* 10 October 1791.

89. Seybolt, *Public Schoolmasters*, 3–19.

90. *Boston Gazette* 13 April 1795.

91. Boston Town Records, 5 April 1784, in *Record Commissioners* 31: 17.

92. *Boston Gazette* 18 March 1784, 13 May 1784, 2 June 1788, 28 May 1789. *New England Chronicle* 2 May 1776; *Independent Chronicle* 27 March 1788, *Columbian Centinel* 27 March 1788, 21 October 1790, 2 April 1791, 8 October 1791.

93. Boston Town Records, 5 April 1784, in *Record Commissioners* 31: 17.

94. Boston Selectmen, minutes, 8 August 1787, in *Record Commissioners* 27: 28.

95. Ibid., 19 May 1790, in *Record Commissioners* 27: 121. On needlework schools see Laurel Thatcher Ulrich, *The Age of Homespun: Objects and Stories in the Creation of an American Myth* (New York: Knopf, 2001).

96. Boston Selectmen, minutes, 31 August 1791, 25 March 1795, in *Record Commissioners* 27: 158, 257.

97. Ibid., 24 December 1795, in *Record Commissioners* 27: 276, 277.

98. Rutman, *Winthrop's Boston*, 181, 207; Warden, *Boston, 1689–1776*, 53–54, 56, 109, 115–116, 118, 120–121. Warden provides an informative discussion on the economic fluctuations in eighteenth-century Boston and the debate during the early decades concerning the public market and the issue of internal economic and market regulations.

99. Petition to the Selectmen for a Town Meeting, Boston Town Papers, 1776.

100. Boston Town Records, 12 February 1777, in *Record Commissioners* 18: 262. The January 1777 act was a response to a petition received by the General Court in November 1776 decrying those who were "lost to all Virtue, and the Love of their Country" as demonstrated by their acts of forestalling and engrossing. The act was repealed in September 1777, although Bostonians continued to pass such regulations, as found in their town records. Massachusetts Archives 181: 351; *Acts and Resolves, Public and Private of the Province of the Massachusetts Bay . . . Vol. V, Acts Passed, 1769–80* (Boston 1886), 811, 1,012, in Handlin and Handlin, "Revolutionary Economic Policy," 12, 15.

101. Boston Taking Book, 1784; Lainhart, *First Boston City Directory*, 33; Allen Crocker to Joseph Crocker, 25 September 1778, in Hannah Mather Crocker, *Reminiscences and traditions of Boston*, Mss 219, 277, R. Stanton Avery Special Collections Department, New England Historic Genealogical Society [NEHGS].

102. *Boston Gazette* 1 January 1781.

103. Handlin and Handlin, "Revolutionary Economic Policy," 22.

104. Boston Town Records, 17 August 1779, in *Record Commissioners* 26: 80; Handlin and Handlin, "Revolutionary Economic Policy," 22. Requests by groups of inhabitants for a regulated marketplace were not new. The "Regulation of Butchers, Hucksters, Forestallers . . . and the Market," for example, was a proposal that periodically resurfaced. Town records before the Revolution suggest that the issue of controls was a divisive one and enforcement not easy. The degree and breadth of concern regarding adherence to regulations appears to have intensified both during and immediately following the Revolution due to the severity of the economic crisis and lack of basic necessities. For cases of earlier attempts at regulation see, for example, Boston Town Records, 14 March 1747, 28 March 1747, 14 May 1751, in *Record Commissioners* 14: 135, 141–142, 196; Boston Town Records, 31 March 1767, in *Record Commissioners* 16: 210.

105. Boston Town Records, 17 August 1779, 14 September 1779, in *Record Commissioners* 26: 80, 87.

106. Petition relating to Hay Engine, February 1790, Boston Town Papers.

107. *Boston Gazette* 17 October 1791.

108. Boston Town Records, 12 August 1779, in *Record Commissioners* 26: 80–81.

109. Ibid., 17 August 1779, in *Record Commissioners* 26: 80.

110. Ibid., 14 September 1779, in *Record Commissioners* 18: 87.

111. Ibid., 27 September 1779, in *Record Commissioners* 26: 91–92. William Molineaux was one of the first members of the Boston Committee of Correspondence in 1773. Warden, *Boston, 1689–1776*, 257.

112. Boston Town Records, 17 August 1779, in *Record Commissioners* 26: 80.

Edward Countryman discusses corporatism and attitudes toward it in various states of the Confederation. "Philadelphians," he notes, "resolved that public control of the marketplace was the very 'spirit of liberty.'" See chap. 5, "Fourteen States," in Edward Countryman, *The American Revolution* (New York: Hill and Wang, 1985).

113. Boston Town Records, 10 March 1783, 25 March 1783, in *Record Commissioners* 26: 294, 301.

114. Ibid., 25 March 1783, in *Record Commissioners* 26: 302–303.

115. Ibid., 300–304. The fines were substantial in that they ranged from six to twelve shillings, which I have estimated, based upon food prices available for the time, would have purchased fish, bread, and vegetables for one meal of a family of four to six persons.

116. Boston Town Records, 18 March 1784, in *Record Commissioners* 31: 10; *Boston Gazette* 23 February 1784.

117. Boston Selectmen, minutes, 2 June 1779, 6 April 1784, in *Record Commissioners* 25: 93, 241.

118. Ibid., 12 April 1780, 8 December 1780, 12 July 1780, 26 June 1782, in *Record Commissioners* 25: 117, 126, 136, 183.

119. Petition of Joseph Stevens and Charles Cole on behalf of themselves and the Fishermen who supply the Boston Market, 2 April 1798, Petition from Stephen Gorham et al. to Selectmen, 24 September 1798, Petition Supporting Solomon Hewes to the Selectmen, 14 October 1798, Boston Town Papers; Boston Selectmen, minutes, 17 September 1798, in *Record Commissioners* 27: 342–343.

120. Boston Selectmen, minutes, 27 December 1802, 23 March 1803, 4 April 1803, 20 July 1803, 23 March 1808, 28 June 1809, in *Record Commissioners* 33: 169, 173, 190, 203, 368, 410.

121. Petition to Selectmen from Christopher Marshall et al. to end outdoor sales in State Street, 28 April 1797, Boston Town Papers.

122. Boston Selectmen, minutes, 21 April 1780, in *Record Commissioners* 25: 117; Boston Taking Books, 1780.

123. *Columbian Centinel* 9 August 1797, 4 March 1795.

124. Boston Town Records, 1 November 1757, in *Record Commissioners* 14: 321–323.

125. Ibid., Boston Selectmen, minutes, 12 October 1785, 19 October 1785, 7 June 1786, 11 October 1786, 18 October 1786, 25 October 1786, in *Record Commissioners* 25: 283, 307, 328–329.

126. Boston Town Records, 13 January 1783, in *Record Commissioners* 26: 287–289; *Boston Gazette* 23 December 1787. The licensed chimney sweeps were "Jonas Barker and Boy, near Winnisimmet-Ferry . . . Charles King, New-North Meeting . . . Charles Smith, Winter's Wharf . . . Lodowick Maloney, Juba Andrew In Green's Lane . . . John Craigan and Peter Vanderboth, Dutch Lane, South-End."

127. *Boston Gazette* 6 November 1780, 25 September 1780, 23 September 1782; *Independent Chronicle* 28 September 1780, 25 December 1788; Boston Town Records, 23 May 1785, in *Record Commissioners* 31: 79; reports of fire constantly appear throughout the selectmen's records. Fire and disease represented the most serious threats to the community.

128. *Independent Chronicle* 13 April 1786; *Boston Gazette* 17 April 1786.

129. Thomas Davis, Boston, to his sister, 30 July 1794 (Ms.2635.6), BPL/RBD; Report of the Committee Chairman, James Sullivan to the Inhabitants of the Town of Boston, December 1795, Committee of the several religious societies in the town (Ms.fBos.795.1), BPL/RBD.

130. *Columbian Centinel* 4 March 1795; Whitehill, *Topographical History*, 50.

131. Roger Lane, *Policing the City: Boston, 1822–1885* (New York: Atheneum, 1971), 7.

132. Untitled document to the selectmen calling for a town meeting [regarding town watch and police], March 1797, Boston Town Papers.

133. Boston Town Records, 30 December 1791, in *Record Commissioners* 31: 272–273; Lane, *Policing the City*, 9.

134. Boston Selectmen, minutes, 25 March 1778, in *Record Commissioners* 25: 62; Mr. William Pooke, The Selectmen having appointed you Constable of the Watch . . . , 28 June 1797, Mr. Jacob Polly, The Selectmen having appointed you Constable of the Watchmen . . . , 20 June 1797, Boston Town Papers, May–December 1797.

135. William Pooke, Report of the Market Watch, June 1797, July 1797, January 1798; Mr. John Low, Report of the Market Watch, 27 July 1795, 28 August 1795, July 1796; Robert Newman, Report of the West Boston Watch, 27 July 1795; Jacob Polly, Report of the North Watch, June 1797. All in Boston Town Papers.

136. Boston Selectmen, minutes, 26 March 1787, 15 August 1787, 26 March 1788, 29 September 1790, in *Record Commissioners* 27: 9, 30, 48, 134–135.

137. Boston Town Records, 22 March 1786, in *Record Commissioners* 31: 107.

138. *Independent Chronicle* 27 June 1793.

139. Ibid.

140. Boston Selectmen, minutes, 26 November 1783, 17 November 1784, in *Record Commissioners* 25: 229, 255.

141. *Columbian Centinel* 1 February 1794, 18 December 1799; *Boston Gazette* 12 October 1781, 7 March 1785, 12 June 1786, 28 December 1795, 2 May 1796, 2 January 1797; *Independent Chronicle* 19 January 1786; Boston Town Records, 24 March 1780, in *Record Commissioners* 26: 120; Boston Town Records, 19 March 1788, 21 May 1788, 24 May 1793, in *Record Commissioners* 31: 168, 176, 333; Boston Selectmen, minutes, 1 January 1783, 19 May 1786, 14 June 1786, in *Record Commissioners* 25: 203, 303, 309; Boston Selectmen, minutes, 20 March 1782, in

Record Commissioners 26, 170; Boston Selectmen, minutes, 3 August 1791, 22 October 1792, 11 June 1794, 13 June 1794, 18 November 1795, in *Record Commissioners* 27: 156, 191, 237, 238, 275.

142. See also Fenn, *Pox Americana*, 46–55, 89–90, 107–108, 264–265.

143. Eldad Taylor, Boston, to his wife, 18 March 1776, "Evacuation of Boston," 231–232; John B. Blake, *Public Health in the Town of Boston, 1630–1822*, Harvard Historical Studies, vol. 72 (Cambridge, Mass.: Harvard University Press, 1959), 127.

144. Boston Town Records, 1 May 1776, in *Record Commissioners* 25: 230.

145. Ibid., 19 July 1776, 31 July 1776, in *Record Commissioners* 25: 3–4, 5.

146. Ibid., 26 August 1776, in *Record Commissioners* 18: 240–241.

147. Ibid., 21 August 1776, 14 September 1776, in *Record Commissioners* 25: 6, 10. A detailed discussion of the inoculation procedure, hospitals, and cleansing may be found in Blake, *Public Health*, 126–131.

148. Boston Town Records, 9 March 1778, 10 March 1778, 11 March 1778, 15 March 1778, in *Record Commissioners* 25: 59, 60.

149. Blake, *Public Health*, 132.

150. Boston Town Records, 28 September 1792, in *Record Commissioners* 31: 305–306.

151. Inoculation costs listed in the town records, 31 August 1792, 2 September 1792, 7 September 1792, Boston Town Papers, 1777–1832; To the Selectmen of the Town of Boston requesting Small Pox Inoculation, 28 August 1792, Request to Selectmen for inoculating families, 25 February 1792, Boston Town Papers; Boston Town Records, 8 October 1792, 22 October 1792, in *Record Commissioners* 31: 307, 308, 309; Blake, *Public Health*, 137–139.

152. Boston Selectmen, minutes, 10 September 1792, 21 September 1792, 22 September 1792, 23 September 1792, 24 September 1792, 1 October 1792, in *Record Commissioners* 27: 212, 213–214, 217.

153. *Columbian Centinel* 5 August 1797; *Boston Gazette* 3 July 1797.

154. An excellent discussion on concepts and use of private and public space in the urban environment in early-nineteenth-century America can be found in Upton, "City as Material Culture," 53–54, 56.

155. Arthur M. Schlesinger, "A Panoramic View: The City in American History," in *The City in American Life: A Historical Anthology*, ed. Paul Kramer and Frederick L. Holborn (New York: G. P. Putnam's Sons, 1970), 17.

156. Warden, *Boston, 1689–1776*, 29.

157. The assessment of patterns of office holding are based upon data I compiled from the Boston Town Records between the years 1770 and 1795. Additional information and charts may be found in Carr-Frobose, "Cultural History of Boston," chaps. 3 and 5.

158. *By-Laws and Town-Orders*, 131, 135; Freeman, *Town Officer*, 76. See also

chap. 5, "Town Meeting Democracy," in Robert E. Brown, *Middle-Class Democracy and the Revolution in Massachusetts, 1691–1780* (Ithaca, N.Y.: Cornell University Press, 1955), 78–99. The assessment of voting patterns for the last two decades of the eighteenth century are based upon data I compiled from the Boston Town Records for the years 1770 to 1800.

159. For further discussion on the 1780s incorporation debates in Boston and comparisons with other towns in the Confederation see Merrill Jensen, *The New Nation: A History of the United States during the Confederation, 1781–1789* (New York: Alfred A. Knopf, 1950), 119–122.

Chapter Four

1. Boston Taking Books, 1784, 1799; Boston Marriages, 1752–1809, in *Record Commissioners* 30: 382, 459; West, *Boston Directory* (1796), in *Record Commissioners* 10: 266. North Street became Middle Street at the intersection of Fleet Street. Malcolm in one instance is listed as living on Middle Street, but all other references list the address as North Street.

2. Boston Taking Books, 1790, 1794, 1799; United States Direct Tax, 1798, in *Record Commissioners* 22: 153.

3. Boston Taking Books, 1780, 1784, 1790, 1794, 1799; *Boston Directory* (1803), 85; *Boston Directory* (1806), 84; *Boston Directory* (Boston: Edward Cotton, 1810), 132; Rohrbach, *Boston Taxpayers in 1821*, 110, 119.

4. Boston Town Records, 13 May 1783, in *Record Commissioners* 26: 314.

5. John J. McCusker and Russell R. Menard, *The Economy of British America 1607–1789: Needs and Opportunities for Study* (Chapel Hill: University of North Carolina Press, 1985), 161, 364, 365.

6. Hadfield, *Englishman in America*, 185. On bankruptcy in the revolutionary era see Bruce H. Mann, *Republic of Debtors: Bankruptcy in the Age of American Independence* (Cambridge, Mass.: Harvard University Press, 2002).

7. Requests for abatement of taxes in the 1786 Boston Taking Book, 27 February 1786, 19 February 1786; Boston Taking Books, 1780, 1784.

8. Boston Town Records, 11 December 1781, in *Record Commissioners* 26: 214.

9. Ibid., 214–215.

10. Shattuck, *Report to the Committee*, 3–5, 26. For the hardships that plagued Boston during the eighteenth century, see Carl Bridenbaugh, *Cities in Revolt: Urban Life in America, 1743–1776* (New York: Alfred A. Knopf, 1955; repr., New York: Oxford University Press, 1971), 18, 41, 48, 73, 76, 100–102, 126, 129, 230, 327 (citations are to the reprint), Warden, *Boston, 1689–1776*, 127–128, and Nash, *Urban Crucible*, 113, 114, 153, 158.

11. Shattuck, *Report to the Committee*, 3–5, 26; United States Bureau of the

Census, *A Century of Population Growth: From the First Census of the United States to the Twelfth, 1790–1900* (Washington, D.C.: Government Printing Office, 1909), 192.

12. James Bowdoin to Thomas Pownall, in Robert A. East, *Business Enterprise in the American Revolutionary Era* (New York: Columbia University Press, 1938; repr., Gloucester, Mass.: Peter Smith, 1964), 214.

13. This figure is based upon calculation of the data in five Boston Taking Books. Sons coming of age would also account for the increase in the number of heads of household. Based upon the average of six persons in each household, the figure of 40 percent growth from in-migration is not unrealistic and possibly conservatively low. The assessors listed the number of children in a family for only 79 heads of household in the 1794 Taking Book. The mean family size for the 79 households listed was 5.5 children. Only four families had fewer than four children and only four families had more than ten children. Although it is not possible to draw firm conclusions on family size for the entire community from only 2 percent of the total heads of household listed, the average of 5.5 children per family is not out of line with Jim Potter's average of four (surviving) children per household based on the 1790 national census. Lemuel Shattuck states that in 1784 there were 7.62 persons per house in Boston and 7.81 per house in 1790. This figure is for total persons, not only children. Boston Taking Books, 1780, 1784, 1790, 1794, 1799; Jim Potter, "Demographic Aspects of the Revolution and Its Aftermath," in Greene and Pole, *Blackwell Encyclopedia*, 565; see also Jim Potter, "Demographic Development and Family Structure," in Jack P. Greene and J. R. Pole, eds., *Colonial British America: Essays in the New History of the Early Modern Era* (Baltimore: Johns Hopkins University Press, 1984), 144–147; Shattuck, *Report to the Committee*, 4–5.

14. The sample group includes all heads of household from the following categories: baker, barber, blacksmith, cooper, cabinetmaker, chaise maker, chairmaker, goldsmith, silversmith, mastmaker, rigger, shipwright, shoemaker, and tailor. Data compiled from the Boston Taking Books, 1784, 1790, 1794.

15. In some instances death accounted for disappearance from the assessment records.

16. A small percentage of those appearing as new heads of household were inhabitants who were either recently widowed or sons come of age and establishing their own households.

17. Boston Taking Books, 1784, 1790, 1794.

18. Ralph V. Harlow, "Economic Conditions in Massachusetts During the American Revolution," *Publications of the Colonial Society of Massachusetts, Transactions, 1917–1919* (Boston 1918): 182–183.

19. Samuel Eliot Morison, *The Maritime History of Massachusetts, 1783–1860* (1921; repr., Boston: Northeastern University Press, 1979), 43; William J. Fowler

Jr., "Marine Insurance in Boston: The Early Years of the Boston Marine Insurance Company, 1799–1807," in Wright and Viens, *Entrepreneurs*, 163–164.

20. Boston Selectmen, minutes, 26 April 1786, in *Record Commissioners* 25: 300; Boston Town Records, 3 May 1786, in *Record Commissioners* 31: 118; Pemberton, "Topographical and Historical Description," 245, 255–256; Whitehill, *Topographical History*, 48–49, 51–52, 62; Oscar Handlin and Mary Flug Handlin, *Commonwealth: A Study of the Role of Government in the American Economy: Massachusetts, 1774–1861* (Cambridge, Mass.: Harvard University Press, 1947; repr. 1969), 76, 78–79; J. Leander Bishop, *A History of American Manufactures from 1608 to 1860*, 3 vols. (Philadelphia: E. Young & Co., 1861; repr., New York: A. M. Kelly, 1966) 1: 241, 497–498.

21. Boston Taking Books, 1784, 1790, 1794.

22. Boston Taking Book, 1799.

23. East writes that Higginson gained his wealth "in Salem in the early war years." Other Bostonians involved in privateering besides Higginson, Russell, and Jones included Joseph Barrell, John Codman, Leonard Jarvis, Mungo Mackey, and James Swan. As with Massachusetts North Shore men, John R. Livingston, originally from New York, "located in Boston during the war for commercial purposes." East goes on to state that "As Boston's war-time commercial interests grew, the town became a center of remarkable activity in the purchase and sale of foreign bills and drafts" and "shares passed rapidly from hand to hand" but that in a market where bills had "fluctuating values" they "might work good or evil for the individual merchant." Wealth was lost and gained. East, *Business Enterprise*, 37–39, 64–65, 66; Morison, *Maritime History of Massachusetts*, 35; Boston Town Records, 11 September 1786, in *Record Commissioners* 31: 130.

24. East, *Business Enterprise*, 52–53; T. H. Breen, in "An Empire of Goods: The Anglicization of Colonial America, 1690–1776," *Journal of British Studies* 25 (1986): 467–499, discusses the growth of a consumer society in eighteenth-century America, paralleling the same development in England. Although his article deals with the eighteenth century prior to the Revolution, the demand for European, and particularly British, goods appears to have not diminished. With the war's end the floodgates of importation once again opened. See also Neil McKendrick, John Brewer, and J. H. Plumb, *The Commercialization of Eighteenth-Century England* (Bloomington: Indiana University Press, 1982).

25. *Boston Gazette* 23 October 1780, 1 January 1781, 9 April 1781, 12 January 1784, 19 April 1784, 11 May 1784, 2 June 1788; Boston Taking Books, 1780, 1784, 1790.

26. Boston Taking Book, 1786. A sulkey was a two-wheeled, one-horse, one-person carriage; a phaeton was a four-wheeled carriage, pulled by one or two horses, with a folding top and seats in front and back; a chaise was a similar lightweight vehicle with only two wheels; and a chariot was a four-wheeled carriage usually used for more formal occasions.

27. Boston Taking Books, 1780, 1784, 1790, 1794; East, *Business Enterprise*, 232; Pinkney, *Christopher Gore*, 16.

28. East, *Business Enterprise*, 35.

29. Robert Treat Paine to Elbridge Gerry, 12 April 1777, quoted by Robert East in *Business Enterprise*, 214; James Warren to John Jay, 27 April 1779, quoted by Robert East in *Business Enterprise*, 227.

30. Eighteenth-century documents relating to tax assessment in Boston present numerous challenges. As G. B. Warden concluded, "procedures of assessment and taxation in Boston were so chaotic and subject to political manipulation that the surviving tax lists are not a valid indication at all of actual distribution of wealth and degrees of inequality." His point is supported by complaints of "inequitable assessments . . . abatement irregularities . . . residency fraud . . . and tax avoidance," discussed by Lewis Rohrbach in his introduction to the published 1821 taxpayers list. Allan Kulikoff utilized the 1790 Taking Book in his study that pointed to an "unequal society" in post-Revolutionary Boston. Lisa B. Lubow compiled information on artisans engaged in the house-building trades from the Taking Books for her study tracing the evolution of capitalist control of the building industry. Jackson Turner Main used the 1780 Taking Book to determine occupational categories, and from 1771 tax sources (not specifically Taking Books) he notes that 61 percent of Bostonians owned some realty and/or personalty. However, he speaks to the questionable accuracy of sources such as tax records in determining absolute wealth. After noting the limitations of available evidence, John W. Tyler has also made use of the Taking Books in his study of post-Revolutionary merchants in Boston. See also G. B. Warden, "Inequality and Instability in Eighteenth-Century Boston: A Reappraisal," *Journal of Interdisciplinary History* 6:4 (Spring 1976): 585–620; Allan Kulikoff, "The Progress of Inequality in Revolutionary Boston," *William and Mary Quarterly*, 3rd ser., 18, no. 3 (July 1971): 375–411; Rohrbach, *Boston Taxpayers in 1821*, 3; Lisa B. Lubow, "From Carpenter to Capitalist: The Business of Building in Postrevolutionary Boston," in Wright and Viens, *Entrepreneurs*, 181–209; Jackson Turner Main, *The Social Structure of Revolutionary America* (Princeton, N.J.: Princeton University Press, 1965), 38–39, 134–135; John W. Tyler, "Persistence and Change within the Boston Community, 1775–1790," in Wright and Viens, *Entrepreneurs*, 99–100, n. 8.

31. At an earlier stage of my research I understood the Taking Books to provide assessments for property owners only, a viewpoint that shaped my original analysis. Recently I have come to the view that it cannot be confirmed that all assessments in these records indicate the ownership of realty. For the purposes of analyzing realty ownership in the current work I used the 1799 Taking Book and 1798 U.S. Direct Tax Census, both of which are extant in their entirety. The resulting database provided a list of who owned realty, a description of the property, where it was located, and the owner's occupation. The 1798 Direct Tax did

not include realty below $100 in value. Had it done so, the percentage of property ownership for Bostonians in 1798/1799 may well have proved higher. For the purposes of analyzing those being assessed for taxes, I used the five Taking Books, which contain all twelve wards. The total heads of household in each were as follows: 1780, 2,212; 1784, 3,265; 1790, 3,117; 1794, 3,397; 1799, 4,437. With the exception of several pages for Ward 12 in the 1799 Taking Book, assessors did not record an assessment of personalty. Assessors applied flat assessment rates to realty (i.e. 25, 100, 150, 200) using a scale of fifty to fifty-three steps, depending upon the year. The numerical assessment was often accompanied by an additional description of the realty. For additional information including charts, see Jacqueline Barbara Carr, "A Change 'as Remarkable as the Revolution Itself': Boston's Demographics, 1780–1800," *New England Quarterly* 73, no. 4 (December 2000): 595–596. Additional transcribed data from the Boston Taking Books can be found in Carr-Frobose, "Cultural History of Boston."

32. The percentages of assessment in the Boston Taking Books were as follows: North End (Wards 1–5) 1784, 47 percent, 1790, 59 percent, 1794, 72 percent, 1799, 78 percent; Central District (Wards 6, 8, and 9) 1784, 59 percent, 1790, 67 percent, 1794, 70 percent, 1799, 65 percent; West End (Ward 7) 1784, 43 percent, 1790, 60 percent, 1794, 64 percent, 1799, 66 percent; South End (Wards 10–12) 1784, 57 percent, 1790, 62 percent, 1794, 65 percent, 1799, 66 percent. All data is compiled from the assessments in the Boston Taking Books for the years 1784, 1790, 1794, 1799.

33. Boston Taking Book, 1799; United States Direct Tax, 1798, in *Record Commissioners* 22: 2–442.

34. Boston Taking Book, 1799; West, *Boston Directory* (1796) in *Record Commissioners* 10: 227, 255; United States Direct Tax of 1798, in *Record Commissioners* 22: 8, 9, 234, 281; Ten of the African-American property owners lived in the West End (Ward 7). These were Prince Watts, soap boiler (who owned two houses and rented one out); Michael Williams, shopkeeper; Boston Faddy, bell-ringer; Julius Holden, tailor; the hairdresser Louis Glapion, who owned property jointly with George Middleton, a former barber employed in 1799 as a coachman; and Samuel Bean, Hamlet Earl, Peter Grant, and John Johnston, laborers. The properties of Watts, Faddy, and Earl bordered each other. Five men lived in the South End. Of these five retail shop owner Juba Hill, servant Thomas Freeman, and laborer John Billings resided in Ward 12. Thomas Freeman owned his property jointly with Joseph Almsly, who appears to have been white. The two men resided together. Cyrus Vassall, a resident of Ward 10, jointly owned a small piece of undeveloped land in Ward 7 with Derby Vassall, a resident of Ward 9. Prince Patterson the carter and William Harris (occupation unlisted) resided in Ward 2 of the North End. Since the 1798 tax did not assess properties with a value below $100, there may consequently be other black property owners not appearing in these records.

Boston Taking Book, 1799; U.S. Direct Tax, 1798, 34, 35, 45, 121, 154, 240, 260, 261, 268, 283, 309, 397; *First Census of the United States, 1790, Massachusetts*; Boston Taking Books, 1780, 1794.

35. Boston Taking Books, 1784, 1790, 1794, 1799. In her study of Boston's carpenters in post-Revolutionary Boston, Lisa Lubow determined that in 1790, 60 percent of the adult males were "laboring proprietors," members of the "middling sort" holding "36 percent of the town's taxable wealth." She further concluded that "of 150 craftsmen trained in carpentry, 77 percent owned property, worth an average of $400." Lubow, "From Carpenter to Capitalist," 181–209.

36. Boston Taking Books 1780, 1784, 1790, 1794, 1799.

37. Ibid.

38. Ibid.

39. Ibid. United States Direct Tax, 1798, in *Record Commissioners* 30: 84; West, *Boston Directory* (1796), in *Record Commissioners* 10: 275; *Boston Directory* (1803), 101.

40. Boston Taking Book, 1784; Boston Selectmen, minutes, 29 August 1781, in *Record Commissioners* 25: 155; List of Persons who subscribed Money to defray the Expence of filling up the Town Dock, 28 January 1784, Boston Town Papers.

41. Boston Taking Books, 1780, 1784, 1790, 1791, 1792, 1794, 1799; Boston Marriages, 1752–1809, in *Record Commissioners* 30: 79; The Names of the Inhabitants of Boston in 1790, As Collected for the First National Census, in *Record Commissioners* 22: 451; West, *Boston Directory* (1796), in *Record Commissioners* 10: 246.

42. "Slops" were inexpensive, ready-made clothes. These were sold to the general public, although originally they were clothes sold specifically to sailors. Boston Taking Books, 1780, 1784, 1790, 1791, 1792, 1794, 1799.

43. For additional information on the system of outwork (also referred to as "putting-out" or "given-out") see also Nancy F. Cott, *The Bonds of Womanhood: "Woman's Sphere" in New England, 1780–1835*, 2nd ed. (New Haven, Conn.: Yale University Press, 1997), 25, 39–40; Christine Stansell, *City of Women: Sex and Class in New York, 1789–1860* (New York: Knopf, 1982; repr., Chicago: University of Illinois Press, Illini Books, 1987), 15–16 (citations are to the reprint). Stansell discusses the evolution of this form of work for women by the nineteenth century. Stansell, 106–119.

44. Morison, *Maritime History of Massachusetts*, 36–37, 96; Hadfield, *Englishman in America*, 185.

45. *Independent Chronicle* 28 February 1788.

46. Edwin J. Perkins, *The Economy of Colonial America*, 2nd ed. (New York: Columbia University Press, 1988), 42.

47. Morison, *Maritime History of Massachusetts*, 43, 48–50.

48. William M. Fowler, "Marine Insurance in Boston: The Early Years of the

Boston Marine Insurance Company, 1799–1807," in Wright and Viens, *Entrepreneurs*, 163–164.

49. Boston Taking Books, 1780, 1784, 1790, 1794, 1799.

50. Ibid.; Lainhart, *First City Boston Directory*, 102; West, *Boston Directory* (1796), in *Record Commissioners* 10: 291.

51. Boston Taking Books, 1780, 1784, 1790, 1794, 1799. Three of the Truemans appear in the 1803 and 1806 Boston directories, two listed as caulkers and one as a shipwright. *Boston Directory* (1803), 123; *Boston Directory* (1806), 123.

52. Boston Taking Books, 1780, 1784, 1790, 1794, 1799. West, *Boston Directory* (1796), in *Record Commissioners* 10: 262; *Boston Directory* (1803), 79; *Boston Directory* (1806), 78.

53. Boston Taking Books, 1780, 1784, 1790, 1794.

54. Ibid., 1780, 1784, 1790, 1794, 1799.

55. Ibid., 1784, 1790, 1794.

56. Billy G. Smith, "The Vicissitudes of Fortune: The Careers of Laboring Men in Philadelphia, 1750–1800," in *Work and Labor in Early America*, ed. Stephen Innes (Chapel Hill: University of North Carolina Press, 1988), 242, 244–245.

57. Morison, *Maritime History of Massachusetts*, 29–30.

58. *Independent Chronicle* 25 May 1780; Ann Smith Lainhart, ed., "Abated Taxes in Boston in 1782," *New England Historical and Genealogical Register* 146 (April 1992): 179.

59. Boston Taking Books, 1780, 1784, 1790, 1794; *Boston City Directory, 1789*, in *Record Commissioners* 10: 290.

60. Boston Taking Books, 1780, 1784, 1790, 1794, 1799. West, *Boston Directory* (1796), in *Record Commissioners* 10: 280, *Boston Directory* (1803), 111; *Boston Directory* (1806), 110.

61. Boston Taking Books, 1780, 1784, 1790, 1794.

62. Ibid., 1780, 1784, 1790, 1794, 1799; Shattuck, *Report to the Committee*, 5–6.

63. William Donnison, accounts, 3 May 1790, 15 November 1791, [?] August 1792, 9 July 1795, 20 November 1795, 27 August 1796, 1 July 1797, 31 December 1796, 24 December 1797, 20 August 1799, in William Donnison account book, 1790–1833 (Mss A 786), R. Stanton Avery Special Collections Department, NEHGS.

64. New Brick Committee Meeting, 25 April 1785, 1 August 1785, 17 August 1785, 6 December 1785, New Brick Committee Book 1761–1800, BPL/RBD; Frederic C. Detwiller, "Thomas Dawes's Church in Brattle Square," *Old-Time New England* 64 (January–June 1979): 7; "The Records of the First Church in Boston, 1630–1868," ed. Richard D. Pierce, *Publications of the Colonial Society of Massachusetts* (1961): 271–274, in Edward M. Griffin, *Old Brick: Charles Chauncy of Boston, 1705–1787* (Minneapolis: University of Minnesota Press, 1980), 177.

65. Boston Taking Books, 1780, 1784, 1790, 1794, 1799; *Independent Gazette* 13 November 1788, 7 April 1791, 30 April 1795; *Boston Gazette* 9 April 1791, 23 September 1782.

66. *Independent Chronicle* 27 March 1788, 23 March 1795.

67. Boston Taking Books, 1780, 1784, 1790, 1794, 1799; *Boston Directory, 1789* in *Record Commissioners* 10: 180; *Boston Directory* (1806), 34; Boston Selectmen, minutes, 28 August 1782, in *Record Commissioners* 26: 191; Robert Mussey and Anne Rogers Haley, "John Cogswell and Boston Bombe Furniture: Thirty-Five Years of Revolution in Politics and Design," in *American Furniture*, ed. Luke Beckerdite (Hanover, N.H.: Chipstone Foundation, 1994), 79–80, 81.

68. Cromwell, *Other Brahmins*, 27.

69. The Taking Books list a number of African-American men as servants, but for the years examined are silent on the occupations of African-American women, who would have been forced into the marketplace by economic necessity. As was true for all women regardless of color, they would have occupied jobs at the bottom of the economic ladder with even some of the opportunities open to white women such as teaching or shopkeeping most likely closed to them at this time.

70. Boston Taking Books, 1784, 1790, 1794.

71. Ibid., 1780, 1784, 1790, 1794, 1799.

72. The assessors listed eighty-eight men by their forename only; an occupation is given for thirty-eight of these listings. Since some of those with first names only may be the same individual, it is not possible to make any positive determinations about this group, except that by and large they worked as servants. One was a barber, one a chairmaker's assistant, one a stagecoach driver, and another a "doctor's employ[ee]." Data compiled from Boston Taking Books, 1784, 1790, 1794.

73. Boston Taking Book, 1786.

74. Ibid., 1780, 1784, 1790, 1794, 1799.

75. *Independent Chronicle* 18 April 1788. See also Jacobs, "History of the Boston Negro," 37–39.

76. W. Jeffrey Bolster, *Black Jacks: African American Seamen in the Age of Sail* (Cambridge, Mass.: Harvard University Press, 1977), 4–5, 70, 158–159.

77. The powdered wigs tied at the nape of the neck with a bow and worn by men during the seventeenth and eighteenth centuries. These were also called periwigs.

78. Boston Selectmen, minutes, 24 June 1778, 1 July 1778, in *Record Commissioners* 25: 70; Boston Taking Books, 1780 1784, 1790, 1794, 1799.

79. Boston Taking Books, 1790, 1794, 1799.

80. The five black barbers who owned property were William Clark and James Morris, both of Ward 8, Cesar Holland and Jonathan Jonah, who lived in Ward 7, and George Miers, a resident of Ward 3. Data compiled from the Boston

Taking Books, 1780, 1784, 1790, 1794. In their work *Black Bostonians*, the Hortons note the important role the barbershop held in the local neighborhood and the black community as a whole. Horton and Horton, *Black Bostonians*, 36–37.

81. For the years spanning 1776 to the end of 1799, a total of 876 female heads of household can be identified through a combination of the Boston Taking Books and town directories, although this number is probably low because of the American Revolution having created a great number of widows. Of the 876 the occupation of slightly under 50 percent is identifiable and includes, in order of number, shopkeepers, boardinghouse keepers, schoolmistresses, the needle trades (mantua makers, "tailoresses" and "sempstresses," milliners), innkeepers, bakers, nurses, and washerwomen. The last two occupations do not appear until the 1799 Taking Book, when four women are listed as "nurse" and three as "washerwoman." For a thought-provoking study of women in Boston and other New England seaport towns during the era see Elaine Forman Crane, *Ebb Tide in New England: Women, Seaports, and Social Change, 1630–1800* (Boston: Northeastern University Press, 1998). Another perspective concerning the impact of the American Revolution on the lives of women, but not specific to New England maritime communities, may be found in Mary Beth Norton, *Liberty's Daughters: The Revolutionary Experience of American Women, 1750–1800* (Boston: Little, Brown & Co., 1980; repr. Ithaca, N.Y.: Cornell University Press, 1996).

82. Money raised by churches in Ward 12 for the soldiers wives & children who are now serving in the Continental Army, November 1777, Boston Town Papers, 1777.

83. Records of requests for tax abatements in the Boston Taking Book, 1786.

84. Boston Taking Books, 1784, 1790, 1794, 1799.

85. *Independent Chronicle* 22 July 1793.

86. Boston Selectmen, minutes, 24 September 1776, 5 February 1777, in *Record Commissioners* 25: 11, 28; Boston Selectmen, minutes, 14 January 1789, in *Record Commissioners* 27: 79.

87. *Independent Chronicle* 1 November 1781, 8 November 1781, 22 November 1781, 11 April 1782, 22 January 1783, 5 January 1786, 1 October 1789, 14 January 1790, 10 March 1791, 18 March 1790, 12 August 1790, 19 January 1795; *Boston Gazette* 28 February 1785.

88. Boston Selectmen, minutes, 12 August 1776, 2 September 1776, 11 September 1776, 6 August 1777, [?] September 1778, 28 August 1780, 21 February 1781, 29 August 1781, 28 January 1782, 21 August 1782, 28 August 1782, 21 January 1784, 14 September 1785, 11 August 1786, 15 August 1786, 13 September 1786, in *Record Commissioners* 25: 6, 8–9, 10, 46, 75, 128–129, 139, 155, 167, 189, 190–192, 235, 279, 320–321, 325; Boston Selectmen, minutes, 17 January 1787, 7 November 1787, 28 November 1787, 30 April 1788, 30 December 1789, 27 January 1790, 22 December 1790, 30 November 1791, in *Record Commissioners* 27: 3,

37, 39, 54, 108–109, 111, 139, 165; Licences granted by the Boston Selectmen for 1784, Boston Town Papers, July 1785; List of Account of [illeg.] Licensed as Retailers and Innholders August 1785, Boston Town Papers.

89. *Boston Gazette* 5 January 1784, 12 January 1784; Boston Taking Books, 1780, 1784, 1790, 1794.

90. Lainhart, *First Boston City Directory*, 26, 39, 44, 46; *Independent Chronicle* 8 November 1781, 3 March 1784; *Boston Gazette* 19 November 1780; Boston Town Records, 16 October 1789, in *Record Commissioners* 31: 209.

91. Boston Taking Books, 1790, 1794, 1799; Boston Selectmen, minutes, 1 September 1784, in *Record Commissioners* 25: 252; West, *Boston Directory* (1796), in *Record Commissioners* 10: 221, 228, 229, 231, 233, 235, 241, 243, 250, 253, 255, 264, 267, 270, 271, 273, 277, 278, 284, 287, 295. On women's education see Norton, *Liberty's Daughters*; Cott, *Bonds of Womanhood*; Linda K. Kerber, *Women of the Republic: Intellect and Ideology in Revolutionary America* (Chapel Hill: North Carolina University Press, 1980); and Joel Perlmann and Dennis Shirley, "When Did New England Women Acquire Literacy?" *William and Mary Quarterly* 3rd ser., 48, no. 1 (January 1991): 50–67.

92. *Independent Chronicle* 5 February 1784; *Boston Gazette* 1 March 1784.

93. Mantua makers were highly skilled dressmakers with training far beyond basic sewing skills. Lainhart, *First Boston City Directory*, 109; *Boston Directory* (1803), 135. The fashionable hats turned out by various milliners did not meet with the approval of everyone, however. In 1786 Harvard College furnished the doorkeeper at the Commencement ceremonies "with a Measure." It seemed that the "present mode of wearing Balloon Hatts [was] attended with disagreeable Effects in public Assemblies." In short, people could not see over or around the overly large fashionable hats of the day. It was therefore "voted to admit no Lady into the Meeting House on Commencement Day whose Hatt shall exceed the breadth of Fifteen Inches." The ladies also received the warning to "dispense with Hoops of an immoderate size." *Boston Gazette* 17 July 1786.

94. Norton, *Liberty's Daughters*, 142.

95. *Independent Chronicle* 20 October 1791; Boston Taking Books, 1790, 1794; West, *Boston Directory* (1796), in *Record Commissioners* 10: 233.

96. Boston Taking Books, 1790, 1794, 1799. Duck is a canvas cloth that was used for clothing, tents, and sails. The factory in Boston primarily produced canvas for sails. Cards were used to untangle the fibers of cotton, flax, and wool to collect and prepare for spinning as in "carding wool." For additional discussion on women in the needle trades and the cottage industry of both garment and shoe production during the early nineteenth century see Cott, *Bonds of Womanhood*; Stansell, *City of Women*; and Mary H. Blewett, *We Will Rise in Our Might: Workingwomen's Voices from Nineteenth-Century New England* (Ithaca, N.Y.: Cornell University Press, 1991), 2–7, 23–29.

97. Boston Taking Books, 1784; Boston Marriages, 1752–1809, in *Record Commissioners* 30: 414; Boston Town Records, 9 March 1778, in *Record Commissioners* 26: 5; Boston Selectmen, minutes, 16 August 1769, in *Record Commissioners* 23: 29; Boston Selectmen, minutes, 21 July 1779, 14 November 1781, in *Record Commissioners* 25: 97, 161.

98. *Independent Chronicle* 1 October 1789, 12 August 1790; Boston Taking Books, 1780, 1784, 1790, 1794, 1799; Boston Selectmen, minutes, 25 July 1781, 11 October 1786, 7 November 1786, in *Record Commissioners* 25: 152, 328, 330. Licences granted by the Boston Selectmen for 1784, Boston Town Papers, July 1785.

99. Boston Selectmen, minutes, 2 September 1776, in *Record Commissioners* 25: 9; *Boston Gazette* 30 April 1781, 31 July 1781.

100. Boston Marriages, 1752–1809, in *Record Commissioners* 30: 454; Boston Births, 1700–1800, in *Record Commissioners* 24: 319, 325; Boston Taking Books, 1780, 1784.

101. David W. Conroy, *In Public Houses: Drink and the Revolution of Authority in Colonial Massachusetts* (Chapel Hill: University of North Carolina Press, 1995), 318. See also Sharon Salinger, *Taverns and Drinking in Early America* (Baltimore: Johns Hopkins University Press, 2002).

102. See also Patricia Cleary, "'Who shall say we have not equal abilitys with the Men when Girls of 18 years of age discover such great capacitys?': Women of Commerce in Boston, 1750–1776," in Wright and Viens, *Entrepreneurs*, 39–61; and Nancy Cott's chapter, "Work," in *Bonds of Womanhood*, 19–62.

103. *Independent Chronicle* 14 December 1780.

104. Boston Town Records, 19 May 1785, in *Record Commissioners* 31: 77.

105. Collections of Massachusetts History Society, vol. 3, 276–277, in Bishop, *History of American Manufactures*, 209–210.

106. Lyman Horace Weeks, *A History of Paper-Manufacturing in The United States, 1690–1916* (New York: Burt Franklin, 1916; repr., 1969), 99–100.

107. *Columbian Centinel* 22 September 1790; *Independent Chronicle* 29 July 1790, 30 April 1795.

108. *Columbian Centinel* 22 September 1790; *Independent Chronicle* 29 July 1790, 30 April 1795; Boston Taking Books, 1780, 1784, 1790, 1794; West, *Boston Directory* (1796), in *Record Commissioners* 10: 257.

109. *Independent Chronicle* 30 April 1795; Boston Taking Books, 1780, 1784, 1790, 1794, 1799; Weeks, *Paper-Manufacturing*, 100; West, *Boston Directory* (1796), in *Record Commissioners* 10: 235; *Boston Directory* (1803), 33; *Boston Directory* (1806), 33; Baptismal Record of Ebenezer Clough, 12 April 1767, in *The New North Church Boston 1714*, comp. Thomas Bellow Wyman, ed. Ann S. Lainhart (Baltimore: Clearfield, 1995), 27; Boston Marriages, 1752–1809, in *Record Commissioners* 30: 124; United States Direct Tax, 1798, in *Record Commissioners*, 22: 125.

110. Gales and Seaton, *Annals of the Congress of the United States 1791–1793* (1849), in Weeks, *Paper-Manufacturing*, 103.

111. Handlin and Handlin, *Commonwealth*, 76, 78–79. See also Bishop on the history of paper hanging in the United States, in *American Manufactures*, 208–211.

112. Handlin and Handlin, *Commonwealth*, 78.

113. Bishop, *American Manufactures*, 241.

114. Ibid., 497–498.

115. *Independent Chronicle* 29 January 1789; Boston Taking Books, 1790, 1794; Bishop, *American Manufactures*, 497.

116. George Washington, Mount Vernon Papers, No. 12, 112, in Bishop, *American Manufactures*, 419–420.

117. John F. Kasson, *Civilizing the Machine: Technology and Republican Values in America, 1776–1900* (New York: Grossman Publishers, 1976; repr., New York: Penguin Books, 1977), 8; *Boston Gazette* 25 April 1791.

118. *Boston Gazette* 24 January 1785.

119. Ibid., 24 January 1785, 31 January 1785.

120. *Independent Chronicle* 6 January 1791; *Boston Gazette* 5 November 1784; Cheever to various English merchants, 15 January 1779, 2 February 1779, 29 September 1781, Caleb Davis Papers 26, 23, in East, *Business Enterprise*, 32–36; Codman and Smith Letterbook, 22 February 1781, in East, *Business Enterprise*, 32; G. E. Meredith, *Descendants of Hugh Amory* (London: 1901), 231, East, *Business Enterprise*, 32.

121. *Boston Gazette* 27 February 1786.

CHAPTER FIVE

1. *Independent Chronicle* 14 February 1788.

2. *Boston Gazette* 11 February 1788.

3. The mechanics organized the parade. Edward Countryman states that merchants and farmers participated at the invitation of the mechanics. Artisan parades, which were "frequent events in the decades that followed" 1788, "rapidly became a way by which artisans would resist what the rulers of the United States were up to, rather than a means for showing agreement with it." Edward Countryman, *The American Revolution*, American Century Series (New York: Hill and Wang, 1985), 226–227.

4. *Independent Chronicle* 14 February 1788.

5. Ibid.

6. Ibid.

7. *Boston Gazette* 11 February 1788.

8. *Independent Chronicle* 14 February 1788.

9. Ibid.

10. *Boston Gazette* 11 February 1788; *Independent Chronicle* 14 February 1788.

11. *Boston Gazette* 11 February 1788.

12. John P. Kaminsky and Richard Leffler, eds. *Creating the Constitution, Sources of the American Tradition* (Acton, Mass.: Copley Publishing Group, 1999), xviii. On the Massachusetts ratification convention, see also Thomas H. O'Connor and Alan Rogers, *This Momentous Affair: Massachusetts and the Ratification of the Constitution of the United States* (Boston: Trustees of the Public Library of the City of Boston, 1987).

13. *Massachusetts Gazette* 8 January 1788; *Massachusetts Centinel* 9 January 1788, in Kaminsky and Leffler, *Creating the Constitution*, 164–166.

14. For an informative discussion on the ways in which celebrations such as this served in creating and shaping a nationalist sentiment, see David Waldstreicher, *In The Midst of Perpetual Fetes: The Making of American Nationalism, 1776–1820* (Chapel Hill: University of North Carolina Press, 1997).

15. *Independent Chronicle* 19 October 1780.

16. *Boston Gazette* 1 March 1784.

17. Ibid., 18 February 1782, 14 October 1782; *Independent Chronicle* 6 July 1780, 18 February 1790.

18. *Independent Chronicle* 26 March 1795, 21 September 1795.

19. *Massachusetts Gazette* 8 January 1788, in Kaminsky and Leffler, *Creating the Constitution*, 165.

20. Gordon S. Wood, *The Creation of the American Republic, 1776–1787*, published for the Institute of Early American History and Culture (Chapel Hill: University of North Carolina Press, 1969), 422. Wood explains that the "frenzied public uproar" against the social club "is inexplicable, and indeed ludicrous, unless viewed within the terms in which contemporaries described social character." Wood discusses the club, what it symbolized, and the fears that existed among the American people during the 1780s (422–425).

21. Wood, *Creation of the American Republic*, 422.

22. *By-Laws and Town-Orders*, 47, 92.

23. In some instances the clerk recorded a count of the inhabitants' votes, though not always. Boston Selectmen, minutes, 28 January 1782, 13 February 1782, 15 February 1782, in *Record Commissioners* 25: 167, 168; Boston Town Records, 11 March 1782, in *Record Commissioners* 26: 228.

24. *Boston Gazette* 12 September 1757.

25. Boston Selectmen, minutes, 8 November 1767, in *Record Commissioners* 20: 111.

26. Boston bylaws forbade the throwing of snowballs under penalty of fine because of the damage that might result. The use of fireworks was also prohibited. Children or servants over the age of twelve and adults caught throwing fireworks could be either fined or placed in the town stocks. Bylaws also required that all

sleighs have bells when driving through the town to prevent accidents. *By-Laws and Town-Orders*, 12–13, 104, 105–106; John Andrews, Boston, to William Barrell, Philadelphia, 6 January 1775, in "Letters of John Andrews," 393; John Barker diary, 18 January 1775, in *British in Boston*, 21.

27. *Recollections of Samuel Breck*, in Scudder, "Life in Boston," 172. Based upon Breck's description of the content of the skits performed, Scudder suggests that the origin of the "Anticks" behavior derives from an old Cornwall mystery play involving such characters as St. George, the Dragon, Father Christmas, the Turkish knight, and the King of Egypt.

28. Boston Selectmen, minutes, 15 December 1784, 22 December 1784, in *Record Commissioners* 25: 256–257.

29. Ibid., 8 April 1778, 21 August 1781, 9 August 1781, 23 November 1785, in *Record Commissioners* 25: 63, 153, 155, 286.

30. *Boston Gazette* 3 May 1789.

31. Virginians built the first colonial theater establishment in British North America in 1716. Twenty years later South Carolinians built a theater in Charleston, and both New York and Philadelphia had theaters by 1750, although in 1682 the Pennsylvania Assembly had passed legislation mandating harsh penalties, including fines, "public condemnation," and even hard labor, for those "whosoever shall introduce into this Province, or frequent such rude and riotous sports and practices as prizes, . . . stage-plays, masques, revels, bull-baiting, [and] cock-fightings." Kenneth Silverman, *A Cultural History of the American Revolution: Painting, Music, Literature, and the Theatre in the Colonies and the United States from the Treaty of Paris to the Inauguration of George Washington, 1763–1789* (New York: Thomas Y. Crowell Co., 1976), 59, 66; Glynne Wickham, *A History of the Theatre*, 2nd ed. (London: Phaidon Press, 1992), 168.

32. Silverman, *Cultural History*, 66.

33. Edmund S. Morgan, "Puritan Hostility to the Theatre," *Proceedings of the American Philosophical Society* 110 (October 1966): 341–342.

34. Silverman, *Cultural History*, 66.

35. William W. Clapp Jr., *A Record of the Boston Stage* (Boston: James Munroe & Co., 1853), 2. For further discussion on perceptions of and attitudes toward the theater in Massachusetts see Jean-Christophe Agnew, *Worlds Apart: The Market and the Theater in Anglo-American Thought, 1550–1750* (Cambridge, Mass.: Cambridge University Press, 1986), chap. 4.

36. Clapp, *Record of the Boston Stage*, 2.

37. *By-Laws and Town-Orders*, 92–93; Clapp, *Record of the Boston Stage*, 2–3; Silverman, *Cultural History*, 67. Silverman notes that in 1762 the Douglass and Hallam theater company (the London Company) attempted to perform in Providence, Rhode Island, which likewise enacted severe antitheater legislation. The Rhode Island law imposed a penalty of £50 per day and £100 on each actor. De-

spite the tactics of winning the approval of governors and other leading officials, troupes were unsuccessful in adding New England to their circuit. Most likely the severe fines imposed in New England kept the acting companies in the middle and southern colonies.

38. Clapp, *Record of the Boston Stage*, 2; Arthur Hornblow, *A History of the Theatre in America from Its Beginnings to the Present Time*, 3 vols. (New York: J. B. Lippincott & Co., 1919) 2: 16.

39. Wickham, *History of the Theatre*, 168; Silverman, *Cultural History*, 59.

40. Ford et al., *Journals of the Continental Congress* 1: 79; Hornblow, *Theatre in America* 2: 17–18.

41. *Columbian Centinel* 4 April 1789.

42. *Independent Chronicle* 23 July 1789; Pemberton, "Topographical History and Description," 253.

43. *Boston Gazette* 4 January 1790.

44. Ibid.

45. *Columbian Centinel* 16 June 1790.

46. *Independent Chronicle* 22 November 1792.

47. *Boston Gazette* 4 January 1790.

48. Ibid.

49. *Columbian Centinel* 12 June 1790.

50. Ibid., 9 June 1790, 12 June 1790.

51. Ibid.

52. *Columbian Centinel* 16 June 1790.

53. *Independent Chronicle* 4 November 1790.

54. *Columbian Centinel* 9 March 1791, 9 April 1791, 11 May 1791.

55. Ibid., 26 October 1791.

56. Ibid., 9 March 1791, 9 April 1791.

57. Ibid., 26 October 1791.

58. Ibid.

59. Boston Town Records, 26 October 1791, 9 November 1791, in *Record Commissioners* 31: 255–266, 267; *Boston Gazette* 31 October 1791.

60. Boston Town Records, 26 October 1791, in *Record Commissioners* 31: 265–268; *Columbian Centinel* 29 October 1791; *Independent Chronicle* 26 March 1789; Boston Taking Books, 1780, 1784.

61. Boston Town Records, 26 October 1791, in *Record Commissioners* 31: 265–268; *Columbian Centinel* 29 October 1791. In January 1792 Mr. Gardiner informed the legislature that three-quarters of those present at the town meeting voted in favor of the petition. *Columbian Centinel* 18 January 1792.

62. *Boston Gazette*, 31 October 1791; *Columbian Centinel* 29 October 1791.

63. *Columbian Centinel* 29 October 1791. The editor of the *Centinel* noted the following in his coverage of the town meeting. "It was the intention of the Editor

to have given an accurate sketch of this debate, but not being able in the afternoon, from the numbers attending to obtain a suitable seat." Still, the *Centinel* provided the best coverage of Boston's three newspapers.

64. Boston Town Records, 26 October 1791, in *Record Commissioners* 31: 267–268.

65. Boston Taking Books, 1780, 1784; *Boston City Directory, 1789,* in *Record Commissioners* 10: 191; *Columbian Centinel* 9 November 1791.

66. *Boston Gazette* 13 October 1791; *Boston City Directory, 1789,* in *Record Commissioners* 10: 32, 72, 82, 87; West, *Boston Directory* (1796), in *Record Commissioners* 10: 237, 269, 276, 279; Rules and Regulations of the Boston Library Society, in *Catalogue of Books in the Boston Library, January 1, 1795,* Early American Imprints, 1st ser., no. 28317.

67. Ellen Susan Bulfinch, *The Life and Letters of Charles Bulfinch, Architect, with other Family Papers* (Boston: Houghton Mifflin Co., 1896), 77.

68. Harrison Gray to his grandson, Harrison Gray Otis, 3 January 1792, in *Publications of the Colonial Society of Massachusetts: Transactions, 1911–1913* 14 (Boston, 1913): 345.

69. Samuel Adams to James Warren, 4 November 1775, *Writings of Samuel Adams,* vol. 3, 1773–1777 (G. P. Putnam's Sons, 1907; repr., New York: Octagon Books, 1968), 235 (citation is to the reprint).

70. *Columbian Centinel* 12 November 1791, 18 January 1792.

71. Ibid.; "The Legislative Proceedings (From the Massachusetts Magazine)," in Hornblow, *Theatre in America* 2: 16–17.

72. *Columbian Centinel* 1 February 1792. In the July 7, 1792, issue of the *Columbian Centinel* an article appears titled "Gardiner on the Theatre." Whether or not Mr. Gardiner "tired the patience of the House" we may never know, but his "learned Speech" was published in June 1792. The *Columbian Centinel* advertised that "For the amusement of such of our readers, who cannot readily come at the Book, we shall insert in the Centinel parts of this entertaining Dissertation . . . which we have the Author's liberty to reprint."

73. *Columbian Centinel* 26 November 1791.

74. Ibid., 26 September 1792.

75. Ibid., 3 December 1791, 21 December 1791.

76. Ibid., 22 December 1791.

77. Ibid., 1 February 1792.

78. Ibid., 3 December 1791, 22 December 1792.

79. Ibid., 3 December 1791, 21 December 1791, 11 August 1792, 15 August 1792.

80. *Independent Chronicle* 15 August 1792.

81. *Columbian Centinel* 8 September 1792.

82. *Boston Gazette* 20 August 1792; *Independent Chronicle* 23 August 1792.

83. *Independent Chronicle* 23 August 1792.

84. Bulfinch, *Charles Bulfinch*, 94; *Boston Gazette* 3 September 1792; *Independent Chronicle* 13 December 1792. Arthur Hornblow lists the group of gentlemen involved with constructing the Exhibition Room as Dr. Charles Jarvis, Joseph Russell, Henry Jackson, Joseph Barrell, and Joseph Russell Jr. He describes the theater as having "a pit, a row of boxes forming three sides of a square, and a gallery, the theatre accommodating about five hundred persons." Hornblow, *Theatre in America* 2: 18, 225.

85. *Boston Gazette* 20 August 1792, 8 October 1792, 15 October 1792, 22 October 1792, 12 November 1792, 19 November 1792, 26 November 1792, 3 December 1792, 10 December 1792; *Columbian Centinel* 22 August 1792, 1 September 1792, 22 September 1792, 6 October 1792; Handbill of the Opening Night of the New Exhibition Room, reprinted in William W. Ball, "Old Federal Street Theatre," *Publications of the Bostonian Society*, vol. 8 (Boston: T. R. Marvin & Son, Printers, 1911): 49.

86. *Boston Gazette* 20 August 1792, 3 September 1792, 20 September 1792; *Columbian Centinel* 12 September 1792, 26 September 1792, 15 December 1792; *Independent Chronicle* 16 August 1792, 22 November 1792, 13 December 1792, 27 December 1792.

87. *Independent Chronicle* 30 August 1792, 6 September 1792, 11 October 1792; *Columbian Centinel* 8 September 1792; *Boston Gazette* 3 September 1792.

88. *Boston Gazette* 3 September 1792.

89. *Independent Chronicle* 13 December 1792.

90. *Boston Gazette* 20 August 1792.

91. Ibid., 3 September 1792.

92. Ibid., 20 August 1792.

93. *Columbian Centinel* 8 September 1792.

94. John Hancock to Senate and House, November 1792, Hancock Papers, MHS, in William Fowler Jr., *The Baron of Beacon Hill: A Biography of John Hancock* (Boston: Houghton Mifflin Co., 1900), 278–279.

95. John Hancock to Senate and House, November 1792, Hancock Papers, MHS, in Ball, "Old Federal Street Theatre," 47–48.

96. *Independent Chronicle* 13 December 1792; *Columbian Centinel* 8 December 1792.

97. *Columbian Centinel* 8 December 1792, 28 December 1792; *Independent Chronicle* 13 January 1792.

98. The next day, Harper placed a notice in the newspaper thanking the members of the audience for their support and for their refusal to accept the return of their admissions. *Columbian Centinel* 8 December 1792, 28 December 1792; *Independent Chronicle* 13 December 1792; Ball, "Old Federal Street Theatre," 50.

99. One of the justices wanted to dismiss Harper because "there had not been

an oath or affirmation of his guilt before the warrant was issued." His counsel then "objected to the legality of the warrant, as contrary to the 14th article of the Declaration of Rights, which requires, that no warrant shall be issued, except upon complaints made upon oath. . . . [T]he complaint upon which the present warrant was issued not being made upon oath, the warrant consequently was illegal." *Columbian Centinel* 8 December 1792; *Independent Chronicle* 13 December 1792.

100. *Columbian Centinel* 28 December 1792.

101. *Independent Chronicle* 3 January 1793.

102. Ibid.

103. *Independent Chronicle* 16 August 1792; 13 December 1792; 27 December 1792; *Boston Gazette* 20 August 1792.

104. *Independent Chronicle* 27 December 1792.

105. *Boston Gazette* 3 September 1792; *Independent Chronicle* 13 December 1792; Boston Taking Book, 1790. This manuscript is a tax assessment document. It includes a listing of values of real property owned by heads of household in 1790, totaling 3,177 men and women. Thus percentage categories are based upon real property only.; Boston Town Records, 3 August 1790, 12 March 1782, 8 May 1792, in *Record Commissioners* 31: 241, 277, 279, 289. The names of the five men assisting Harper and Powell are listed in Hornblow, *Theatre in America* 2: 18.

106. Boston Town Records, 26 October 1791, 12 March 1792, 21 December 1792, in *Record Commissioners* 31: 266, 276, 314; *Boston Gazette* 3 October 1791; *Columbian Centinel* 27 March 1793; Boston Taking Book, 1790; Records of Suffolk Deeds [pertaining to deed transactions relating to the Federal Street Theater], MHS; *Boston City Directory, 1789*, in *Record Commissioners* 10.

107. *Columbian Centinel* 22 December 1792; *Independent Chronicle* 27 December 1792.

108. Boston Town Records, 9 November 1791, in *Record Commissioners* 31: 267–268, 313–314; *Independent Chronicle* 27 December 1792.

109. Boston Town Records, 21 December 1792, in *Record Commissioners* 31: 313–315.

110. *Columbian Centinel* 22 December 1792; *Independent Chronicle* 27 December 1792.

111. *Independent Chronicle* 27 December 1792.

112. Ibid., 7 March 1793.

113. *Columbian Centinel* 27 March 1793, 3 April 1793; *Columbian Centinel* 28 March 1793.

114. *Boston Gazette* 14 January 1793, 21 January 1793, 28 January 1793, 18 March 1793, 25 March 1793, 8 April 1793, 22 April 1793, 6 May 1793, 27 May 1793; *Columbian Centinel* 23 March 1793, 30 March 1793, 15 May 1793, 25 May 1793, 20 May 1793, 23 May 1793, 29 May 1793, 5 June 1793, 1 February 1794, 22 February 1794. The six trustees appointed to the theater included the three

men who from the beginning fought so hard for the repeal of the 1750 act: Joseph Russell, Perez Morton, and Charles Bulfinch. *Boston Gazette* 15 April 1793.

115. Bulfinch, *Charles Bulfinch*, 95.

116. *Columbian Centinel* 5 February 1794.

117. Pemberton, "Topographical and Historical Description," 255.

118. *Columbian Centinel* 1 February 1794, 22 February 1794.

119. Ibid., 30 May 1795, 13 June 1795, 24 June 1795.

120. Ibid., 24 June 1795.

121. *Independent Chronicle* 26 May 1791; *Boston Gazette* 30 May 1791, 28 December 1795, 18 July 1796; *Columbian Centinel* 27 July 1791, 26 May 1794, 14 June 1794; "Bowen's Columbia Museum," handbill (Boston: D. Bowen, 1798), *Early American Imprints*, no. 33443, 33444, 2nd ser.

122. *Boston Gazette* 28 December 1795.

123. Ibid., 9 January 1786, 23 January 1786, 15 January 1787, 22 January 1787, 23 July 1787, 13 September 1790, 25 April 1791; *Columbian Centinel* 17 April 1786, 22 September 1790, 11 December 1793, 2 August 1794; *Independent Chronicle* 18 September 1788, 11 December 1788, 8 December 1791.

124. *Columbian Centinel* 14 June 1798, 14 February 1798.

125. Letter to the Selectmen of Boston from John Noel, Mayor of Savannah, 29 November 1796, Boston Town Papers, January 1797; Clapp, *Record of the Boston Stage*, 49; *Columbian Centinel* 24 May 1794, 2 July 1794.

126. To the Gentlemen Selectmen of the Town of Boston, Petition relative to [the] Theatre, May 1796, Boston Town Papers, January–June, 1796; Boston Taking Books, 1796, 1799; Boston Town Records, 11 May 1776, in *Record Commissioners* 31: 431.

127. *Independent Chronicle* 8 September 1796; *Columbian Centinel* 14 September 1796.

128. *Boston Gazette* 9 May 1796; Hornblow, *Theatre in America* 2: 254–355.

129. Boston Taking Book, 1799; Clapp, *Record of the Boston Stage*, 42, 50.

130. *Independent Chronicle* 5 February 1798; *Columbian Centinel* 2 February 1798.

131. *Independent Chronicle* 5 February 1798; *Columbian Centinel* 2 February 1798; Pemberton, "Topographical and Historical Description," 255.

132. *Columbian Centinel* 14 February 1798.

133. Ball, "Old Federal Street Theatre," 62, 64; *Publications of the Colonial Society of Massachusetts: Transactions 1900–1902* 7 (Boston: 1905): 210.

134. *Independent Chronicle* 8 September 1796, 14 February 1798; *Columbian Centinel* 28 December 1796, 8 February 1798.

135. On the controversy over legalization of theater and on its relation to liberalism and incorporation of the town of Boston, see T. A. Milford, "Boston's Theater Controversy and Liberal Notions of Advantage," *New England Quarterly* 72, no. 1 (1999): 61–68.

Epilogue

1. West, *Boston Directory* (1796), in *Record Commissioners* 10: 217–220. West notes that his introduction, "A General Description of Boston," is "extracted *by permission*, from the Rev. Dr. Morse's Gazetteer of America, a work now in the press, and which will be published in the course of the present year."

2. Writers' Program of the Works Progress Administration in the State of Massachusetts, comp., *Boston Looks Seaward: The Story of the Port, 1630–1940*, Boston Port Authority (Boston: Bruce Humphries, 1941), 68.

3. West, *Boston Directory* (1796), in *Record Commissioners* 10: 217–220.

4. *Independent Chronicle* 14 February 1788.

5. George H. Moore, *Notes on the History of Slavery in Massachusetts* (New York: D. Appleton & Co., 1866), 228–236. Moore discusses this law and provides the names of those men and women listed in the public notice. The notice listed places of origin as New Hampshire, Connecticut, Rhode Island, New York, New Jersey, Pennsylvania, Maryland, Virginia, North Carolina, South Carolina, Nova Scotia, the West Indies, Africa, France, and Britain. He also notes that the state law may have been tied to concerns about the harboring of possible fugitive slaves. See also Litwack, *North of Slavery*, 16.

6. WPA, *Boston Looks Seaward*, 70.

7. Whitehill, *Topographical History*, 84–86.

8. L. H. Butterfield et al., eds., *Diary and Autobiography of John Adams*, vol. 3 (Cambridge, Mass., 1961), 193–194, in Edmund S. Morgan, *The Meaning of Independence: John Adams, Thomas Jefferson, George Washington* (New York: W. W. Norton & Co., 1976), 6–7.

Bibliography

A NOTE ON UNPUBLISHED PRIMARY SOURCES

A substantial portion of the primary source material used in this work consists of unpublished records kept by the town of Boston between 1775 and 1800. The Boston Taking Books located in the Rare Book Room of the Boston Public Library provided an important foundation for my work, as did the loose papers on town matters found in the Rare Book Room's collection of Boston Town Papers. The Taking Books utilized include volumes from 1780, 1784, 1790, 1794, and 1799 in their entirety (Wards 1 through 12). The years 1785, 1786, 1787, 1788, 1791, 1792, and 1796 were fully examined but selectively analyzed, as records for all twelve wards are not extant. The Rare Book Room also holds the Adlow Collection, which contains licences issued by the town, bills, and summonses. The study of the Boston's poor in chapter 3 draws upon the manuscript containing the Records of the Boston Overseers of the Poor for the early 1790s, which is housed at the Massachusetts Historical Society, as are the Matthew Ridley Papers. The Hannah Crocker Papers and account books of William Donnison are located in the collections of the New England Historic Genealogical Society. The letters of Thomas Davis and William Bant and the records of the New Brick [church] Committee may be found in the Rare Book Room of the Boston Public Library.

PUBLISHED PRIMARY SOURCES

Adams, Samuel. Samuel Adams to Jeremy Belknap, Boston, 30 March 1795. *Collections of the Massachusetts Historical Society*, 1st ser., 4: 83.

Anonymous. "Letters to Gardiner Greene." *Massachusetts Historical Society Proceedings* 13 (June 1873): 56–63.

Barker, John. *The British in Boston: Being the Diary of Lieutenant John Barker of the*

King's Own Regiment from November 15, 1774 to May 31, 1776. Notes by Elizabeth Ellery Dana. Cambridge, Mass.: Harvard University Press, 1924.

Boston Record Commissioners. *Reports of the Record Commissioners of the City of Boston*. 31 vols. Boston, 1876–1904.

———. *Boston Births, 1700–1800*. Vol. 24, 1894.

———. *Boston Marriages, 1700–1751*. Vol. 28, Boston 1898.

———. *Boston Marriages, 1752–1809*. Vol. 30, Boston 1903.

———. *Miscellaneous Papers*. Vol. 10, Boston 1886.

———. *Boston Town Records 1729–1742*. Vol. 12, Boston 1885.

———. *Boston Town Records 1742–1757*. Vol. 14, Boston 1885.

———. *Boston Town Records 1758–1769*. Vol. 16, Boston 1860.

———. *Boston Town Records 1770–1777*. Vol. 18, Boston 1887.

———. *Boston Town Records 1778–1783*. Vol. 26, Boston 1895.

———. *Boston Town Records 1784–1796*. Vol. 31, Boston 1903.

———. *Boston Town Records 1796–1813*. Vol. 35, Boston 1905.

———. *Selectmen's Minutes 1701–1715*. Vol. 11, Boston 1884.

———. *Selectmen's Minutes 1764–1768*. Vol. 20, Boston 1889.

———. *Selectmen's Minutes 1769–1775*. Vol. 23, Boston 1893.

———. *Selectmen's Minutes 1776–1786*. Vol. 25, Boston 1894.

———. *Selectmen's Minutes 1787–1798*. Vol. 27, Boston 1896.

———. *United States Direct Tax of 1798 and United States Census of 1790 For Boston Only*. Vol. 22, Boston 1890.

Boston City Directory, 1789. Boston: John Nerman, 1789. In *Reports of the Record Commissioners*, vol. 10.

Boston Directory. Boston: John West, 1803.

Boston Directory. Boston: Edward Cotton, 1806.

Boston Directory. Boston: Edward Cotton, 1810.

Boston Gazette. 1774–1795.

Bradford, S. Sydney, ed. "The Common British Soldier: From the Journal of Thomas Sullivan, 49th Regiment of Foot." *Maryland Historical Magazine* 62 (September 1967): 219–253.

Butterfield, L. H., Marc Friedlaender, and Mary-Jo Kline, eds. *The Book of Abigail and John: Selected Letters of the Adams Family, 1762–1784*. Cambridge, Mass.: Harvard University Press, 1975.

———. Wendell D. Garrett, and Marjorie E. Sprague, eds. *Adams Family Correspondence*. Vol. 2. Cambridge, Mass.: Harvard University Press, 1963.

———, eds. *Diary and Autobiography of John Adams*, Vol. 3. Cambridge, Mass., 1961. In Edmund S. Morgan, *The Meaning of Independence: John Adams, Thomas Jefferson, George Washington*. New York: W. W. Norton & Co., 1976.

Bibliography

By-Laws and Town Orders of the Town of Boston, Made and passed at Several Meetings in 1785 and 1786 and Duly approved by the Court of Sessions. Early American Imprints, 1st Ser., no. 19515. Boston: Edmund Freedman Printing Office, 1786.

Bynner, "Topography and Landmarks of the Provincial Period." In Justin Winsor, ed., The Memorial History of Boston including Suffolk County, Massachusetts 1630–1880. Vol. 2, The Provincial Period, 491–532. Boston: James R. Osgood & Co., 1882.

Carter, Clarence Edwin, ed. The Correspondence of General Thomas Gage with the Secretaries of State, and with the War Office and the Treasury, 1763–1775. Vol. 2. New Haven, Conn.: Yale University Press, 1933.

Carter, William. A Genuine Detail of the Several Engagements, Positions, and Movements of the Royal and American Armies; with an Accurate Account of the Blockade of Boston: Boston, n.p., 1938.

Chastellux, Marquis de. Travels in North America in the Years 1780–1781–1782. New York: n.p., 1828.

Columbian Centinel (Boston), 1790–1795.

Connecticut Courant (Hartford), 1775.

Connecticut Gazette (New London), 1775.

Constitutional Gazette (New York), 1775.

Cunningham, Anne Rowe, ed. Letters and Diary of John Rowe, 1759–1762, 1764–1779. Boston: W. B. Clarke & Co., 1903.

Edes, Peter. A Diary of Peter Edes, The Oldest Printer in the United States, Written During His Confinement in Boston, by the British, One Hundred and Seven Days in the Year 1775, . . . Written By Himself. Bangor, Maine: Samuel S. Smith, Printer, 1837.

The Essex Gazette (Salem), 1775.

Ford, Worthington Chauncey, Gaillard Hunt, John C. Fitzpatrick, and Roscoe R. Hall, eds. Journals of the Continental Congress, 1774–1789. Vol. 1. Division of Manuscripts. Library of Congress. Washington, D.C.: Government Printing Office, 1904.

Freeman, Samuel. The Town Officer: or the Power and Duty . . . As Contained in the Laws of Massachusetts. 7th ed. Boston: J. T. Buckingham, 1806.

Gray, Harrison. Harrison Gray to his grandson, 3 January 1792. Publications of the Colonial Society of Massachusetts: Transactions, 1911–1913 14 (Boston: 1913): 344–345.

Gremain, Lord George. A Plan of Boston in New England with its Environs. London, c. 1775.

Hulton, Anne. Letters of a Loyalist Lady: Being the Letters of Anne Hulton, Sister of Henry Hulton, Commissioner of Customs at Boston, 1767–1776. Cambridge, Mass.: Harvard University Press, 1927.

Independent Chronicle (Boston), 1776–1795.

The Journals of Each Provincial Congress of Massachusetts in 1774 and 1775, and of the Committee of Safety. Boston: Dutton Wentworth, 1838.

Lainhart, Ann Smith, ed. *First Boston City Directory (1789), Including Extensive Annotations by John Haven Dexter (1791–1876).* Boston: New England Historic and Genealogical Society, 1989.

———, ed. "Abated Taxes in Boston in 1782." *New England Historical and Genealogical Register* 146 (April 1992): 178–180.

———, ed. Thomas Bellow Wyman, comp. *The New North Church Boston, 1714.* Baltimore: Clearfield, 1995.

Leach, John. "A Journal Kept by John Leach, During His Confinement by the British, in Boston Gaol, in 1775." *New England Historical and Genealogical Register* 19 (July 1865): 255–263.

Massachusetts Gazette (Boston), 1774.

New England Chronicle (Cambridge), 1775–1776.

New Hampshire Gazette (Portsmouth), 1775.

Newell, Timothy. "A Journal Kept During the Time That Boston Was Shut Up in 1775–6." *Collections of the Massachusetts Historical Society,* 4th ser., 1 (1852): 261–276.

New York Journal (New York), 1775.

Oliver, Andrew, and James Bishop Peabody, eds. *The Records of Trinity Church, Boston, 1728–1830.* In *Colonial Society of Massachusetts Collections,* Vol. 56. Boston: Colonial Society of Massachusetts, 1982.

Paine, Samuel. "Letter of Samuel Paine Upon Affairs at Boston in October, 1775." *New England Genealogical and Historical Register* 30 (July 1876): 369–373.

Parker, Samuel. *Charity to Children Enforced.* Boston, 1803.

Pemberton, Thomas. "A Topographical and Historical Description of Boston, 1794; By the Author of the Historical Journal of the American War." *Massachusetts Historical Society Collections,* 1st ser., 3 (1794): 241–304.

Percy, Hugh Earl, Duke of Northumberland. *Letters of Hugh Earl Percy from Boston and New York, 1774–1776.* Edited by Charles Knowles Bolton. Boston: Charles E. Goodspeed, 1902.

Providence Gazette (Providence), 1775.

Records of the Church in Brattle Square with Lists of Communicants, Baptisms, Marriages, and Funerals, 1699–1872. Cambridge, Mass.: University Press, John Wilson and Son, 1902.

Reed, William B. *Life and Correspondence of Joseph Reed: Military Secretary of Washington at Cambridge.* Vol. 1. Philadelphia: Lindsay and Blakiston, 1847.

Robertson, Douglas S., ed. *An Englishman in America 1785: Being the Diary of Joseph Hadfield.* Toronto: Hunter-Rose Co., 1933.

Rohrbach, Lewis Bunker. *Boston Taxpayers in 1821.* Boston: True and Greene, 1922; repr., Camden, Maine: Picton Press, 1988.

Sargent, Winthrop, comp. and ed. "Letters of John Andrews, Esq. of Boston, 1772–1776." *Massachusetts Historical Society Proceedings* 8 (July 1865): 316–413.

Stevens, Benjamin Franklin, ed. *General Sir William Howe's Orderly Book at Charlestown, Boston and Halifax, June 1775 to 1776 26 May*. Kennikat American Bicentennial Series. London: Benjamin Franklin Stevens, 1890; repr., London: Kennikat Press, 1970.

Strickland, J. E., ed. *Journal of a Tour in the United States of America, 1794–1795*. New York: New York Historical Society, 1971.

Taylor, Eldad. "Evacuation of Boston, 1776, By An Eye Witness." *New England Genealogical and Historical Register* 8 (July 1854): 231–232.

Thacher, James. *Military Journal During the American Revolutionary War, From 1775–1783*. Boston: Richardson and Lord, 1823.

U.S. Bureau of the Census. *A Century of Population Growth: From the First Census of the United States to the Twelfth, 1790–1900*. Washington, D.C.: Government Printing Office, 1909.

Upham, William P., ed. "Extracts from Letters Written at the Time of the Occupation of Boston by the British, 1775–6." *Historical Collections of the Essex Institute* 13, no. 3 (July 1876): 153–231.

U.S. Department of Commerce and Labor, Bureau of the Census. *First Census of the United States, 1790, Massachusetts*. Washington, D.C.: Government Printing Office, 1908; repr., *Heads of Families at the First Census of the United States Taken in the Year 1790, Massachusetts*. Bountiful, Utah: Accelerated Indexing Systems, 1978.

———. *Second Census of the United States, 1800, Massachusetts*. Washington, D.C.: Government Printing Office, 1908; repr., *Heads of Families at the Second Census of the United States Taken in the Year 1800, Massachusetts*. Bountiful, Utah: Accelerated Indexing Systems, 1978.

West, John. *The Boston Directory Containing the Names of the Inhabitants, their Occupations, Places of Business, and Dwelling-Houses*. Boston: Manning and Lering, 1796. In *Reports of the Record Commissioners*, vol. 10.

SECONDARY SOURCES

Abbott, Carl. "The Neighborhoods of New York, 1760–1775." *New York History* 55 (1974): 35–55.

Agnew, Jean-Christoph. *Worlds Apart: The Market and the Theater in Anglo-American Thought, 1550–1750*. Cambridge: Cambridge University Press, 1986.

Alexander, John. *Render Them Submissive: Responses to Poverty in Philadelphia, 1760–1800*. Amherst: University of Massachusetts Press, 1980.

Bibliography

Ball, William. "Old Federal Street Theatre." In *The Bostonian Society Publications*, Vol. 8, 43–91. Boston: T. R. Marvin & Son Printers, 1911.

Benton, Josiah Henry. *Warning Out in New England, 1656–1817*. Boston: W. B. Clarke, 1911; repr., Freeport, N.Y.: Books for Libraries Press, 1970.

Bishop, J. Leander. *A History of American Manufactures from 1608 to 1860*. 3 vols. Philadelphia: E. Young & Co., 1861. 3rd. ed. Revised with an introduction by Louis M. Hacker. New York: A. M. Kelly, 1966.

Blackmar, Elizabeth. "Rewalking the 'Walking City': Housing and Property Relations in New York City, 1780–1840." *Radical History Review* 21: 131–48.

Blake, John B. *Public Health in the Town of Boston, 1630–1822*. Harvard Historical Studies, Vol. 72. Cambridge, Mass.: Harvard University Press, 1959.

Blanck, Emily. "Seventeen Eighty-Three: The Turning Point in the Law of Slavery and Freedom in Massachusetts." *New England Quarterly* 75, no. 1 (March 2003): 24–51.

Blewett, Mary H. *We Will Rise in Our Might: Workingwomen's Voices from Nineteenth-Century New England*. Ithaca, N.Y.: Cornell University Press, 1991.

Bolster, W. Jeffrey. *Black Jacks: African American Seamen in the Age of Sail*. Cambridge, Mass.: Harvard University Press, 1977.

Bouldry, Howard E. *A Plan of the Town of Boston and the Charleston Peninsula in New England, 1775*. Boston, 1969.

Breen, T. H. "An Empire of Goods: The Anglicization of Colonial America, 1690–1776." *Journal of British Studies* 25 (1986): 467–499.

Bridenbaugh, Carl. *Cities in Revolt: Urban Life in America, 1743–1776*. New York: Alfred A. Knopf, 1955; repr., Oxford: Oxford University Press, 1971.

Brown, Richard. "The Confiscation and Disposition of Loyalists' Estates in Suffolk County, Massachusetts." *William and Mary Quarterly*, 3rd ser., 21, no. 4 (October 1964): 534–550.

Brown, Robert E. *Middle-Class Democracy and the Revolution in Massachusetts, 1691–1780*. Ithaca, N.Y.: Cornell University Press, 1955.

Brown, Wallace. *The King's Friends: The Composition and Motives of the American Loyalist Claimants*. Providence, R.I.: Brown University Press, 1965.

Bulfinch, Ellen Susan. *The Life and Letters of Charles Bulfinch, Architect, with Other Family Papers*. Boston: Houghton Mifflin Co., 1896.

Cappon, Lester J., and Barbara Bartz Petchenik, eds. *Atlas of Early American History: The Revolutionary Era, 1760–1790*. Published for the Newberry Library and the Institute of Early American History and Culture. Princeton, N.J.: Princeton University Press, 1976.

Carr, Jacqueline Barbara. "A Change 'as Remarkable as the Revolution Itself': Boston's Demographics, 1780–1800." *New England Quarterly* 73, no. 4 (December 2000): 583–602.

Bibliography

Carr-Frobose, Jacqueline. "A Cultural History of Boston in the Revolutionary Era, 1775–1795." Ph.D. diss., University of California, Berkeley, 1998.

Cash, Philip. *Medical Men at the Siege of Boston, April 1775–April 1776: Problems of the Massachusetts and Continental Armies.* Memoirs of the American Philosophical Society. Philadelphia: American Philosophical Society, 1973.

Clapp, William W., Jr. *A Record of the Boston Stage.* Boston: James Munroe & Co., 1853.

Cleary, Patricia. "'Who shall say we have not equal abilitys with the Men when Girls of 18 years of age discover such great capacitys?': Women of Commerce in Boston, 1750–1766." In Conrad Edick Wright and Katheryn P. Viens, eds., *Entrepreneurs: The Boston Business Community, 1700–1850,* 39–61. Boston: Massachusetts Historical Society, 1997.

Conroy, David W. *In Public Houses: Drink and the Revolution of Authority in Colonial Massachusetts.* Chapel Hill: University of North Carolina Press, 1995.

Cook, Edward M., Jr. *The Fathers of the Towns: Leadership and Community Structure in Eighteenth-Century New England.* Johns Hopkins Studies in Historical and Political Science. Baltimore: Johns Hopkins University Press, 1976.

Cott, Nancy F. *The Bonds of Womanhood: "Woman's Sphere" in New England, 1780–1835.* 2nd ed. New Haven, Conn.: Yale University Press, 1997.

Countryman, Edward. *The American Revolution.* New York: Hill and Wang, 1985.

Cox, Caroline. *A Proper Sense of Honor: Service and Sacrifice in George Washington's Army.* Chapel Hill: University of North Carolina Press, 2004.

Crane, Elaine Forman. *Ebb Tide in New England: Women, Seaports, and Social Change, 1630–1800.* Boston: Northeastern University Press, 1998.

Cromwell, Adelaide M. *The Other Brahmins: Boston's Black Upper Class, 1750–1950.* Fayetteville: University of Arkansas Press, 1994.

Dayton, Cornelia H., and Sharon Salinger. "Mapping Migration into Pre-Revolutionary Boston: An Analysis of Robert Love's Warning Book." Paper presented at the McNeil Center for Early American Studies, University of Pennsylvania, Philadelphia, Pa., September 10, 1999.

Detwiller, Frederic C. "Thomas Dawes's Church in Brattle Square." *Old-time New England* 64 (January–June 1979): 7.

Dudley, Dorothy. *Theatrum Majorum.* Cambridge, 1876. In Colonial Society of Massachusetts, *Music in Colonial Massachusetts, 1630–1820.* Vol. 1. *Music in Public Places.* Boston: Colonial Society of Massachusetts, 1980. (Proceedings of a conference held May 17–18, 1973.)

East, Robert. *Business Enterprise in the American Revolutionary Era.* New York: Columbia University Press, 1938; repr., Gloucester, Mass.: Peter Smith, 1964.

Fenn, Elizabeth A. *Pox Americana: The Great Smallpox Epidemic of 1775–1782.* New York: Hill and Wang, 2001.

Bibliography

Fischer, David Hackett. *Paul Revere's Ride*. New York: Oxford University Press, 1994.

Fowler, William, Jr. *The Baron of Beacon Hill: A Biography of John Hancock*. Boston: Houghton Mifflin Co., 1980.

———. "Marine Insurance in Boston: The Early Years of the Boston Marine Insurance Company, 1799–1807." In Conrad Edick Wright and Katheryn P. Viens, eds., *Entrepreneurs: The Boston Business Community, 1700–1850*, 151–179. Boston: Massachusetts Historical Society, 1997.

Frey, Sylvia R. *The British Soldier in America: A Social History of Military Life in the Revolutionary Period*. Austin: University of Texas Press, 1981.

Frothingham, Richard, Jr. *History of the Siege of Boston and of the Battles of Lexington, Concord, and Bunker Hill*. Boston: privately printed, 1849; repr., Boston: Little, Brown & Co., 1903.

Gilchrist, David T. *The Growth of Seaport Cities: 1790–1825*. Charlottesville: University Press of Virginia, 1967. (Proceedings of a conference sponsored by the Eleutherian Mills-Hagley Foundation, March 17–19, 1966.)

Greene, Evarts B., and Virginia D. Harrington. *American Population Before the Federal Census of 1790*. New York: Columbia University Press, 1932; repr. Gloucester, Mass.: Peter Smith, 1966.

Greene, Lorenzo Johnston. *The Negro in Colonial New England*. New York: Atheneum, 1968.

Griffin, Edward M. *Old Brick: Charles Chauncey of Boston, 1705–1787*. Minneapolis: University of Minnesota Press, 1980.

Hale, Edward E. "The Siege of Boston." In Justin Winsor, ed., *The Memorial History of Boston including Suffolk County, Massachusetts, 1630–1880*. Vol. 3, *The Revolutionary Period: The Last Hundred Years*, 67–118. Boston: James R. Osgood & Co., 1881.

Handlin, Oscar. *Boston's Immigrants: A Study in Acculturation*. Rev. ed. Cambridge, Mass.: Harvard University Press, 1959.

Handlin, Oscar, and Mary Flug Handlin. *Commonwealth: A Study of the Role of Government in the American Economy Massachusetts, 1774–1861*. Rev. ed. Cambridge, Mass.: Harvard University Press, 1947.

———. "Revolutionary Economic Policy in Massachusetts." *William and Mary Quarterly*, 3rd ser., 4, 1 (January 1947): 3–26.

Harlow, Ralph. "Economic Conditions in Massachusetts During the American Revolution." *Publications of the Colonial Society of Massachusetts: Transactions, 1917–1919* (March 1918): 163–192.

Hayden, Robert. *The African Meeting House in Boston: A Celebration of History*. Companion Press Book. Boston: Museum of Afro-American History, 1987.

Henretta, James A. "Economic Development and Social Structure in Colonial Boston." *William and Mary Quarterly* 12 (January 1965): 75–92.

Herndon, Ruth Wallis. *Unwelcome Americans: Living on the Margin in Early New England*. Philadelphia: University of Pennsylvania Press, 2001.

Holbrook, Stewart H. *The Old Post Road: The Story of the Boston Post Road*. American Trails Series, ed. A. B. Guthrie Jr. New York: McGraw-Hill Book Co., 1962.

Hornblow, Arthur. *A History of the American Theatre in America from Its Beginnings to the Present Time*. 3 vols. New York: J. B. Lippincott & Co., 1919.

Horton, James Oliver, and Lois E. Horton. *Black Bostonians: Family Life and Community Struggle in the Antebellum North*. New York: Holmes & Meier Publishers, 1979.

Jacobs, Donald Martin. "A History of the Boston Negro from the Revolution to the Civil War." Ph.D. diss., Boston University, 1968.

Jensen, Merrill. *The New Nation: A History of the United States during the Confederation—1781–1789*. New York: Alfred A. Knopf, 1950.

Jones, Douglas Lamar. "The Transformation of the Law of Poverty in Eighteenth-Century Massachusetts." In *Law in Colonial Massachusetts, 1630–1800*. Boston: Colonial Society of Massachusetts; distributed by University Press of Virginia, 153–190.

Jones, E. Alfred. *The Loyalists of Massachusetts, Their Memorials, Petitions and Claims*. London: Saint Catherine Press, 1930.

Kaminsky, John P., and Richard Leffler. *Creating the Constitution*. Sources of the American Tradition. Acton, Mass.: Copley Publishing Group, 1999.

Kasson, John F. *Civilizing the Machine: Technology and Republican Values in America, 1776–1900*. New York: Grossman Publishers, 1976. Repr., New York: Penguin Books, 1977.

Kerber, Linda K. *Women of the Republic: Intellect and Ideology in Revolutionary America*. Chapel Hill: University of North Carolina Press, 1980.

Kirker, Harold, and James Kirker. *Bulfinch's Boston, 1787–1817*. New York: Oxford University Press, 1964.

Knights, Peter R. *The Plain People of Boston 1830–1860: A Study in City Growth*. Urban Life in America Series, ed. Richard C. Wade. New York: Oxford University Press, 1971.

Kulikoff, Allan. "The Progress of Inequality in Revolutionary Boston." *William and Mary Quarterly*, 3rd ser., 18, no. 3 (July 1971): 375–411.

Lane, Roger. *Policing the City: Boston, 1822–1885*. New York: Atheneum, 1971.

Leveseque, George A. *Black Boston: African American Life and Culture in Urban America, 1750–1860*. New York: Garland Publishing, 1994.

Litwack, Leon F. *North of Slavery: The Negro in the Free States 1790–1860*. Chicago: University of Chicago Press, 1961.

Lubow, Lisa B. "From Carpenter to Capitalist: The Business of Building in Postrevolutionary Boston." In Conrad Edick Wright and Katheryn P. Viens, eds., *Entrepreneurs: The Boston Business Community, 1700–1850*, 181–210. Boston: Massachusetts Historical Society, 1997.

MacEacheren, Elaine. "Emancipation of Slavery in Massachusetts: A Reexamination 1770–1790." *Journal of Negro History* 55, no. 4 (October 1970): 289–306.

Machor, James L. *Pastoral Cities: Urban Ideals and the Symbolic Landscape of America*. Madison: University of Wisconsin Press, 1987.

Main, Jackson Turner. *The Social Structure of Revolutionary America*. Princeton, N.J.: Princeton University Press, 1965.

Mann, Bruce H. *Republic of Debtors: Bankruptcy in the Age of American Independence*. Cambridge, Mass.: Harvard University Press, 2002.

McCusker, John J., and Russell R. Menard. *The Economy of British America, 1607–1789: Needs and Opportunities for Study*. Chapel Hill: University of North Carolina Press, 1985.

McKendrick, Neil, John Brewer, and J. H. Plumb. *The Commercialization of Eighteenth-Century England*. Bloomington: Indiana University Press, 1982.

Middlekauff, Robert. *The Glorious Cause: The American Revolution, 1763–1789*. New York: Oxford University Press, 1982.

Milford, T. A. "Boston's Theater Controversy and Liberal Notions of Advantage." *New England Quarterly* 72, no. 1 (1999): 61–68.

Moore, George H. *Notes on the History of Slavery in Massachusetts*. New York: D. Appleton & Co., 1866.

Morgan, Edmund. "Puritan Hostility to the Theatre." *Proceedings of the American Philosophical Society* 110 (October 1966): 340–347.

Morison, Samuel Eliot. *The Maritime History of Massachusetts, 1783–1860*. New York: Houghton Mifflin Co., 1921; repr., Boston: Northeastern University Press, 1979.

Morris, Richard. "Urban Population Migration in Revolutionary America: The Case of Salem, Massachusetts, 1759–1799." *Journal of Urban History* 9, no. 1 (November 1982): 3–30.

Mussey, Robert, and Anne Rogers Haley. "John Cogswell and Boston Bombe Furniture: Thirty-Five Years of Revolution in Politics and Design." In Luke Beckerdite, *American Furniture*, 73–105. Hanover, N.H.: Chipstone Foundation, 1994.

Nash, Gary. "The Social Evolution of Preindustrial American Cities, 1700–1820, Reflections and New Directions." *Journal of Urban History* 13, no. 2 (February 1787): 15–145.

———. *Forging Freedom: The Formation of Philadelphia's Black Community, 1720–1840*. Cambridge, Mass.: Harvard University Press, 1988.

———. *The Urban Crucible: Social Change, Political Consciousness, and the Origins of the American Revolution*. Cambridge, Mass.: Harvard University Press, 1979.

Nell, William C. *The Colored Patriots of the American Revolution*. Boston: Robert F. Wallcut, 1855; repr., New York: Arno Press, 1968, from a copy in the Moorland-Spingarn Collection, Howard University, Washington, D.C.

Nichols, Charles. "Samuel Salisbury: A Boston Merchant in the Revolution." *Proceedings of the American Antiquarian Society*, 2nd ser., 35 (April 1925): 46–63.

Norton, Mary Beth. *The British-Americans: The Loyalist Exiles in England 1774–1789*. Boston: Little, Brown & Co., 1972.

———. *Liberty's Daughters: Revolutionary Experience of American Women, 1750–1800*. Ithaca, N.Y.: Cornell University Press, 1996.

O'Brien, William, S.J. "Did the Jennison Case Outlaw Slavery in Massachusetts?" *William and Mary Quarterly*, 3rd ser., 17, no. 2 (April 1960): 219–242.

O'Connor, Thomas H., and Alan Rogers. *This Momentous Affair: Massachusetts and the Ratification of the Constitution of the United States*. Boston: Trustees of the Public Library of the City of Boston, 1987.

Perkins, Edwin J. *The Economy of Colonial America*. New York: Columbia University Press, 1988.

Perlmann, Joel, and Dennis Shirley. "When Did New England Women Acquire Literacy?" *William and Mary Quarterly*, 3rd ser., 48, no. 1 (January 1991): 50–67.

Pinkney, Helen R. *Christopher Gore: Federalist of Massachusetts, 1758–1827*. Waltham, Mass.: Gore Place Society, 1969.

Potter, Janice. *The Liberty We Seek: Loyalist Ideology in Colonial New York and Massachusetts*. Cambridge, Mass.: Harvard University Press, 1983.

Potter, Jim. "Demographic Aspects of the Revolution and Its Aftermath." In Jack P. Greene and J. R. Pole, eds., *The Blackwell Encyclopedia of the American Revolution*, 565–568. Cambridge: Basil Blackwell, 1991.

———. "Demographic Development and Family Structure." In Jack P. Greene and J. R. Pole, eds., *Colonial British America: Essays in the New History of the Early Modern Era*, 123–126. Baltimore: Johns Hopkins University Press, 1984.

Price, Jacob M. "Economic Function and the Growth of American Port Towns in the Eighteenth Century." *Perspectives in American History* 8 (1974): 123–186.

Quimby, Ian M. G., ed. *The Craftsman in Early America*. Wilmington, Del.: Henry Francis du Pont Winterthur Museum, 1984.

Rothman, David J. *The Discovery of the Asylum: Social Order and Disorder in the New Republic*. Boston: Little, Brown & Co., 1971.

Rutman, Darret B. *Winthrop's Boston: A Portrait of a Puritan Town, 1630–1649*. Chapel Hill: University of North Carolina Press, 1965; repr., W. W. Norton & Co., 1972.

Schlesinger, Arthur M., Jr. "A Panoramic View: The City in American History." In Paul Kramer and Frederick L. Holborn, eds., *The City in American Life: A Historical Anthology*, 13–36. New York: G. P. Putnam's Sons, 1970.

Scudder, Horace E. "Life in Boston in the Provincial Period." In Justin Winsor, ed., *The Memorial History of Boston including Suffolk County, Massachusetts, 1630–1880*. Vol. 2, *The Provincial Period*, 437–490. Boston: James R. Osgood & Co., 1882.

———. "Life in Boston in the Revolutionary Period." In Justin Winsor, ed., *The Memorial History of Boston including Suffolk County, Massachusetts, 1630–1880*. Vol. 3, *The Revolutionary Period*, 149–188. Boston: James R. Osgood & Co., 1882.

Seybolt, Robert Francis. *Public Schoolmasters of Colonial Boston*. Cambridge, Mass.: Harvard University Press, 1939.

Shammas, Carole. "The Space Problem in Early United States Cities." *William and Mary Quarterly*, 3rd ser., 57, no. 3 (July 2000): 505–542.

Shattuck, Lemuel. *Report to the Committee of the City Council Appointed to Obtain the Census of Boston for the Year 1845*. Boston: John H. Eastburn, 1846; repr., New York: Arno Press, 1976.

Shurtleff, Nathaniel B. *A Topographical and Historical Description of Boston*. Boston: Alfred Mudge and Son, 1871.

Silverman, Kenneth. *A Cultural History of the American Revolution: Painting, Music, Literature, and the Theatre in the Colonies and the United States from the Treaty of Paris to the Inauguration of George Washington, 1763–1789*. New York: Thomas Y. Crowell Co., 1976.

Smith, Billy G. "The Vicissitudes of Fortune: The Careers of Laboring Men in Philadelphia, 1750–1800." In Stephen Innes, ed., *Work and Labor in Early America*, 221–251. Chapel Hill: University of North Carolina Press, 1988.

———. *The "Lower Sort": Philadelphia's Laboring People, 1750–1800*. Ithaca, N.Y.: Cornell University Press, 1990.

Spector, Robert M. "The Quork Walker Cases (1781–83): Slavery, Its Abolition, and Negro Citizenship in Early Massachusetts." *Journal of Negro History* 53, no. 1 (January 1968): 12–32.

Stansell, Christine. *City of Women: Sex and Class in New York 1789–1860*. New York: Alfred A. Knopf, 1982; repr., Chicago: University of Illinois Press, Illini Books ed., 1987.

Stark, James H. *The Loyalists of Massachusetts and The Other Side of The American Revolution*. Boston: W. B. Clarke Co., 1910; repr. Bowie, Md.: Heritage Books, 1988.

———. *Antique Views of Ye Towne of Boston*. Boston: Morse-Purce Co., 1907.

Thwing, Annie Haven. *The Crooked and Narrow Streets of the Town of Boston, 1630–1822*. Boston: Marshall Jones Co., 1920.

Bibliography

Tyler, John W. *Smugglers and Patriots: Boston Merchants and the Advent of the American Revolution.* Boston: Northeastern University Press, 1986.

———. "Persistence and Change within the Boston Business Community." In Conrad Edick Wright and Katheryn P. Viens, eds., *Entrepreneurs: The Boston Business Community, 1700–1850*, 97–119. Boston: Massachusetts Historical Society, 1997.

Ulrich, Laurel Thatcher. *The Age of Homespun: Objects and Stories in the Creation of an American Myth.* New York: Alfred A. Knopf, 2001.

Upton, Dell. "The City As Material Culture." In Anne Elizabeth Yentsch and Mary C. Beaudry, eds., *The Art and Mystery of Historical Archaeology: Essays in Honor of James Deetz*, 51–74. Boca Raton, Fla.: CRC Press, 1992.

Waldstreicher, David. *In The Midst of Perpetual Fetes: The Making of American Nationalism, 1776–1820.* Chapel Hill: University of North Carolina Press, 1997.

Warden, G. B. *Boston 1689–1776.* Boston: Little, Brown & Co., 1970.

———. "Inequality and Instability in Boston." *Journal of Interdisciplinary History* 6, no. 4 (Spring 1976): 585–620.

Warner, Sam Bass, Jr. *The Private City: Philadelphia in Three Periods of Its Growth.* Philadelphia: University of Pennsylvania Press, 1968.

Weeks, Lyman Horace. *A History of Paper-Manufacturing in the United States, 1690–1916.* New York: Burt Franklin, 1916; repr., 1969.

Wells, Robert V. "Population and Family in Early America." In Jack P. Greene and J. R. Pole, eds., *Colonial British America: Essays in the New History of the Early Modern Era*, 39–52. Baltimore: Johns Hopkins University Press, 1984.

White, Shane. *Somewhat More Independent: The End of Slavery in New York City, 1770–1810.* Athens: University of Georgia Press, 1991.

Whitehill, Walter Muir. *Boston: A Topographical History.* Cambridge, Mass.: Harvard University Press, 1959; repr., 1968.

Wickham, Glynne. *A History of the Theatre.* 2nd ed. London: Phaidon Press, 1992.

Wood, Gordon, S. *The Creation of the American Republic, 1776–1787.* Published for the Institute of Early American History and Culture. Chapel Hill: University of North Carolina Press, 1969.

Wright, Conrad Edick, ed. *Massachusetts and the New Nation.* Boston: Massachusetts Historical Society, 1992.

Writers' Program of the Works Progress Administration in the State of Massachusetts, comp., *Boston Looks Seaward: The Story of the Port 1630–1940.* Sponsored by the Boston Port Authority. Boston: Bruce Humphries, 1941.

Wulf, Karin A. *Not All Wives: Women of Colonial Philadelphia.* Ithaca, N.Y.: Cornell University Press, 2000.

Index

Wade, Joseph, 157
wages, 121
Waldo, John, 55
Walker, Quock, 76
Walley, Thomas, 104
Wallis, Samuel, 94
Ward, Betty, 106
Ward, John, 138
wards, 47–48, 49, 68, 71, 97–98
warehouses, 65, 129, 233
Warner, Daniel, 164–65
warning out, practice of, 5, 98–102,
    104–6, 263n44
Washington, George, 28, 33, 35, 36,
    135, 248n122; birthday celebrations
    for, 195; street named for, 53; visit to
    Boston, 6
Washington Street, 53
Washington Tavern, 56
watchmen, 95, 132–33
water, 15, 140
Water Street, 75
Waters, Josiah, 138–39
Watertown, Mass., 40, 88
Watts, Prince, 5, 171, 173
Webber, Seth, 162
Welch, John, 93
Wells, Susannah, 178
Wentworth, Phillip and Phineas, 153
West Boston Bridge, 47
West Church, 39, 68
West End, 9, 45, 229; African-Ameri-
    cans in, 76–79, 232, 257n115; asylum

institutions in, 82–83; geography and
land use, 47, 68, 70–74; map, 69;
wards of, 48; wealthy householders
in, 155
West India trade, 73, 74, 183
West, John, 229
Weymouth, Mass., 40
wharves, 47, 57, 166, 229, 230, 251n49
Whigs, 23, 37
White Horse Tavern, 56, 177, 197
White, William, 117
Whittemore, Amos and William, 185
widows, 80, 96, 110, 158; American
    Revolution and, 174, 280n81; as tav-
    ern keepers, 180
Williams, James, 137
Williams, Molly, 124
Williams, Thomas, 74, 75
Willon's Lane, 68
Willoughby, Elijah, 22
Wing's Lane, 154
Winnisimmet Ferry, 47, 65, 68
Winslow, Violet, 174–75
winter entertainments, 198
Winter Street, 55, 182
women, trades employed in, 173–81,
    187, 231–32, 279n69, 280n81
Woodman, Abigail, 92, 176, 177
Worcester, Mass., 21, 55
workhouse, 77, 82, 97, 111, 166

yellow fever, 135, 138